An American Family

An American Family

The Great War and Corporate Culture in America

Ferdinando Fasce

Translated by Ian Harvey

The Ohio State University Press
Columbus

English translation published 2002 by The Ohio State University.

Library of Congress Cataloging-in-Publication Data
Fasce, Ferdinando, 1951–
    [Famiglia a stelle e strisce. English]
    An American Family : the Great War and corporate culture in America /
    Ferdinando Fasce ; translated by Ian Harvey.
        p. cm.
Includes bibliographical references and index.
ISBN 0-8142-0908-4 (hardcover : alk. paper)—ISBN 0-8142-5100-5 (pbk. : alk. paper)
    1. Working class—United States—History.
    2. United States—Social conditions. I. Title.

HD8072 .F34 2002
331.89'04733'097467—dc21
                                    2002007839

The translation of this book has been funded by SEPS.
Via Val d'Aposa, 7 40123 Bologna, ITALY
39 051 271992 telephone / 39 051 265983 fax / seps@alma.unibo.it email
www.seps.it

Cover design by Dan O'Dair
Printed by Thomson-Shore Inc.

The paper used in this publication meets the minimum requirements of the
American National Standard for Information Sciences—Permanence of Paper
for Printed Library Materials. ANSI Z39.48-1992.

9   8   7   6   5   4   3   2   1

Contents

Introduction

This book looks at the relations between management and workers in a particular American company in the era of the First World War. The focus is on the methods of coordination and integration of human resources, on communication systems, and on the rules and values transmitted by the company management to the shop floor through a combination of production imperatives, mobilization catchphrases, new engineering know-how, and welfare techniques. The book will, however, also seek to reconstruct the reactions of the workers and the role that intermediary structures played in this system. We shall thus be looking at the everyday reality of a large company, captured at the point of intersection between the wishes of management and actual reality at a decisive moment in the life cycle of that company.

The case we are studying is not Ford or any of the other American companies that one might associate with the great American industrial fortunes. Perhaps even those who have read attentively and in full the two great *summae* of U.S. labor and business history published in the 1980s and 1990s by the leading experts of the relative disciplines will have difficulty remembering the passing references to this company that both books contain. The references to Scovill—the name of the company we are talking about—were inevitable because, in terms of assets, Scovill would have been placed in 172nd position if there had been at the time a *Fortune* list of the top five hundred industrial companies in the country. In the words of Charles W. Cheape, it was "one of five hundred or a thousand companies that have shaped and dominated the core industries of the American economy in the last century." Undoubtedly, however, it lacked the high profile of those companies that were revolutionizing the market with their new products and innovative sales techniques, changing means of production with the development of a mass system of manufacturing, and transforming organizational forms through their contacts with outstanding figures in the field of managerial innovation such as Taylor and his disciples. Its relative anonymity was reinforced by the fact that it was firmly rooted in a medium-sized town in Connecticut. Mary McCarthy, as she looked back on her childhood on the other side of the country, thought of Waterbury as embodying the quintessence of the selfsame province from which she came ("at a guess Seattle, as far as I remember it, was no more backward than Waterbury, Connecticut").[1]

Close contact with such an apparently provincial and nondescript object of study has necessarily caused some documentary and methodological problems, as well as a certain amount of frustration. I occasionally forgot, as I emerged blinking into the daylight after consulting the reports of the various federal commissions (on industry or immigration) held in the first twenty years of the twentieth century, having failed to find any trace of either the company or the town, that I had chosen Scovill precisely because of its anonymity. My idea was to take a large company at the time of Taylorism and Fordism and study it from the inside, to look at the way it treated its workers, and in particular the communicative and cultural aspects of these relations, but I was careful to avoid any company that was an unquestioned leader in technological innovation and nationwide labor policy.

Long before deciding on Scovill, I had been aware of a need that had emerged in the years between the 1970s and the 1980s in the most advanced American research, and that also found an echo in those Italian scholars who were studying the history of the working class and the working-class movement. This was the need to enlarge the horizons of labor history, to move toward an increasingly effective and realistic assessment of the role played by the world of labor in the face of the power mechanisms at work in society as a whole. Coming as I was from an analysis of the high points of working-class self-activity such as the Industrial Workers of the World and, more generally, from an examination of the factory through workers' eyes,[2] I believed it would be possible to satisfy this need, not by moving out of the factory (toward politics, ethnic studies, or other variables), but rather by focusing on it more closely through an alternative lens. This was to be provided by management sources, which, with some outstanding exceptions, labor historians up to the end of the 1980s had rarely touched.[3] In order to enlarge my view of the rest of the social system, my idea was to examine this microcosm in its reaction to the epoch-making event of the First World War.

Various impulses lay behind the decision to deal with the war era. First, there was the fact that the American literature on corporate welfare, on the working class, and on the processes of what was at times the "coercive" integration of immigrants, indicated this phase as a watershed in the systematic redefinition of labor policy and mechanisms of control over the workforce. Despite numerous radical differences of approach, interpretation, and political orientation, this literature found ample factual corroboration in business and organizational research dealing with the emergence and consolidation of the modern corporation, as well as in the literature on the redefinition of the relationship between the public and private spheres brought about during the first two decades of the twentieth century. This literature disclosed an unprecedented circulation of resources and ideas between the two spheres, beginning at the turn of the century and culminating in the mobilization for war. Corporate liberalism, corporate capitalism, and "organized capitalism" were the expressions used to define this process in studies investigating the formation of the military-industrial complex, the penetration of political and legal structures by the economic potentates, the development of a hegemonic vision by the corporate world, and the progressive (and much disputed) emergence of federal power as a relatively independent player on the national political and social scene.[4]

Second, I was struck by a remarkable blind spot in historiography: It seemed that precisely the country that provided the most fundamental insights into the history of the mentality and construction of collective memory in the Old World during and after the war [5] was, on close examination and with very few, albeit praiseworthy, exceptions,[6] the country that was least studied in this respect. There was clearly a need for a more in-depth study of propaganda and the changes in popular mentality inside the United States to examine the role played in this context by the business world.[7]

The need for a careful look at the connections between structural and cultural components was also suggested by two lines of study that emerged in the 1980s: On the one hand, the studies that investigated the history of mentality and the collective imagination by focusing on the so-called "incorporation of America," and, on the other, the sociological and anthropological research into "corporate culture," that is, into the attempts by management to formulate and spread among its workers a system of rules, practices, and shared values.[8]

Once I was clear in my mind that I should try to study what had happened in a major American company during the war and concentrate on the intentions of those managing the company, the messages they conveyed, and the dynamics that this set in motion, I chose first of all the general geographical area and then a company within that area. Connecticut seemed to be particularly suitable because it had been the center of the national armaments industry; it had been the source of 54 percent of arms

and munitions produced in the country in 1917–18, and it was here that
some of the widest-ranging and most advanced (and best documented)
forms of mobilization in the entire country were developed. I hit upon
Scovill because it was one of the few major companies in the state that
combined a leading role in manufacturing war material, a long historical
tradition—which would make it possible to identify a potential dialectic of
continuity and discontinuity set off by the world conflict—and a sizeable
archive.[9]

Unfortunately, however, the archives proved to lack two essential
sources for the historian: balance sheets (only a few years had survived, and
even these were riddled with gaps) and the minutes of the board meetings
(which were completely missing). The rest of the material, however,
including circulars, bulletins, confidential reports, and items of incoming
and outgoing commercial correspondence, was rich enough (albeit disor-
ganized, especially in relation to the management of the plant) to encourage me to continue in the hope that I would find alternative solutions—at
least for the missing parts of the balance sheets. With this problem
resolved, thanks in part to financial journals, and an old unpublished company history that had been kept in the archives, I then moved on to the
state archives on mobilization, other papers about mobilization to be
found in the National Archives, various odds and ends of local history preserved in the archives and institutions of Waterbury, Hartford, and Yale,
local newspapers, and, finally, oral sources.

Given the limited nature of the union material available—restricted to
some episodic references contained in the minutes of annual conferences
of the state and national federations or in some articles in national union
and workers' journals—the oral sources represented the principal direct
channel for letting the voice of the workers be heard. What I have used
comes from a collection of tapes recorded by Jeremy Brecher kept at the
Mattatuck Museum in Waterbury and about ten interviews I made personally, with the help of Brecher, in the Italian community Waterbury and
with those who had returned to Pontelandolfo (Benevento), the town from
which many of the inhabitants of the local Little Italy had emigrated. A
combination of the company material, the mobilization sources, and the
documents of bodies such as the Federal Department of Justice and the
Connecticut Department of Labor shed ample light on the behavior and
interests of the workers.

The framework of the book took shape almost of its own accord around
the concentric rings that formed the various types of sources. While firmly
focused on one particular case, the book also makes an effort to show what
was happening in the rest of the country. It starts from the office of the plant

manager (because this is the locus that the company archive covers best) and moves outward to the city and the state. What emerges is a network of concrete and symbolic relations that involved management and workers, a system of individual and collective rules and emotional investments deployed by social actors whom the investigation follows as they move between the shop floor, the neighborhood, and the other arenas of private and social life. By emphasizing the idea of corporate culture and deciding to view things from above, the intention is not to hide but rather to disclose by means of contrast forms of resistance and occasionally opposition that were hidden in the interstices of the scene. Likewise, I have attempted to show, in all its contradictions, the organizational learning process that management underwent as the company found itself gradually taking on an institutional role that went beyond the purely economic sphere. This role led it to occupy public spaces where the collective rituals of mobilization for war were played out and to enter the private sphere of working families, through the various mechanisms of certification and discipline connected with the draft and other aspects of civilian and military life.

My concern for providing a description made up of minute details arose out of the intent to construct a plausible history in which the working class and capital, that is, the famous abstract mass caught in an abstract grip (which Selig Perlman referred to as dangerous hypostases), might be resolved into the individuals and groups that comprised them in everyday life. The result was the discovery—but only at the end of a process of analysis—that, contrary to what Perlman thought, the grip in which the workers were held really was vise-like. Which is not, of course, to underestimate the professional, ethnic, and gender divisions that existed within the world of the working class, the phases of class formation and disruption it went through over time, or the relative privileges that a section of the working class tried to defend. Nor does it mean disregarding the gray zones and the active role that some segments of the company structure, which found themselves both in real and ideological terms caught between labor and capital, played in the incipient process of expanding the coordination and organizational functions of the company to gain any possible benefits from the mechanisms of stratification, co-optation, and control associated with this process.[10]

In order to follow these dynamics in their concrete evolution, I have tried as far as possible to insert into the narrative the subtle relationship of unity and distinction between Scovill and the national picture, and between the shop floor and the values and broader issues facing America at the time. The purpose of the notes is to highlight the specific historiographical filters (business history, the history of technology, labor history, and work and ethnic studies) through which the archive material has passed. We shall come back to the more general points shortly. First, however, I would like to illustrate how the book is structured.

It is divided into four chapters. The first chapter gives a basic outline of the history of Scovill, its labor policy, and its systems of supervision and communication over a period of a century, until the outbreak of the war: This long prologue is necessary to gain a picture of both the continuities (typical of a provincial company run by a family of managers and in part owners with a decades-long history in the company) and the radical changes the firm underwent during the war. The second chapter looks at the impact the war contracts had on the company; these led to an enormous amplification of resources and consequently to a need for differentiation in the structure and reinforcement of the mechanisms of command and coordination. At the same time, it also sheds light on the gradual expansion of the company's sphere of influence to include various parts of workers' lives, from health to recreation. As the third chapter shows, this process became both more evident and more intense after the United States entered the war, eventually becoming a prescriptive organizational model of behavior, extended in theory to the whole of the labor force. It can be summed up in the term "employee-citizen," loyal to country and company. The long, contradictory process whereby the company management's forms of involvement of workers in production, education, and recreation were continued even after the Armistice is the subject of the last chapter. The tensions that had built up during the war and especially in the reconversion phase exploded in two large-scale strikes that put an end to a period of peace that had lasted for almost two decades. The workers' defeat in the second and decisive conflict and the arrival of the recession of 1920–21 led to a drastic reduction in the workforce, as well as a rolling back of the social policies formulated by the company during the war period. The main strategy, however, was to selectively maintain some of the organizational and cultural features developed by the company management—in terms of self-awareness, coordination, and communication functions—as a way of holding together the "family" of the workers.

This study thus confirms the conclusions of the now classic works by Brody, Nelson, Montgomery, and Dubofsky on the centrality of the war as a period of transition in American corporate labor policy. The inside perspective and the emphasis on the cultural aspects of these policies applied to a major company, albeit one that was not in the forefront of technological and organizational developments (and one that retained some of the typical managerial characteristics of a family firm), place the focus firmly on the radical nature and controversial complexity of this transition. This puts a definite end to the linear vision that sees the advent of the Tayloristic factory as a purely technical phenomenon or at least one that was played out in a pre-determined sequence. If we focus once again on the crucial nature of the war (and its structural effects on the life of the company) and examine the workshop through the eyes of the company as a whole, the picture takes on a much more complex outline. Technological and technical-organizational innovation becomes part of a broader framework, a "factory regime," that affects production but also goes beyond it, drawing on a varied arsenal of instruments and occasionally appearing capable of satisfying at least some of the material and cultural needs of the workers. As part of the undoubted (and decisive) acceleration that the war contracts gave to the process of ongoing rationalization, a mass of traditions established by use took shape, as well as bureaucratic rules and attempts to moderate them or personalize them through "clan-like" forms of involvement, such as the company bulletin or welfare policies. Added to these were previously unused mechanisms to integrate workers, mechanisms of a highly mytho-symbolic nature forged in the war propaganda laboratory.[11]

In their attempts in the immediate postwar period to voice their collective views, the workers made an appeal based on the most universal core of patriotic ritual, that is, those promises to expand social and political citizenship that were, according to some militant workers, contained in Wilson's democratic rhetoric. In this attempt the fragments of labor culture (or counterculture) that the analysis has identified and that took the form of the troubled dynamics of adaptation and resistance, crystallized in the everyday life of the factory into open opposition to excessive corporate power. Their antagonism, the result of a temporary ability on the part of workers, driven by the militants of the left, to bring together ethnicity and class, exposed the essentially manipulatory and exploitative nature of the patriotic catchphrases, the bureaucratic rules, and the commitments undertaken by management toward the workers.[12]

The reaction of the company to the workers' initiative clearly showed the continuity between war and reconversion. It consisted in what, according to Howell John Harris, could be called unitary corporatism: a power structure in which the company, as a result of a specific economic, political and social, local and state environment, incorporated a growing amount of resources and new functions that in the past had been supplied from outside, in part taking the place of market, community, and public institutions in matters of command and social control, and managing to thwart, or at least to select and re-work to its own ends, any attempt to call into question or mediate privileges that may have come from one part of the local and state (or federal) context. It is well known that, during the war and in the immediate postwar period, this unitary corporatism co-existed, on a national level, with situations in which, in a climate of great social ferment and extreme factory conflict, there was a significant growth in the organized presence of workers and some extremely contradictory efforts at mediation between capital and labor on the part of the federal government. The twenties saw a severe reduction in the power of the unions and the dismantling of any residual mediation by government.[13]

The formal strengthening of the internal command structure along bureaucratic lines, selectivity in labor policies, and a de facto compromise between the bureaucratic spirit on the one hand and the traditional abuses of the intermediary structures on the other—these features of the company in the twenties, with which the book concludes, are fully confirmed in other case studies of corporate culture that have recently seen, for the first time, experts on labor and business history converging on company sources. They confirm the picture that has begun to emerge in the most recent studies of the welfare movement. This phenomenon, despite the hesitations of manufacturers worried about overspending and in some cases about appearing "paternalist," seems to have found a stable place in the industrial history of the country in the first quarter of the century. Its spread and effectiveness did, however, fluctuate considerably even before the Great Depression brought it to a halt, although this did not prevent a widespread return of interest in these policies during the Second World War and the subsequent decades.[14]

The general profile of the big company that emerges from this case study—a basically organic system, structured according to hierarchies that over time became formally more vertical (also and especially in the internal distribution of benefits), and capable of concentrating its power in a way that appears at times limited only by market trends—seems to sum up the three prevailing pictures of the corporate world in the period prior to the stock market crash and the New Deal drawn separately by labor, business, cultural, and political history. The company emerges from the workshop of Scovill as a central institution in the American economic structure of the twentieth century, by virtue of the mechanisms of production of strategic and management decisions, and the coordination of resources that it managed to develop. It also takes on the semblance of an apparently irreplaceable presence, even if for some its self-assertion as a model of government is frankly disturbing, of the system of values and the mechanisms of command and integration in contemporary American society. Last but hardly least, it resembles a prism in which individuals and groups that belonged to distant worlds, and in some cases opposing camps, met and occasionally clashed daily.[15]

In light of the documentary evidence presented here, however, each of these three images begins to waver a little, and issues and problems are raised that lie outside the province of this work. In terms of production and structural rationalization, the history of Scovill suggests a much more tortuous and arduous path than that which business history has often delineated. It also suggests the need for further research on the interaction between technical progress, economic growth, and the distribution of power and consensus produced by the second industrial revolution. Finally, it points to the largely unexplored question of the impact of the expansion of white-collar functions.[16]

Now that I have been able to show that I was not completely alone in the years I spent in the workshop of a brass factory, I should perhaps also mention that a book did appear in the United States (although unfortunately only after I had completed my research), which might have made me feel even less lonesome. An American scholar had chosen Scovill as one of three case studies in an important inquiry she conducted, largely inspired by the school of Alfred Chandler, into the transformation of American company communication systems in the age of rationalization, between the 1880s and 1920. Although our themes and approaches are different, it was comforting to find that the writer was in agreement with a series of observations about the nature and pace of organizational change at Scovill, which I have developed in several articles published over the past few years in Italy and abroad and which have formed the basis for this book.[17]

Without the skillful assistance of the archivists Florence B. Lathrop (Baker Library), Mark Jones (Connecticut State Library), and Ann Smith (Mattatuck Museum), this book would have never seen the light of day. Philip W. Bishop, the author in the early 1950s of an unpublished history of Scovill kept at Baker Library, was equally instrumental in pointing me in the direction of sources crucial to this research. To Jeremy Brecher I owe the gift of his wonderful friendship and most of what I know about the Naugatuck Valley, while Al Scopino, Jr., shared with me his knowledge of Scovill's history. Mansel Blackford, Austin Kerr, John Rumm, and Carmen Sirianni generously provided suggestions and insights on corporate culture. Catherine Collomp, Marianne Debouzy, Howell Harris, Richard Oestreicher, and Daniel Rodgers read and commented astutely on several preparatory drafts of the material contained in this book. Throughout the research David Montgomery and Rudolph Vecoli have been an unfailing source of encouragement and inspiration for my work, providing invaluable methodological suggestions and unearthing labor and ethnic sources unknown to me.

Closer to home, Anna Maria Martellone provided me with cultural and scientific support at two key moments in the long process of my research; Bruno Cartosio, Susanna Garroni, Matteo Sanfilippo, and Elisabetta Vezzosi have never stopped showing me their friendship and helping me with their competence in American history; Manlio Calegari and Claudio Costantini have kindly put aside their early modern Genoese historical interests to talk with me about my favorite things; and Tiziano Bonazzi has persuasively shown me that a historian should never follow the dubious wisdom of the saying "it is better to travel hopefully than to arrive."

Last, but hardly least, I wish to acknowledge the financial assistance of the Italian Ministry of Education and the Center for American Studies in Rome, whose help made this research possible.

This is the English translation of the book, originally published in 1993, that won the 1995 Organization of American Historians Foreign-Language Book Prize. The only changes that the author has made for this American edition concern the introduction and the endnotes, which have been updated and edited to fit an American and international audience. The author gratefully acknowledges the financial contribution provided by the Segretariato Europeo per le Pubblicazioni Scientifiche (SEPS) that made the translation possible.

I

Brass Valley

1. A CENTURY OF BUTTONS

In the autumn of 1914, the British government awarded the Bethlehem Steel Corporation, one of the world's leading steel manufacturers, the first order for war material given to a company on the other side of the Atlantic. The order was for arms and munitions to a total value of almost $50 million. For the part relating to grenade fuses, Bethlehem turned to the Scovill Manufacturing Company in Waterbury (Connecticut).[1] Over a century old, Scovill was one of the longest-standing industrial companies in America and one of the few to boast a certain amount of experience in military production of this type. At the moment of taking on an order that was to radically change its countenance, the company was in the middle of a process of technological and organizational transformation that had started at the turn of the century. In order to sketch a profile of these transformations, we need first to take a rapid look back at the company's long history.

Right from its very foundation in 1802, Scovill had been at the cutting edge of developments in the so-called Brass Valley. This was the name given to the Naugatuck Valley on account of the type of factories that were concentrated there. The Naugatuck Valley was a strip of land less than thirty miles long that cut across Connecticut and had its center of gravity in Waterbury, the fourth largest city in the state in terms of population and the third largest industrial center. The area had some of the typical features of an industrial district, given its high degree of specialization and its almost monopolistic control over one industry. At the start of the twentieth century, 90 percent of rolled brass and brass wire manufactured in the United States came from here. By the outbreak of war in Europe, the proportion was firmly fixed at 80 percent. Such a level of concentration in one area had no equal in any other sector. To mention only a few examples: In

1

1900 Pennsylvania, the steel state par excellence, supplied only 54 percent of national production, and only 45 percent of shoes were made in Massachusetts, the leading state for footwear.[2]

Most historians and sociologists who have studied the Naugatuck Valley agree that the abundant reserves of water concentrated around the Naugatuck River and the area's dense woodlands are the topographical factors that explain the original industrial settlement. Water was the prime motive power, and timber the combustible material for the annealing processes necessary between one operation and another. There is another factor, however, that should not be disregarded, and that is the legacy of techniques, operational practices and trading channels passed on from the considerable craft tradition of button making, clock making, and the manufacture of various utensils, which had flourished in the area since the 1790s. It was out of this reservoir of artisans, workers, and traders that merchants and businessmen such as the Scovill brothers emerged in the early nineteenth century. The sons of a rich merchant and landowner, they started their button-making company with a workforce of some ten permanent workers, going on to embrace market horizons that went beyond local borders to include the rest of New England.

From the point of view of know-how, the decisive factor in the definitive transition to the factory system was the arrival in the 1820s and 1830s in the Naugatuck Valley of some skilled English workers with long experience in button making. They had been hired by observers sent by Scovill and other companies that were starting up in the area to study the production techniques and market structures of Waterbury's competitors in the Old World. Long-term contracts of $900 a year, at a time when an unskilled workman and a laborer earned, respectively, $6.00 and $2.50 a week for jobs that were unstable, were by no means exceptional for these "jobbers" or contractors. They were given this name because they took on, ran, and paid the rest of the workforce on an hourly basis with money subtracted from their own wages.

These English immigrants who were experts in button making were soon joined by others with skills in working in foundries and metal rolling, attracted to Brass Valley by its most enterprising manufacturers. Some of these manufacturers focused their business on casting and rolling, that is, the first two stages of production before the finished product. Companies like Scovill, on the other hand, continued to make buttons as their basic product, but introduced casting and rolling to restructure the production cycle—an early example of cost-saving vertical integration.[3]

Between the 1840s and 1850s, thanks to the adoption in 1833 of a protective tariff—the result of pressure exerted on the federal government by

Connecticut's businessmen—national products managed to overcome the British competition. The basic problem remained their extreme dependence on the importation of raw materials, a crucial cost factor. Only in the 1870s did the copper mines and refineries in the Lake Michigan area, protected since 1869 by a strong tariff, emerge as a production center capable of replacing the leading centers of world production, Devon and Cornwall, in satisfying the growing demand coming from the Naugatuck Valley. During this same period the rich zinc deposits in Wisconsin, New Jersey, and Missouri started to be exploited, laying the foundations for a reduction in the imports from Germany and Belgium, which had until then covered the area's entire need. The massive effect of raw materials on costs was to remain a distinctive factor in the industry. By the end of the nineteenth century they represented a share that varied between 64 and 67 percent of the total, compared to 42 to 50 percent in the iron industry, 42.5 percent in cotton, and 27.2 percent in mechanical engineering. The high quality of the product, the basically high prices, and the limited volume (the unit of weight for brass is the pound, not the ton as in the steel industry) complete the picture of the structural characteristics of the sector from the commercial point of view.[4]

Talking about brass, a reporter from a Boston trade paper, who visited Waterbury at the end of the 1860s, wrote, "but for it, the city would be no city . . . you hear it, smell it, feel it everywhere." The total identification of the city with its product was sealed in 1876, at the moment when the local delegation for the centennial exhibition in Philadelphia was being coordinated, with an adaptation of the Horatian motto—*Quid aere perennius* (What is more lasting than brass?). This motto was proposed by Frederick J. Kingsbury, one of the leading local bankers and president of Scovill. Kingsbury and other similar figures were part of a complex network of family relations (Kingsbury had married one of the heirs to the Scovill family), property strategies, and interlocking directorates, which constituted one of two factors of integration in this industrial district. Certainly it was the factor that most firmly underpinned the strong sense of stability that the entrepreneurs of the valley never failed to manifest in public. Exemplary in this respect was the board of directors of another important brass company in the city, Waterbury Brass. This was a real focal point of local interests: not only Kingsbury sat on it but also the members of the CitizensBank and the Waterbury SavingsBank and all the principal brass manufacturers.[5]

Parallel to this complex system of interlocking directorates was another instrument of integration, itself a reflection of the tremors that began to be felt in the sector in the last quarter of the century. In this stormy phase of deflation all the problems left unsolved in the period since the middle of the nineteenth century came out into the open as attempts were made to consolidate personal relations among brass manufacturing associations through pacts and formal relationships, in order to ensure price control and fair shares of the market among the different enterprises. The first cartel in the history of America, the American Brass Association (the official name given to the coordinating body of the industry in 1853), went through several crises. Three factors contributed to this. The first was the expansion of the brass market and the emergence of the first forms of competition outside the valley, which posed the most serious threats in terms of price cuts. Second, fluctuations in the costs of raw materials began to make themselves felt. These were linked to the difficulties American manufacturers had in adjusting to the international copper and zinc markets. A final factor was the highly unpredictable trends in the overall economic cycle due to the international financial situation and the cutthroat competition prevailing in key sectors such as the railroads and the steel industry. All this necessarily had repercussions on Scovill and the other enterprises in the Naugatuck Valley. Solidity and good profit margins were a constant in the reports on Waterbury's companies in the 1880s drafted by Dun and Bradstreet. Yet internal correspondence inside Scovill and between its management and other manufacturers in the area betrayed growing anxiety about the ever present combined dangers of overproduction and extreme price cutting.[6]

In the 1890s fear of sanctions under the Sherman antitrust law accelerated the drive to find a solution that would give greater guarantees of unity among producers than the rules of voluntary association in the industry, invariably broken both with regard to prices and especially with regard to production and sales quotas. Hence came the proposal to introduce a holding, a formula that was beginning to become more popular at that time in various sectors, including one very close to brass, namely the barbed wire industry. Supporters of the idea were enterprises that made foundry semi-finished products (bars and ingots) and rolled brass (plates, wire, bars, and pipes). These were all products that came in for much tighter competition than the finished products made by Scovill. Although not one of the most convinced champions of the initiative, Scovill took part in the preparatory stages of setting up the new company through two representatives. One was Kingsbury, who was by now standing largely on his own, having for years dedicated increasingly less time to the company whose president he was and ever more to playing the role of the wise old man, the arbiter of internal disputes within the American Brass Association. The other was Chauncey P. Goss, who had stood at Kingsbury's side as his number two man in the company's top management for more than thirty years, as treasurer and general manager, responsible for marketing policies in a company he had entered as assistant bookkeeper during the Civil War.

The negotiations were concluded by the end of 1899 and saw the creation of a holding with 6,100 workers and $6 million in capital—the American Brass Company—that had Ansonia, a town close to Waterbury, as its headquarters. The influential journal *Iron Age* was not exaggerating when it greeted the new company, which had a market share of some 40 percent, as a "powerful factor" on the American industrial scene.[7]

After much discussion, Scovill, which at the time had over two thousand workers and a capital of $1.6 million, decided not to join this new structure. Undoubtedly an important factor in this decision was the fear of being swallowed up by particularly strong and aggressive rolled brass–making companies. Scovill was afraid that a company that every year added hosts of new products to the buttons and lamps it already produced might be seen as a mere appendix, as subordinate to the holding's complex strategies of vertical integration. Scovill's aim was rather to reinforce the traditional niches it occupied by virtue of owning some exclusive patents. It was trying to reinforce them and to integrate them, responding to the challenges coming from a varied demand, which reflected the combined effects of increasing electrification, the development of the telephone, and the demand for ever more personalized goods and components.

The most convinced advocate of independence was Chauncey P. Goss, and it was no accident that he took over the presidency of the company from Kingsbury in 1900. Indeed, the banker had looked upon the setting up of the American Brass Company favorably, and had even participated actively in the latter stages of that operation. However, the handover of power within Scovill took place in an apparently friendly atmosphere. Kingsbury and his banks kept their interests in the company, and the banker continued to be one of the seven members of the board of directors. The board also included, besides Goss, three men the new president could trust: his eldest son Edward (who had joined the board in 1898), the secretary Mark Sperry, and an old administrative collaborator, T. R. Hyde, a member of the Scovill family and another wealthy citizen of the town.

Given the incomplete nature of the data on the company's shares, it is impossible, however, to make a clear evaluation of any possible contractions in Kingsbury's block of shares and especially the relationship that existed in this context between the old and the new president. Certainly the treasurer must have considerably increased his own quota compared to the situation at the beginning of the 1880s, when he possessed no more than about ten out of fourteen thousand shares, compared to the fourth of the total controlled, either directly or through his banks, by Kingsbury. According to some sources, already at the beginning of the century Goss possessed a quota somewhere between a sixth and a fifth of the total and continued subsequently to increase his large investment in Scovill's shares, eventually controlling almost a third of the capital by 1910.[8]

At all events his strategic line was clear. Scovill confirmed its own inclination toward what we might today call "flexible specialization." Already at the end of the 1880s a walk through his room of models turned into a "visit to a museum," given the plethora of products it contained (buttons and thimbles, mail boxes and cameras). The important thing then was to increase the company's ability to provide personalized versions in medium- and small-to-medium-sized batches. It was also necessary to strengthen the sales structure, which, to reach their hundred or so customers (artisans, builders, wholesalers, and mechanical and electromechanical companies), was already having to expand more than normal in the metallurgical sectors, through three agencies located in strategic cities such as Boston, New York, and Chicago. Finally, from a manufacturing point of view, Goss counted on the capacity, which the company had amply demonstrated, to plan and construct new machinery and equipment internally to respond rapidly to such a varied and fragmented demand.[9]

2. THE SECRET OF PROGRESS

This capacity placed Scovill firmly in the "American system of manufacturing." This expression, used in the middle of the nineteenth century by a British industrial commission on a visit to some American arsenals, summed up the surprised admiration the commissioners felt for the strong innovative thrust of production processes founded on the interchangeability of parts and on specialized machine tools. The homeland of Eli Whitney, Samuel Colt, and the less famous, but probably more important, bicycle manufacturer Albert Pope, Connecticut had made this tradition one of its distinguishing marks. This strong vocation for technological change had made the Connecticut Yankee, who was both an idealized and a caricatured version of the ordinary state citizen, into a standard figure in national folklore. "I think I'll come up with some kind of machine to make something" was the most frequent motto to accompany this image, which acquired full literary dignity in Mark Twain's figure of the "Connecticut Yankee at King Arthur's Court," who thought of himself as being capable of making "all sorts of labor-saving machinery. . . . Why, I could make anything a body wanted—anything in the world, it didn't make any difference what; and if there wasn't any quick new-fangled way to make a thing, I could invent one."[10]

Twain's Connecticut Yankee, sent off to Camelot in 1883, would have felt perfectly at home four years earlier if he had walked around the various departments of Scovill with the correspondent from *Scientific American*. In an article that appeared in the December 1879 issue of this prestigious journal, the reporter put great emphasis on the complex processes of mechanical manufacturing used in the Waterbury company. These were divided into two parts, corresponding to the two main families of products: buttons and lamps. In each section, further divided into departments, first various general machine tools were used for pressing operations (lathes, milling machines, planes, and drilling machines) and then specially designed automatic machines for making the finished product. The workforce was made up to a considerable extent of women. In the nineteenth century, brass and buttons were considered typical women's occupations, and Scovill embodied this tendency perfectly. Already in 1831 women, who were in general young, unmarried, and American-born, made up more than half of the button department. In the second half of the century, their presence increased (31 percent of the total in 1850, 34.3 percent in 1892), as the factory gradually expanded to include further departments and functions, making and manufacturing new products or new versions of old products. At the same time, the phenomena of "dilution" and mechanization advanced in mechanical manufacturing, to the point where a worker in the early 1880s was to say that "Today the trade is so broken up that it takes eight men to finish the same job" that fifteen years earlier required only one.[11]

Who invented and built the automatic machines that so impressed the reporter from *Scientific American* and that made Waterbury one of the cities with the highest annual index of new patents in the whole country? "Mechanics who were workers for the company," was the answer given by the journalist. They formed part of a varied milieu of people engaged in technical discussion and experimentation who embraced very different social groups and income brackets, but who were in some way united in their interest in innovation. This common interest is what brought together, for example, on the one hand, Blake and Johnson, manufacturers of automatic and semiautomatic lathes and drilling machines, and on the other, John Van Deusen, a mechanic and skilled carpenter with twenty years of experience. A convinced teetotaler like his masters, a regular attendee at the local society for scientific readings, fervently enthusiastic about "the bewildering multiplicity of articles that excite our profoundest admiration" of the universal exhibitions, it was the veteran Van Deusen who built the new machines. These were the same machines that would, as the Blake and Johnson catalogue assured its readers, simplify operations, thus making it possible to assign one worker simultaneously to several machines, and to achieve a previously unthinkable work rate. They were designed by a colleague of Van Deusen's, who was soon to set up his own business in order to exploit his patents directly. Likewise, the inventor of a special system for attaching buttons to clothes was a former worker who was put in charge of the Scovill button department after having started as an errand boy and risen up through the ranks. Goss himself had begun as a clerk and had gone on to become an administrative manager, but his natural talent for mechanics had also led him to patent new tools and machine parts.[12]

A varied group of technical and social figures acted then as an intermediary between the part of the factory where there was a growing division of labor and the part where the organizational pattern of industrial skills that had dominated nineteenth-century mechanical engineering still prevailed. Belonging to this group were foremen, highly skilled workers—whom the process of innovation tended to remove from direct transformation and concentrate in the tooling department—and entrepreneurs who had made their way up through the ranks.

In a company like Scovill the craft tradition was most clearly reflected in the two closely integrated factors of informality and delegation. Nothing can illustrate this point better than a letter written in October 1887 by the secretary (the third highest position in the company, after the president and the Treasurer) Mark Sperry. He was in charge of the administrative and financial management of the company and was replying to an electrical company in Colorado that had written to ask for information about Scovill's shop rules. One should remember that at that time the Waterbury company had 870 workers, making it a large-scale business compared to the 200 workers employed by an average-sized company in the same sector and the slightly more than 300 working in the steel or cotton industry at the beginning of the century. Sperry wrote:

> We have never had any shop rules printed. There is a general understanding that 10 hours constitutes a day's work, and that the hands are expected to do a day's work if they get a workday's pay. Each department is under the direction of a foreman, in whom we trust, and who sees that the hands are industrious and attend to their business. If they do not do it he sends them off and gets others. The managers of the Co. do not deal directly with the hands. They simply deal with the foremen, and if they do not like the way the hands under a foreman work they bounce the foreman and get another. We do not think printed rules amount to anything unless there is somebody around

constantly to enforce them, and if such a person is around, printed forms can be dispensed with.[13]

Scovill was certainly in good company: for example, in the Whitin Machine Works, the biggest manufacturers of textile machines, even as late as the 1890s, there was no evidence of any direct written communications between management, foremen, and workforce. However, both the engineering periodicals and the annual reports issued by various states' labor bureaus on the strike situation show that the subject was under discussion. Trade journals carried a wide-ranging debate on the subject of written regulations (about schedules, discipline, and conduct at work). Against a background of time cutting and the beginning of systematic discussions about how to increase productivity, rules were being introduced into the mechanical engineering industry, asserting the employers' right to decide on the work rate and workload for all, ignoring the traditions of the trade and exploiting the potential of the machines to the fullest. Even among manufacturers, especially those who had come up through a long apprenticeship in the workshop and who often ran medium- or small-to-mediumsized businesses, there were voices contrary to these so-called "new rules." The discussions in the technical periodicals echoed reports issued by state bureaus of labor that talked about ever increasing conflicts between company and worker on this question.

Until then the only sectors that had known any kind of formal communication between management and workers were the big cotton concerns of Lowell and the railroad companies. In the cotton industry this took the form of a printed sheet of paper that from the 1840s onwards was affixed outside the entrance to departments crammed with Yankee girls from the nearby countryside. Their gender, lack of skill, and age made them a "dependent" workforce by definition, who therefore needed protection and paternalistic, and if necessary formal, discipline. So they were told about the importance of punctuality, the need to obey their bosses, and their duty to conduct themselves in a morally correct way both at work and in the company-owned boarding houses where they slept. In the case of the railroads, on the other hand, special financial and "physical" factors (distance, security, size, and unusual synergies) had led since the end of the 1850s to the creation of complex bureaucratic pyramids that issued written instructions aimed at individual working positions. But here, too, the climate of unbridled competition for new markets in the West in the 1880s led to increasing efforts to tighten up and apply with more decision the rules regarding lines of command, workloads, and bans on drinking or smoking at work—bans that the strictest companies and officials tried to extend beyond the work sphere.[14]

The only mention of the problem of alcohol in regulations in force at that time in the metal manufacturing industry was to be found in a company that wrote that "anyone leaving the shop during working hours and going into the saloon will be discharged." This was published by the *American Machinist,* which hastened to add "the last rule is hardly necessary for machine shops under ordinary circumstances but the shop in question is located next door to a flourishing 'gin mill' which seems to have had too many allurements for the workmen." On questions such as these Scovill appeared to be willing to turn a blind eye. Even at the beginning of the twentieth century, when a newly hired engineer put up a notice in the foundry department prohibiting all beer drinking during working hours, the casters went to the head of the department, whom they knew well because they had grown up together, told him what had happened, and ended up being offered free beer for a week in the saloon across the road from the factory. Likewise, at the end of the 1880s, in his correspondence with some customers, the secretary and one of his assistants openly admitted that some orders were "at a standstill" because a worker, "the man upon whom we rely for such new work . . . being still on a drunk . . . has been on a week's racket and has just returned, somewhat the worse for wear and tear. We will try to get him to do the work next week." To make him come back they even sent him a pleading telegram: "Need you badly. When will you be back?"[15]

Obviously the management would have preferred to follow the example set some years earlier by another company in the town, where the sudden departure of a skilled mechanic, who "went off to have a good time," had opened the doors for one of his younger colleagues to obtain a permanent job. However, and here we see how only in the light of this second message from Sperry does the first one about the lack of rules take on any real meaning, there were, in a context of informality and delegation, many foremen and workers who were absolutely indispensable, especially in view of the variety of the company's products. There is ample evidence of this to be found in the correspondence between the Scovill management and its customers about trends in orders. This evidence also makes it possible to reconstruct, using the words of the company management, the hierarchy of technical authority, still reflecting the craft tradition, which we find confirmed in the handbooks and pay statistics of the time.

Pay levels and technical and professional skills in this sector, whose high levels of average pay made it relatively attractive, were distributed along a descending curve that largely mirrored the path taken by the product in the sequence from raw material to finished product. This shows how complex, and in many ways internally divided, the world of skilled workers was during this transitional phase. At the top there was the foundry caster, who earned up to $2,000 a year (a fifth of the salary paid to the top management post, occupied by treasurer Goss); his two assistants earned $900. Their tasks were to prepare the molds and to lift up the crucible with the molten metal, which the molder had to stir with a stick and then pour into the molds. The next phase saw the five-man rolling team at work, whose annual wages were between $800 and $1,070. Both these stages of production had remained essentially unchanged for decades. As we have seen, the world of mechanical engineering, on the other hand, was changing radically. This was shown by the expansion of the tooling department: Created by Scovill in 1874 with twelve workers, twenty years later the workforce had almost quintupled. The wages earned by these skilled workers ranged from $900 to $1,000, while the pay for the foreman of a normal mechanical engineering department did not exceed $900, and only the boss of a section such as brass rolling earned as much as $2,000. As for the semiskilled and unskilled hands, their wages ranged from $555 (for those working at the annealing furnaces and who had seniority) to $290 (for women working the machines). In between these there were wages of $475 and $425 as maximum rates for, respectively, male machine workers and laborers. These figures are all based on an average of about three hundred working days of ten hours apiece.[16]

The words most commonly used to describe the work of skilled workers, often not without open hostility on the part of those who wanted to see their position in the production cycle scaled down, were "art" and "secret." Of course, these were features common to the rest of the metal manufacturing industry, but here they took on a very special quality. This was due to the chemical composition of the materials, which made metallographic research much more difficult than similar work in, say, the steel industry. In the words of an observer in the early 1890s, "this brass is such a 'fickle' metal, so to speak, being at one and the same time hard and another soft." The metal, the observer continues, is at least as "fickle" as the person working it, who decides on the right temperature for the casting "on the basis of the color and the behavior of the surface of metals in the crucible," and who "thinks he possesses the only true and orthodox system of producing first-rate castings." This was noted resentfully by the authors of the first technical handbooks, who reported the "lack of regularity" in the operation, sometimes carried out at night to better shield these "mysteries" from prying eyes.[17]

Another basic feature of this organizational framework was the fact that it was less a technical than a social construct. It was the effect of some skilled workers carving out a space for themselves within a complex dynamic characterized by a combination of factors: downward exclusion, an economy made up of gestures and knowledge designed to defend the immaterial resource of skill against those higher up, and a negotiation about identity, again conducted with their masters, where respectability and responsibility were the crucial bargaining chips. Hence the programmatic declarations of the United Brass Workers' Association of North America, one of the leading brass unions in the 1880s: it reported how "the welfare of the American worker" was being "jeopardized by the importation . . . of hordes of unskilled workmen composed in the main of the dregs of foreign pauper asylums." But then in order to make quality products the new winding machines, whose usefulness was recognized by the union within a positive vision of technological progress, needed to be entrusted to the most skilled workers. Without them the process "is fraught with many difficulties [and] . . . is seldom successful." Success could be guaranteed by the relationships that were being created between employers and unions: the former were "ever more numerous" at the picnics organized by the latter, "cementing the bond which exists between them and their workmen"; hence the appeal to "let all things be harmonious and in order. . . . Work in unison is noble, in discord a disaster."[18]

In this respect Waterbury could consider itself a model city, and would have been so even without the mediation of the moderate and corporative United Brass Workers' Association, around which the collective interests and identities of this group of workers were able to coalesce. This was the picture painted by the Bureau of Labor Statistics of Connecticut in 1885. Although it did not pass unscathed the crucial test of the following year, when much of the country was hit by a wave of strikes, the "general tone . . . of cooperation" and the "community of interests" between capital and labor in the city were confirmed by the relative lack of conflicts and the limited strength of organized workers and their unions.

Admittedly, in 1886 there was a sudden growth in the presence of the Knights of Labor in the town, with six new chapters out of a total of thirteen founded between 1883 and 1893. Similarly, in the space of a few months there were six strikes, whereas the town's statistics had previously shown only two strikes over the whole period from 1881 to 1885. But both these phenomena were short-lived. The Knights soon saw their chronic problem in the city—the problem of continuity—dissolve in the more general crisis suffered by the organization nationwide, and it then disappeared completely with the 1893 depression. The number of strikes, too, was very low, compared not only to the forty-three cases in nearby New Haven, which in 1880 had three times the population of Waterbury, but also compared to the thirteen strikes in Danbury and the twenty-six in

New Britain. These two towns were roughly half the size of the brass capital and had a reputation, especially New Britain, for low levels of workers' militancy.

In Waterbury there were two strikes that involved the tobacco workers, who were, together with the building workers, the most united and aggressive segment (and indeed both struggles started with a request for a wage increase and ended with a victory for the workers). Only one conflict involved the woodworkers and five the brass industry. At the center of these struggles were mechanical engineering workers, such as polishers, or workers belonging to borderline areas between these and the foundry, such as trimmers. Both fought, and in each case unsuccessfully, against pay cuts and the "new rules" that threatened to dilute their tasks ever more.[19]

In general these battles lasted only a few days and were not reported in the local papers. Similarly reluctant to mention such events was the anonymous author of a long report published at the end of 1887 at the request of the Connecticut Bureau of Labor Statistics in a section of the annual report dedicated to "discontent among the laboring classes." The brief profile of the author and numerous features of both lexis and content that this article shared with some writings published under the name of Kingsbury during that same period suggest that behind this anonymous "capitalist and manufacturer" was the banker himself. Indeed, he was not above intervening in the debate on social questions, taking up a profoundly conservative position, which he reiterated in this article. After the conclusion of the first, short strike in the history of the company, which otherwise remained completely untouched by the fleeting blaze of militancy in 1886, Kingsbury's basic convictions about the "worker born and reared in Connecticut" seemed to have remained unshaken. In the banker's view, he was "honest, ambitious, and independent," interested in bettering his individual condition, as was amply demonstrated by the thousands of houses owned by the state's workers, and had been sensible enough never to yield to the threats and pressures of external agitators.[20]

This refrain—about the bond of experience that united the state, and especially the town, in a world beset by industrial conflict—was to be heard frequently at the meetings of the local Young Men's Christian Association (YMCA), a Bible-reading and welfare association. Precisely at this time, the YMCA, with the help of considerable amounts of business financing (in Waterbury, as in the rest of the country), was giving itself a new look. Increasingly the Bible-reading sessions were either accompanied or replaced by courses or lectures on social questions and on technical and professional subjects, music concerts, and sports programs for young men inspired by the message of so-called "muscular Christianity." The YMCA was closely linked to the Congregational church, and Kingsbury and Goss offered their financial support both to the church and the recreational association to promote leisure programs or talks on the work ethic and self-help, thus consolidating "personal contact between employers and employees" (that is, foremen and skilled workers who were either American- or English-born WASPs). These contacts were, according to the State Labor Bureau, the keystone of social peace in the town.[21]

However, cooperation and independence, the qualities attributed to and requested from the Connecticut worker, were not always virtues he or she could reconcile with ease. The fifth of brass workers (more than two-thirds of whom were skilled workers) who owned their own houses were by no means willing to accept the cuts in salary or increases in productivity at the same pay demanded by the companies. That would have undermined their ability to pay their mortgages as well as their dignity as "thinking machines," as the casters liked to call themselves. The daily life of Scovill—with its constant tug-of-war between managers and the foundry department—bears witness to these tensions. The opportunities for increasing production volumes and precision of parts created by innovations in mechanical manufacture turned the foundry into a bottleneck. It was no accident that it was the casters who, from 8 to 11 October 1887, were the first to go out on strike, as we have already mentioned. The only surviving account of this event is a letter from Sperry to a New York customer, in which he explains the delay in delivery: "We have had a strike in the casting shop and lost our German silver caster, and it is not easy to get another one immediately, as a good deal of skill and experience is necessary to make good German silver castings."[22]

A few years later the remaining casters had to accept the company's decision to abandon the organizational structure that had been in place since the middle of the century. Within this system the casters worked under orders from a foreman with whom they shared long experience of the craft for a fixed daily wage paid by the company. If they did not come from families of foremen and skilled workers, however, helpers and assistants were hired under the strict control of the skilled workers. Yet, in 1889, as a cost-saving measure, the system of contracting—which had disappeared from Scovill sometime around the year 1850—was reintroduced to replace this organizational module. In various places there were signs of a return to this system in the 1880s as an explicit way of dividing the workers' front, and in fact the unionized workers generally turned down this form of work organization.

According to the contracting system, the company paid the contractor, who took responsibility for the rejects, a sum proportionate to the sellable product calculated in pounds. The only example of a Scovill contract that has been handed down to us fails to give a very precise idea of how the mechanism worked, because it only gives the overall figure paid to the pieceworker in a year ($23,296 for 1894) and says nothing about how much the caster had to deduct from that sum to recompense his assistants. Nor does it reveal how this particular pieceworker and others, who we know had managed to reduce costs, were successful in this enterprise. In other words, we do not know whether they, like the Yankee contractors in some metal manufacturing companies in neighboring New Haven and other parts of New England, had had to cut times and the wages they paid out (for piecework) to their assistants. What is certain is that the apex of the pyramid had noticeably narrowed, with a small number of highly qualified casters working simultaneously on several furnaces (and in several teams).

What favored the final acceptance of these conditions was the 1893 depression, which prolonged by several months the seasonal employment of casters. The physical environment in which they worked was so unhealthy—amidst vapors and metal exhalations—that it was impossible to work in the warmest months of the year. The environment was also responsible for what in the following century would be identified as "brass founders' ague," a serious condition that meant the working lives of those who did this job were much shorter than those of a toolmaker or machine builder. But in the 1880s and 1890s such questions were hardly ever raised in public. The complaint that "brass work is very injurious to health. The polishers and molders are all the time breathing the vapors or the particles that are floating around in the air"—a charge made in 1883 by a skilled worker who also pointed out that the average age of casters was 35 years of age—was buried among the pages of the monumental national inquiry conducted by the Senate into the relations between "capital and labor." But it is difficult to imagine that the casters of Scovill did not take these problems into account, especially under the threat of severe economic depression, as they adapted themselves to the new pay conditions.[23]

Unable to fully appropriate the workers' know-how in order to make it into a simple appendix to the company's assets, the company allowed the craft to hold on to its secrets for the time being. In exchange, through contracting, the casters yielded in part to the economic demands of the company and thus deepened the social divisions within the world of labor.

3. A CHANGING CITY

How would a latter-day version of Washington Irving's Rip Van Winkle, who had fallen asleep at the time of the casters' strike and woken up twenty years later, have found Waterbury on his awakening? Unfortunately neither the Henry James of the *American Scene* nor the observers of the Dillingham Commission, both travelers through early-twentieth-century Connecticut, stopped off at the brass capital. Nevertheless, what the immigration commissioners noted about New Britain can readily be applied to Waterbury. In the words of the Immigration Commission:

> The introduction of machinery, with its attendant opportunity to make use of low-priced labor, has made the employment of the immigrant not only possible but highly profitable. . . . In the case of all the races the opportunity for steady employment offered by the factories was the principal cause for their coming. . . . Most of the immigrants have entered the lower, more unskilled occupations where the lowest wages are paid.[24]

What the commissioners were referring to were the so-called "new" immigrants, many of whom were Italians. Waterbury had been a city of immigrants at least since the middle of the century; even as early as then, a fourth of the population (mostly Irish, who made up 20 percent of the residents) had been born outside the United States. By 1890, over 70 percent of the inhabitants were first- or second-generation foreigners, and again the Irish made up the largest group (40 percent of the total). Having started as laborers engaged in digging work or in the construction of canals, the jobs that had originally attracted them to Waterbury, they had in the meantime moved on to working in watchmaking and brass factories. In particular, working in a brass factory paid much better and offered greater job stability. And now, after years of working on the lowest employment levels, they were beginning to make their way up the ladder and were becoming foremen.[25]

The Irish community was not only growing professionally: with their strength in numbers, their unity, and their sociability, reflected in their various churches and friendly societies, the Irish had also made progress inside the Democratic Party. From the Civil War onward, for an almost uninterrupted period of over twenty years, the town had had a Democratic mayor. Ousted by the Republicans in 1891, the Democrats returned to City Hall two years later with the help of the Irish electoral machine, which managed to install an Irish draper as first citizen.[26]

Twenty years later the Irish still constituted the strongest ethnic group, with 21 percent of a total population made up of two-thirds immigrants and their children. Next were the Italians (14 percent) and then, some distance behind, the Russians (7.7 percent), the French Canadians (5 percent), and the Germans (4 percent). The Italians had come to the Naugatuck Valley in small groups in the 1870s and especially the 1880s and had grown

TABLE 1.

Waterbury Inhabitants by Country of Birth (1890–1920)

Country of origin	Years			
	1890	1900	1910	1920
a) Native-born (U.S. parents, foreigners, and "mixed"	24,108	29,953	46,828	60,187
b) Foreign-born	8,908	15,366	25,438	29,174
Canada	1,362	2,266	1,901	2,015
England/Wales	724	982	1,243	1,086
Germany	887	1,195	1,433	1,010
Ireland	5,402	5,866	5,838	4,507
Italy	308	2,007	6,567	9,232
Lithuania	*	*	*	3,674
Poland	102	*	*	1,629
Russia	123	1,265	5,600	3,209
Others	-	1,785	2,856	2,812
c) U. S. Blacks	186	540	775	951
Total	33,202	45,859	73,041	90,312

Source: Compiled from U.S. Census Office, Census Reports Population for the years in question, Washington, D.C., Government Printing Office, 1891, 1901, 1913, 1922

* In the years marked with an asterisk, the Lithuanians were listed as Russians and the Polish as Russians, Germans, or Austrians.

visibly in numbers, here and in the rest of the state, between 1890 and 1910 (Table 1).

Following the unwritten law of "queueing" that applied among the various ethnic and social groups, they had taken the place of the Irish first as street laborers and then increasingly in the most humble tasks in the brass factories.[27]

Among the towns in the area of Sannio and Irpinia that, through an elaborate system of migratory chains, had most contributed to the Italian settlement in Waterbury were Avigliano (Potenza) and Pontelandolfo (Benevento). Beset by an endemic agrarian crisis, Avigliano exemplified what Francesco Saverio Nitti called the situation of "extreme poverty" that existed in Basilicata. Razed to the ground by the Piedmont army in 1861 because it was considered a den of bandits, and then fifteen years later the scene of the unsuccessful anarchic insurrection staged by the Banda del Matese, Pontelandolfo seemed to be the living embodiment of the long historiographical debate about the relationship between banditry, social uprisings that either failed or failed to happen, and emigration.[28]

TABLE 2.
Workforce, Capital, and Index of Machinery Investment

Year	Workforce	Capital	Index of machinery investment (1890=100)
1890	1,200	390,000	100
1900	2,000	1,600,000	375
1910	3,500	4,051,000	1,000

Source: Scovill's annual balance sheets, SCII, vols. 253, 254, and 284A, Bishop "History of Scovill," pp.130ff.

The opportunities that arose due to the increased size of companies and the phenomena of "dilution" and mechanization worked like a magnet on this inexhaustible reservoir of hands. For a company like Scovill, which saw its workforce leap from 1,200 workers in 1890 to 2,000 at the beginning of the century and 3,500 to 4,000 in the following decade, it was clearly more profitable to expand the ranks of its laborers, as long as they continued to be cheap, rather than to mechanize transport operations. Technological investments involved introducing automatic and semiautomatic machines, a move that sparked some debate among managers about the relationship between the construction and preparation costs (involving long periods and highly skilled work) they required and the resulting savings in skilled work. At level 100 in 1890, the index for these investments rose to 375 in 1899, and tripled again ten years later (Table 2). This opened up, especially for the immigrants, the opportunities to get jobs as semiskilled machine tenders already mentioned by the members of the Dillingham Commission.[29]

4. GRAPHS AND CIRCULARS

There were undoubtedly many Italians working for Scovill at the beginning of the century. The 1901 *City Directory* records the presence of about a hundred, almost 10 percent of the company's 1,150 workers (out of an overall workforce of 2,000). This represented a considerable increase from the two or three names found ten years before. Yet there is little point in looking for more detailed evidence of the presence of Italians, or more generally of other ethnic groups, in the company documentation covering that period. President Goss had other problems on his mind, and these had to do with the trend of a changing national market and questions of production and internal management. Goss, who had almost forty years of experience in bookkeeping and especially in maintaining contacts with sales agents and customers, retained his positions as treasurer and general manager, deciding to deal with the production side in person, with the help of Sperry. Both came from Connecticut Yankee merchant families, had started working for the company almost at the same time, and had followed the company's fortunes from a managerial position during Kingsbury's presidency. The Goss-Sperry duo had introduced important changes: they had standardized and brought order into the procedures to follow with customers, modified the bookkeeping system, and introduced new ways of getting through the growing number of files. Influenced by accounts handbooks and by the acceleration in communications brought about by the telegraph, in the 1880s Goss and Sperry had laid down rules about the heading and form of messages, with the aim of making them shorter and easier to file. At the same time upper management (the treasurer and secretary) started requesting basic monthly reports from the heads of the most important production sectors (the foundry, the rolling mill, and the button and lamp sections). This information was used, as in all other American companies in the last quarter of the nineteenth century, to try to monitor the efficiency of the production processes—"monitor" because in effect it was a retrospective examination of the costs of the various phases under three headings: payroll, materials, and overhead.[30]

Were these measures sufficient to deal with the radical problems of coordination and planning that the growth of the company's resources posed to a structure that, at the beginning of the century, was still largely decentralized? Was it enough to have a president-treasurer (and general manager) and a secretary to keep the plant under control without any unified technical management, a plant made up of sections and departments that hired and managed human resources on their own initiative, and manufactured and shipped their products almost as if they were autonomous divisions *ante litteram*? Convinced of the need to plug the numerous holes that various problems with speed of delivery and quality control mercilessly exposed, Goss, once he had become president, turned to his sons, Edward and John, for help.

Edward had entered the company as a twenty-year-old draftsman, with a diploma in mechanical engineering from the prestigious Massachusetts Institute of Technology and experience in the technical drafting room of a large local foundry at the end of the 1880s. In 1898 Goss put his son on the board of directors and, once he himself had risen to the position of president, appointed Edward assistant treasurer. Thus for the first time the way was clear for a graduate engineer, who was also a member of the American Society of Mechanical Engineers, to become part of the economic management of the company. One can only presume that he was not without some knowledge of the various movements in organizational innovation

(which affected engineers and, to a lesser extent, accounting experts) generally known as systematic management.

The elderly manager looked to his second son to resolve the organizational and management problems of the workshop. John seemed to have
been heading in this direction ever since his school days. In his dealings
with John, Goss had followed the common custom of many Connecticut
metal manufacturers and given his son a technical training that consisted
of equal parts of attending a leading engineering school and direct experience working in the family firm. Shortly after graduating from the Sheffield
School, the engineering school at nearby Yale, in the mid-1890s, John had
been sent as an apprentice to the tooling shop in the button department.
He went through most of the manufacturing departments, and finally
reached the position of assistant to the supervisor in the lamp section.
Then, when his superior reached retirement age in 1904, he was considered
mature enough to replace him. From that moment on, at first hardly
noticeably, but then in a way that became increasingly evident, life in this
section of manufacturing operations and gradually in all the rest of the
production system came under the influence of the rationalization initiatives of this young engineer.[31]

At the time he was attending the Sheffield School, the syllabus did not
offer any management training courses, so it is difficult to say whether he
learned anything about management there. The fact is that John Goss
introduced into workshop practice at Scovill, at least in the relations
between management and foremen, one of the principles of systematic
management that at the turn of the century was spreading in the metal
manufacturing industry: the large-scale, regular, and widespread use of
written communications. It was this innovation that most clearly marked
the break in the everyday running of the company that coincided with the
arrival of John Goss in the ranks of management.[32]

In strictly technological terms, the ten years prior to the outbreak of the
First World War saw a continuation and intensification of the aforementioned efforts to renew the stock of machinery. The introduction of automatic threading machines, electric welding, and mechanized assembly
made it possible to reduce the traditional operations of manual assembly
and finishing that in 1885 still took up about 37 percent of total work-
hours. They also made it possible to intensify the labor-saving efforts
already noted by the federal commission on labor problems at the end of
the century. The commission, for example, pointed out that the introduction of the steam press had reduced the operations of shearing and spin-
ning of the plates to an eighth of the time required for the corresponding
manual operation. No less important was the process of electrification. It

had started in 1900 with the installation of an electric generator applied to a furnace and had gradually been extended to include machine tools, so that by 1910 electrical energy had become one of the main items of company expenses.[33]

John Goss tried to insert these processes into a framework of rules and procedures in order to guarantee integration and centralized control of the factory in terms of structural organization, administration, and discipline. The two hundred or more circulars that he sent to foremen between 1904 and 1909 of which we have copies give clear evidence of this. At the same time they also reflect how, at a time when the name of Taylor was beginning to be mentioned beyond the narrow world of specialist engineering conferences and was making an impact on ever wider business circles, a company with some thousands of workers really functioned.

The first point that emerges is indeed the almost total absence of something that embodied one of the principles of Taylorism in the true sense of the word, namely detailed instructions to workers about how to carry out a particular task. On this point foremen seemed to enjoy broad margins of discretion, the result of the structural peculiarities of Scovill's products (the crucial nature of the raw materials, the high quality of the products, and especially the high degree of variability in the nature and size of the orders). Such characteristics did not encourage managerial initiatives toward the predetermination and excessive standardization of production processes carried out strictly according to Taylor's principles. These margins, however, were to be found within the increasingly narrow basic parameters that Goss tried to define from day to day in his technical circulars. Amounting to more than half of the total, these technical circulars emphasized the need to verify carefully the quality of the incoming materials, to manage them as well as the rejects with caution, to monitor whether the finished product met with the customers' specifications, and to consult with the technical management (that is, Goss himself) immediately in case of difficulty.

An additional 10 percent of messages dealt with the problems of the relations between the various company sections that arose out of the amalgamation of departments that had previously been separate and the breaking up of others into new independent departments in the wake of mechanization and the division of labor.

These phenomena and the continual enlargement of the company had far-reaching managerial repercussions. These are reflected in the circulars Goss sent out about workers' behavior and discipline—roughly about a third of the total. An illuminating example is the memo Goss sent to his father, in his role as general director. This memo shows the extent to which the mentality of management had changed on the technical level but also how it had changed even more on the management level compared to the spirit of delegation evinced by Sperry twenty years before. The main complaint was the following:

> Responsibility unchecked rests entirely upon the department superintendents and their subordinates to systematize or leave unsystematized those details which are vital to the payroll scheme and many things are allowed to pass in a department, which in themselves at the time may not seem important, but which unchecked have become precedents in that department and at present are unquestionably the cause of large losses to the company.[34]

The young engineer was referring to the internal mechanism regulating hiring, the effective presence of the workers in the department, and the payroll. According to an established practice among companies at that time, it was the job of the foreman to hire the workforce. The criteria and methods adopted in making the decision were exclusively his province, and his decision was final. As a rule, he had already decided before the candidates presented themselves at the factory gates, based on personal acquaintance and informal contacts within the various ethnic communities, and this usually brought him in a dollar or two. The official act of hiring was sanctioned by the general management office, where the foreman introduced the worker and informed the clerks about the rate of pay he had decided on and piecework or day work, depending on the type of activity. On this basis, with the use of cards, compiled every day by the department timekeeper (who depended on the foreman), which were handed in to the clerks, the office paid the weekly wage.

From the moment he was hired, the worker came under a series of overlapping gazes that were meant to supervise his movements within the company walls. At the beginning of each shift, in order to pass through the gates he came under the scrutiny of the guards, who issued him with an entry permit. Once he had reached his department, he was taken under the wing of the foreman or his assistant, who told him what to do, while the timekeeper filled in his card at the beginning and end of every day and handed it in to the managing office. The timekeeper or the foreman also monitored the workforce as it left the department, which they could only do after the siren had sounded and with a permit (or a special pass if they were leaving early) countersigned by the foreman. The worker then went back to the factory gates, where he was once again checked by the guards before being allowed to leave the factory.

Needless to say, things were a little more confused than this reconstruction would suggest. This version is made up of bits of reality and the image of reality that an external observer or someone who had never left his comfortable managerial armchair might have. For one thing, in the words of Goss, "our present pass 'system' is a farce, worse than useless." At the gates, mixed together with the regular workers, there are "many people . . . that do not belong here and find their way to the different rooms and hallways in quest of work."[35] This happened very often, especially when there was a sudden (and uncontrolled) need for hands to cope with an unexpected order. In this case the foreman "forgot" to take the newly hired hand to the office, which then saw cards arriving and claims being put in for wages by people whose names were not on the payroll. Frequently these included sons and acquaintances of a company employee, who gained entry on the pretext of delivering lunch to someone during the midday break and were then allowed to work for some time without anybody outside the department knowing about it.

On the other hand, even the regular workers were able to take advantage of the numerous cracks that opened up in the organizational structure, although the only effect of this was to reinforce the completely personal power exercised by the foreman in his own domain. He had it in his power to operate a system of bribes, to extort "favors" from workers in exchange for getting a good job or being let off for being late, leaving early, or even being absent altogether. The system also depended on the guard or the timekeeper being prepared to turn a blind eye. As Goss had perhaps realized during the years he had spent on the shop floor, and as in any case he was told by informers placed strategically in various parts of the factory, the clerks were unable to do anything about these informal negotiations that took place every day between the workforce, the guards, the timekeepers, and the foremen. Facilitated by the size and anonymity of a workforce that ethnically speaking was becoming increasingly less homogeneous and less visible, this set of practices clashed with management's attempts to go beyond the simple preparation and handing over of pay envelopes and to create a consistent system of payment that would reflect and regulate actual behavior in the factory.

First of all, John Goss wanted to tighten up the defense of the factory perimeter. The guards had to be more vigilant, and he saw a system of printed passes signed by the foremen (in duplicate, one for the department and one for the office) as the way to avoid "day hands leaving early and being paid full time . . . anyone getting in easily after hours without a record of his presence, and . . . anyone coming in who did not belong here." Second, he sought to stop the timekeepers and foremen from reaching agreements with the hands unbeknownst to the management (Goss wrote to the foremen that the timekeepers' habit of talking to the workers "presumably about their work," was "very bad for the morale of any room which allows it").[36] Finally, his plan was to introduce standardized cards with wage rates, presence, and time worked per day: everything in multiple copies and distributed to all departments, workers, and offices.

These initiatives complemented other stopgap measures such as an absolute ban on women and children bringing meals to their relatives, and were only really put into effect with any degree of success after 1908, when the death of the man in charge of the button department made it possible to unify all manufacturing operations under one manager for the first time in the history of Scovill. The post was given to John Goss, who a year later was appointed superintendent of the whole plant, a position that put him one step below his brother Edward, who in turn had just been made general manager in place of his father. Their father maintained the post of president and treasurer, while Sperry added the title of vice-president to that of secretary.

At this point, in addition to reinforcing his technical office (comprising draftsmen, designers, and production assistants), the plant manager took the most important step in bringing the process of hiring workers and especially their attendance at work under control by creating the central time office. The task assigned to this office was not, as its name might suggest, to lay down working times, which remained the prerogative of the foremen; its objective was rather to control as effectively as possible the work of the timekeepers, to prepare and distribute the time cards, to make sure that the foremen gave them back duly filled out, and to avoid any intermediaries violating too blatantly the laws passed by the Connecticut legislature in 1905 and 1907 on the question of hiring and employing minors. According to these regulations, young people under the age of 16 could be hired only on condition that they showed a certificate testifying that they had attended a state school up to the age of 14.

The difficulty of keeping those who officially did not belong to the company outside the gates and keeping legitimate workers inside the departments until the sounding of the official signal was a real problem and one that could not easily be resolved by sending out a circular or setting up a new office. This is at least what can be deduced from reading Goss's notices on both these points; even after the centralization of command in the plant, these problems continued to preoccupy the management. Rationalization came up against an apparently inexhaustible number of variations on the theme of conflict of responsibility (where one canceled the other out). If the guards were accused of giving out "collective" passes to speed up the flow of people coming into the plant, and thus generating much confusion, they for their part reported the theft of pass pads by workers who always remained unknown. Another complaint was that they were given exit permits that were "blank . . . with absolutely nothing written on them" or with suspicious signatures or that had been presigned by the foremen. This was sometimes a way of masking the tendency of the supervisors themselves to leave the department before they ought to. Even the introduction of time clocks in some departments between 1909 and 1910 was an insufficient measure to avoid throngs of people forming at the gates before the siren went off. In fact, management often received indications that the clocks themselves had been tampered with and were not working properly. To avoid lines and crowds of people Goss encouraged intermediaries to deploy techniques worthy of a Panopticon ("any foreman can see how many of his hands are gathered at the gates, by watching the gates at these hours from some point where he cannot be seen"). And then, in a rare outburst of impatience, he threatened to take "some other, more drastic measures" should these fail.[37]

These difficulties did not, however, prevent the concentration of authority on other levels, above all in accounting. In 1910 an administrative body named the general cost office was set up, again falling under the direct jurisdiction of John Goss. To get it underway the service turned to a consultant in company accounting, one of the first examples of a professional figure hired by the company on a temporary basis. With its request to the foremen to fill out preprinted monthly questionnaires about administrative trends in the department, the cost office gave a significant impulse to the introduction of an information flow from the bottom to the top. Besides this there were also the first, still very timid attempts to abandon the previously observed practice and to proceed to the preventive definition of standard costs that the production units had to maintain.

No less important was the form of these communications. They confirmed the now general use of two closely related innovations: typing and carbon paper. Typing had started quietly in the 1880s with only one typewriter in the whole factory; as it spread it also contributed to the gradual process of the feminization of clerical work (in 1910 women made up a quarter of white-collar workers in Waterbury, who in turn were less than 4 percent of all workers). Circulars, time cards, and bookkeeping reports all highlighted the importance of the new system of reproduction, which made it possible to get rid of blotting paper and letterpresses. Furthermore, when submitting this kind of information to managers and the board of directors, the company made early use of graphs and statistics, a way of presenting data that was to spread even more in the war years.[38]

Another part of the factory that saw the use of consultants during that same period was the foundry; by the turn of the century there were already several Sheffield School chemical engineering graduates working on its products. Other brass companies (albeit in the sector of semifinished products) were some years ahead of Scovill in this field. For them the need to change the rules of the game so as to be able to meet the demand for larger volume, higher quality, and faster production times had become ever more pressing. American Brass opened the way with a rudimentary laboratory in which as early as 1903 the undisputed authority in the field, the chemist William H. Bassett, introduced the use of the microscope in testing brass materials and products. A proper research department was not set up until the early 1910s. Precisely at that moment Scovill, too, created a structure capable of competing with Bassett's. The task given to the four chemists hired full-time by Goss was to force the casters to adopt written formulas for the preparation of the furnace loads. One can get an idea of the technical and management problems encountered in these efforts to render the sector as "scientific" as chemistry or electro-technics by taking a look at the section on "difficulties in brass molding" introduced by the trade magazine *Foundry* at that time. Full of references to "secrets," "mysteries," and "enigmas," it nevertheless implied a future that appeared to have already begun, thanks to experiments in two directions. On the one hand, there was the as yet embryonic attempt to use oil crucibles instead of the usual pit crucibles on which the craftsmen, thanks to loads that could not exceed 100–150 pounds (compared to the 860 pounds the new crucibles could contain), had built their ability to control the quantity produced. On the other hand, molding machines began to appear in the brass industry, which, as in steel and automobile manufacture, made it possible to save on operators and to replace traditional skills.[39]

If the offensive launched against the casters in the last decade of the nineteenth century had been carried out on a strictly economic and managerial level, without affecting the actual content of the craft, and if it could rely on crucial bridgeheads inside the craft itself in the figure of the contractor, the campaign conducted in the years immediately preceding the First World War was designed to force a technical wedge into that world. This happened through a combination of know-how coming out of the polytechnics and the willingness of some contractors to collaborate with management on the details of operating practices.

Clearly this could not be an easy process. However, it was facilitated at Scovill by old Goss's customarily shrewd use of family resources inserted and trained at the heart of this craft-based factory. The president's third son, Chauncey P., Jr., who had started as an apprentice in the foundry in 1899, was to be the man who led the transformations in that department. While working in the foundry he had acquired the habit of patiently "stealing" as much knowledge as possible, a subtle training that involved never asking direct questions lest they rouse the suspicions of the more senior casters. At the same time, he had tried to bond with the most recently employed skilled workers, those who were learning the trade and eager to get on. They were gradually transformed (as had happened to rollers in the steel industry) from contractors into foremen, becoming part of the formal company hierarchy that was slowly taking shape in the foundry. The key figure in this development was William Monagan, an Irishman who started working in 1893, at a time when, in the words of Chauncey P. Goss, Jr., "the caster . . . worked things out according to his own ideas. Everybody was happy and everybody made top wages."[40] Twenty years later Monagan was head of this department, given the position by the president's own son, who had held it himself for several years and had then become superintendent of all production processes prior to manufacturing operations (casting and rolling) under the orders of his brother John.

On the other hand, the fact that people continued to call him affectionately "Chan," a moniker given him during his apprenticeship in the department, reflects the caution with which the third of the Goss brothers acted. He tried to avoid shattering completely the long-standing "anthropomorphic" balance and mechanisms that governed the working of the department. He was, for example, the department head we saw earlier disowning the rather overzealous (and teetotal) engineer, for fear of upsetting production.[41]

This formed part of the overall picture of the advancing modernization at Scovill that was being brought about by men such as John Goss, men who were concerned with striking a proper balance between highly contrasting impulses. If on the one hand there were technological and market opportunities and constraints, on the other there was the culture to which they belonged as provincial engineers who were nonetheless abreast of developments in systematic management and who were anxious to legitimize their role in the workshop. Another feature was the established dynamics of the trade in which they themselves had to a certain extent been formed. The company needed efficiency, it is true, but, given the peculiar technological features of the brass industry, this had to be achieved within a context of flexibility and versatility, suggesting the need for a selective redefinition and not a complete abandonment of traditional organizational practices. Proof of this can be found in the tone used by John Goss in the circulars sent out to the foremen. These betrayed his intent to clarify the lines and content of the chain of command, but without forcing the situation, except in extreme cases. Especially in the early phase of these administrative and disciplinary innovations, there were frequent invitations to discuss the solutions proposed in the circular, or again emphasis was placed on the fact that "everybody's good faith is beyond all dispute." More generally, the willingness to avoid putting bureaucracy before common sense bears witness to a gradual approach to change that reflects both the structural elements of the company's product and market and the internal continuity and progressive growth of management typical of a family firm, characteristics that were far from uncommon within the industrial panorama, at least until the beginning of the twentieth century.

5. WORKERS AND THE MIDDLE CLASS

We have already caught some glimpses of resistance, highlighted even more by the very procedures designed to break it down. But were there also open manifestations of opposition by the workers? After the short strike by the casters in the latter half of the 1880s, Scovill was only marginally affected by a long national strike in 1901 by machinists belonging to the International Association of Machinists (IAM), which failed in Waterbury. In this case an immediate *cordon sanitaire* had been erected between the various companies in the valley, who exchanged blacklists of strikers to avoid the same people being rehired. The defeat only partly tarnished the image of growing strength evinced by the metal unions, with the participation of some Scovill workers during that year's Labor Day parade. With the return of prosperity at the turn of the century, not even Waterbury had managed to avoid the wave of unionization that spread across Connecticut and the country as a whole. According to the only available estimates of members, based on certainly overoptimistic workers' sources, the union organizations, led mostly by militant Irishmen, doubled their membership in the period between 1898 and 1903, reaching a figure somewhere between eight and nine thousand (out of a workforce of almost fifteen thousand for the whole city). However inflated these figures may be, there can be no doubt that, as is proved by several sources (union and public), at least in terms of the number of organizations, the city belied its reputation for a lack of interest in popular and working associations, and on a state level leaped from tenth (1890) to fourth position, immediately behind Hartford, New Haven, and Bridgeport.[42]

Of particular importance was the presence of brass organizations, which included the Lady Brass Workers (two hundred members, about a sixth of those occupied in the sector) and the Metal Polishers Union, the local chapter (with more than six hundred members, again about a sixth of male workers) of a national union affiliated with the American Federation of Labor (AFL). Both contributed decisively to the basically egalitarian efforts to control wage dynamics within the sector in a political battle whose reform orientation was particularly marked in the case of the Metal Polishers Union. Formally a craft union, in actual fact it grouped together various trades and skills, even acting in some cases as a point of reference for recently immigrated and low-skilled workers. Its goals included public control of the big monopolies, the municipalization of utilities, the direct election of all public officials, and the abolition of antiunion injunctions that the state and federal courts handed down in the event of labor disputes. In this respect the brass workers were acting in line with the efforts that labor had made in Connecticut at the beginning of the century to destroy the antiunion climate that prevailed in state public bodies. At the root of this antiunion climate was the control exercised by the most conservative Republicans on the state legislature, thanks to an electoral system that, together with that of Rhode Island, represented the most spectacular case of unequal and unrepresentative distribution of seats. An American version of Britain's "rotten boroughs," they rewarded rural areas and the conservative WASP elite.[43]

Between 1901 and 1902, the attempts to apply union pressure on leaders of the progressive forces in the Democratic Party led to four workers and reform-oriented union members becoming mayors in towns close to Waterbury: Hartford, Bridgeport, Derby, and Ansonia. But this period that saw an opening up of the state political scene, starting from the margins, was to be short-lived. Victims of the major national campaign to establish the open shop, which also reached Connecticut in 1903 in the unfailing form of the so-called Citizens' Alliances (which united the silent majority of the lower-middle and middle class to the business class), these progressive and proworker administrations were ousted almost immediately. As the century went on, the state reinforced its reputation as one of the regions of America where it was most difficult to organize unions.[44]

One Citizens' Alliance, which included in its number the Republican alderman Edward Goss and his brother John, was set up in Waterbury in 1903 on the occasion of the longest and most violent labor conflict in the city's history. The strikers were streetcar workers employed by the Connecticut Railway and Lightning Company, the most powerful state corporation in the industry, whose headquarters and capital were outside the city. The 210 days of struggle, which culminated in the killing of a policeman and the governor sending in the National Guard, ended in a crushing defeat for the workers.

This defeat had come about in a climate of extreme tension in a city that was alarmed and divided, and it set off a process that weakened and undermined the forces of organized labor, soon making Waterbury once again the home of the "open shop," where there were no union contracts. At first the Democratic city council, still led by the Irish mayor elected ten years before, had not disguised its sympathies for the strikers, but had then changed course when the conflict had become particularly fierce. The mayor's initial decision to side with the streetcar workers in their fight against a company that did not belong to the city seemed to echo the logic of coalitions set up to fight against business interests extraneous to the local community that was typical of the Gilded Age. Now as then, this precarious solidarity was strengthened by the ethnic and family ties between strikers, small merchants, and local politicians, in this case mostly Irish.

Concerned that there might be a repetition of the disorders that had accompanied the strike, the local WASP business elite, which was already lined up in the Citizens' Alliance against the "excesses" of the workers, decided, once calm had been restored, to move onto the offensive. The aim was to redesign the framework of oligarchic power in the city, founded on the coexistence of a manufacturing world firmly under the control of the Connecticut Yankees and a political system in which the Irish "machine" was firmly established. To make this change it was necessary to stimulate and accelerate the process of the "deplebeianization" of the local political structure, which had already taken its first steps with the municipal statutes of 1895 and 1902, approved on the occasion of the adjustments to the boundaries of the city decided in that period. On the basis of these statutes, real political power shifted from the local council to the mayor and the executive bodies of the Board of Finance and the Board of Public Safety. These bodies provided openings for representatives of the business and professional world as consultants working side by side with the administrators in the name of an "impartial" ideal of efficiency.[45]

This same ideal, together with the motto "law and order," was the key word in the violent election campaign during which, only a few months after the conclusion of the tragic labor conflict, the leading brass industrialists openly entered the political arena. Conducted in heated tones, with a clear social polarization that the city had never experienced before, the election ended with a victory for the Republican ticket, headed by an executive of American Brass. The losers were representatives of a ticket that had split the Democratic Party and the Irish community. In place of the party "old guard" who had governed the city since 1893, the most progressive union forces and their allies within the Democratic structure had managed to gather support around a working-class, popular formation. The watchwords used by the Democratic candidates, a fifth of whom were workers, had once again counseled and broadened the "public" strategy of the Metal Polishers. In response a sizable share of the traditional middle-class Irish vote moved over to join the ranks of the Republican Party. The Republicans also managed to draw support from traditionally Democratic

American-born workers who were worried by the specter of economic crisis summoned up by businessmen in case "anarchy" won.

Once in office, the new city council expanded the powers of the two boards of finance and public safety and further enlarged the police force, which had already tripled in number shortly before the election of the outgoing aldermen. Further, it set up commissions for the more efficient running of the local government machine. The Goss brothers were prominent in the front ranks of those on such commissions who regularly succeeded in throwing out proposals for the municipalization of utilities such as electricity. In short, the 1903 elections shaped the basic framework for the political future of the city. And even "respectable" Democrats, those who were less involved in the world of organized labor and who returned to power in the city in 1907, were forced to operate within this framework.[46]

In the meantime there was a steady decline in union strength. Here, more harshly than elsewhere, the Metal Polishers suffered the effects of the interminable jurisdictional disputes that, in the wake of the constant modifications in workplace organization, put them in opposition to other unions, and the result helped to favor the employers' objective of establishing an open shop. By 1908 this union, which at the turn of the century filled halls with "enthusiastic meetings" and participated actively in the impressive annual Labor Day demonstrations, numbering in its ranks also Scovill workers, had disappeared from the City Directory. On the other hand, the Directory did reflect another phenomenon worthy of attention: the sharp increase in the number of ethnic organizations of "new" immigrants, outstanding among which were the seventeen Italian mutual aid societies. The city's first celebration of Columbus Day in 1910 saw them marching in the parade, headed by the small class of merchants and professionals that was becoming established in the community. This middle class in the making drew from the main local newspaper a judgment about the group that differed sharply from that expressed in the press at the beginning of the century. The Italians were no longer the unruly fellow countrymen of the brigand Musolino (whose alleged presence in Connecticut had aroused fear and apprehension also in Waterbury at the beginning of the twentieth century) and the anarchist Bresci; they had now become "a temperate race," capable of producing lawyers and doctors.[47]

Besides such professionals, in a network of interclass relations of solidarity and hierarchy there were unskilled industrial workers and laborers who belonged to the various ethnic societies. Here they found the first bulwark against unemployment and poverty, a factor of cohesion second only to that supplied by a family extended to include old and new friends tied to their towns of origin. Ethnic societies could, at times, exist side by side with the union, but more often they preceded and survived them. If one scans the local directory, one comes across Scovill workers among the founding members of the first Italian organization in Waterbury, the Vittorio Emanuele Society, even as soon as the early 1890s, long before the arrival in the city of the Metal Polishers. Twenty years later, the union had disappeared, but the Vittorio Emanuele Society still numbered various wage earners among its officers. Likewise, there were workers from various brass companies among the officers of the Society Operaia Aviglianese of Soccorso when it was founded in 1910.[48]

The City Directory also points to another possible alternative to union organizations, namely mutual aid funds, affiliation with which was incompatible with membership in a union and which were constituted in the various companies with funds set up using money deducted from pay and redistributed in the event of accidents, illness, permanent handicap, or death. To belong to this scheme a worker had to have had a certain minimum number of years of service with the company, while the payment of benefits depended on good conduct and regular payment of dues.

Written statutes, normally drafted by the managers of the fund and promoters of the initiative, in agreement with the company management, laid down the criteria for the allocation of funds. They were framed by foremen, skilled workers, or clerks, the social groups that had started these schemes and for whom they were originally intended. The interest for the company lay in tying the best resources to the firm, as is proved by the fact that 72 percent of thirty-seven mutual aid plans set up in Connecticut by 1890 were for skilled workers. Modest or even nonexistent was the direct financial contribution supplied by the Waterbury companies, or indeed the 70 percent of companies that had programs of this kind in the country by 1907. Generally they limited themselves to making available accounting and managerial services. It is also true that significant amounts (on the order of several million dollars) were invested in this field only by large corporations such as U.S. Steel, which were engaged in broad programs of welfare: health care, social work, integration, and social control. While their concern for the problem of accidents and corporate mutual aid certainly grew out of an awareness of the dangerousness of the manufacturing processes, what was more important for the corporations was the need to consolidate their presence in working communities throughout the country, to ward off the possibility of autonomous organization by the workforce, to tie the most valuable human resources to the company, and to foster a positive self-image. The beginning of public relations and welfare campaigns served to protect the large corporations from accusations leveled at them by middle-class reformers and to preempt the first attempts being made in various individual states at public regulation of the question of compensation payments to workers.[49]

In the Naugatuck Valley only American Brass, the company closest in size to the national corporations, at the beginning of 1913 supported a sickness fund that enjoyed a limited financial contribution from the company with a formal pension scheme, whose application was, however, always at the discretion of the management. The plan had two thrusts. On the one hand, it provided for old-age pensions for executives and clerks who were at least sixty-five years old and who had worked for the company for at least twenty-five years. For manual workers with at least fifteen years of service who were unable to continue working because of accident or illness, disabilities pensions were planned. With this measure the company preceded by a few months the law on compensation for accident also passed in Connecticut in 1913, a few years after states with more advanced social legislation such as Wisconsin and Massachusetts.[50]

In the first decade of the century Scovill limited itself to allowing its workers to collect fees for a mutual aid society in which the company apparently had no say. Between 1905 and 1907, however, there are traces of pensions and insurance coverage paid out, on an absolutely discretional basis, to long-serving foremen and workers. An informal principle of seniority, as a criterion for constructing a still very primitive internal labor market, was the rule the company observed during the 1907 recession. A circular sent out by Goss asked the foremen to take into due consideration individuals' needs and company seniority in drawing up the list of redundancies that in the seven-month period between November 1907 and the following June cut personnel by 15 percent.[51]

Goss, however, went no further than this, remaining true to his conservative and highly individualistic version of social Christianity. This he had acquired during his long spell in the YMCA, where he continued to be a leading officer. Honest work, self-help, and the ethic of success, for which the lecturers at the Waterbury YMCA sought precedents even in Epicurus and confirmation in the "industrious" Indians on the reservations, represented the cornerstones of his social vision. His aversion to practices that smacked of paternalism was too strong for him to even think, at least for the time being, of systematic welfare programs. In his view they threatened to drain the company's finances, weakened individual initiative, and would undermine the direct line in the hierarchy.[52]

Nevertheless, precisely the need to actively involve intermediaries in the process of redefining privileges led Goss to come to terms with an emerging instrument in the armory of welfarism, the one that probably least made him feel that he was betraying his convictions. In various parts of the country attempts were being made to close the ranks of the control structure, and on company initiative foremen's associations were springing up that addressed the question of the technical training of foremen and their use of their free time. In 1911 one such association was set up in Waterbury, at Scovill's direct competitor, Plume and Atwood. Goss had already been thinking about the possibility for some time before this. And there were indeed questions of numbers, ethnic composition, and internal structuring of the supervision apparatus that raised serious problems about how to run such a structure as it underwent rationalization.

In 1913 there were about 150 to 160 company employees who were in charge of sections, departments, or rooms, at a ratio of $1/24$ with the rest of the workforce. By comparison, in sectors that were about to become mass industries and where command was more incorporated into technology, such as the automobile industry, the ratio was $1/30$ and, in some departments, $1/50$ (although shortly after this Ford also realized that, without a strengthening of the intermediary structure, not even the assembly line could alone guarantee the desired levels of production). Scovill's lesser degree of technological integration, its flexibility, and a certain persistent empiricism (a factor linked to the predominance of the personalized production of medium- and small-to-medium-sized batches) were coupled with a large number of control figures, who were moreover split by profound professional differences and differences of company seniority and pay. Although they all wore white collars, the daily pay of intermediaries ranged from eleven dollars for the section head with most seniority, to two dollars for a recently appointed foreman. To underscore the very different levels of employment stability, moreover, section heads and department foremen were paid a fixed weekly wage (like clerks), while assistant foremen, although they enjoyed better conditions than those of the unskilled workers under their control, received hourly (or daily) pay, just like the workers (or like the lower clerks, such as timekeepers).

Another factor was the process of formalizing the structure set up by Goss. He had gone back to the old tripartite division into sections, departments, and rooms, codifying it and adapting it to changes in the organization, and this had the effect of heightening his subordinates' perception of internal distances. Not to mention the fact that, besides the WASPs and the Northern European immigrants, who continued to represent the majority of the intermediaries, there was an at least 30 percent contingent of Irishmen.[53]

What measures needed to be taken to ensure that "in manufacturing company of the size of Scovill . . . with all its various subdivisions of Departs, Rooms, etc. and the large number of Superintendents and Assistants," there was "a united and enthusiastic feeling amongst all of its responsible men"? In the two-year period 1908–9 Goss talked about this subject on several occasions with a group made up of six of the most trusted foremen, almost all of whom had been with the company for at least twenty years. They were headed by Alfred J. Wolff, who had started working in the company's tool room as an adolescent in the early 1870s, together with his brothers Adrian and Lucien. A member of the municipal school commission, captain of the Connecticut National Guard, and a mason, at first sight Wolff seemed to embody the typical profile of an Anglo-Saxon foreman or skilled worker in the 1880s. In other words, his language and religion could easily have made him pass as a member of the upper management on a local council, in a Congregational church, or in the YMCA. The only difference was, however, that even in the case of a senior worker in the company the picture had become more complicated, and seniority in the company no longer mirrored directly or was reinforced by ethnic or religious ties. A French immigrant, Wolff was not a member of the YMCA because, like Monagan (another member of this select group of the company's faithful), he was Catholic and preferred the social activities of his own parish. Not to mention the fact that, conversely, John Goss had now started to pursue status in the public sphere in a way that removed him, outside the workplace, from those directly under him. Although he maintained his family's proverbial reserve and sobriety, unlike his father he began to move in the new circles reserved for the local elite, such as the country club and even the New York Railroad Club. He had been introduced into this club by his marriage to an heir of a railroad family, the same interests that had routed the streetcar workers in 1903.[54]

The situation was further complicated by the paradox that, faced with the reality of ever increasing social distances, the horizons and objectives of integration pursued by the director of the plant could not stop, as they had in the past, at those directly below him. Through men like Wolff, and especially Monagan, John Goss sought to reach the lower hierarchical echelons, where it was more likely that the assistant foremen and the laborers could join forces informally against top management on a day-to-day basis. After all, they were the people who represented the company in the eyes of the many immigrants—or "birds of passage"—who arrived like parcels sent from Pontelandolfo, attached hinges by machine for a few years at Scovill, and then went back to their home country and possibly even turned up again a few years later outside the factory gates, without having left any trace in the company. Goss expressed the wish that a "united and enthusiastic feeling amongst all its [Scovill's] responsible men . . . could be aroused to a greater degree probably in all its employees."[55]

All this forced management to look for a channel of socialization between the various levels in the hierarchy directly rooted in the company. For Wolff and his colleagues who formed the small group convened by Goss, this was an occasion to formally seal the tacit pact of loyalty to the company once more, receiving twofold assurances: upward, in terms of the redefinition of their managerial role, and downward, or horizontally, in terms of the internal problems of power and mutual adaptation that the new shape of the supervision structure entailed. Passing through the intermediary stages of putting on an annual dinner and outing, the foremen then went on to create the Scovill Foremen's Association (SFA) in 1913. The aims of the association were typical for such bodies: "To promote more intimate intercourse and social relations amongst its members . . . to promote a broader interchange of ideas amongst its members and other employees . . . to train and instruct its members in technical and shop matters . . . to promote the material interest of the members and their employers." Predictably, this programmatic founding document ended with a note of thanks to Goss, included officially on the board of the SFA, and to the management as a whole, who had always encouraged the foremen's initiatives, granting them time and providing them with premises for their meetings. Besides the "ordinary" members, in other words the foremen and their assistants, the statute also referred to "associate" members, or "any manager or person recommended by the management," and "honorary" members, "any person recommended by the general management of Scovill . . . because of long time and faithful services or because of unusually valuable services to the Co."[56]

The affiliation procedures established a dividing line that largely corresponded to whether or not an employee wore a white collar. They were designed to bring together the various functions of supervision, further filling their ranks of supervisors, along the axis of seniority or professional merit, with engineers, clerks, and even some of the more skilled workers. Strictly excluded from this circle by fundamental differences in roles, pay conditions, and job security, coupled in turn with ethnic stigmas, were laborers and semiskilled workers. In 1914 semiskilled workers earned on average $10.00 to $11.00 a week. This was more or less the same as a recently appointed assistant foreman (whose chances of keeping his job in the event of a crisis were at any rate higher, not to mention the opportunities he had of progressing in his career), but much lower than the salaries of clerks (around $17.00, which was also the average pay for a toolmaker) and naturally lower than the salary received by the foremen, which ranged from a minimum of $19.50 to a maximum of $48.00.[57]

The SFA thus lent fresh symbolic meaning to already established factors of status and tended to reinforce the dependent middle-class identity of all the "old hands" without formal qualifications. It was people of this ilk that Edward and John Goss, exactly like Henry Ford, preferred to put in positions of control and technical assistance, reserving graduates and holders of diplomas for use only in the chemical laboratory. In this way the rigor and sense of responsibility of a craft culture deprived of its collective class moral code had to transform imperceptibly into the professional pride of a class of supervisors and engineers who had grown up largely in the workshop. In Goss's view this pride needed to be nurtured with the awareness—based on a mixture of conservative social Christianity and engineering science—of the technical and social service that this productive (and intellectual) class performed for modernity, placing itself midway between capital (identified with the world of finance) and labor (identified with hands and machine tenders). This was the subject that the superintendent (and co-owner) of the factory, whose knowledge of manual labor was based on practical experience and who liked to call himself an industrialist rather than a capitalist, would regularly choose as his theme in the opening addresses he gave at the annual foremen's dinner held by the SFA.[58]

Through rituals like banquets and outings the company organism began to come closer to the new forms of middle-class consumption and social behavior that were emerging in the metropolises, while still exercising the discretion and prudery of generations that had grown up in Victorian provincial America. In New York the new middle class of clerks and middle managers found in their free time a partial compensation for the decline in their independence and property-owning capacities, for the blurring of ethnic divisions, and for the tensions generally provoked by the appearance on the scene of the first independent professional women. On a more modest scale, as befitted the provincial context, such mechanisms, which offered both identification and differentiation, probably operated at the SFA annual dinner. With its menu printed in gold letters promising cream of celery aux crotons, it initiated even the most uncouth to the exoticism (in language and food) that had found its way onto middle-class tables in the last twenty years of the nineteenth century. The leisure time picnic was a further way of lending a shared meaning to otherwise divergent occupational and existential paths. There was sufficient space under the company banner for the nostalgia of farmers from the valley who had ended up in the factory, the echoes of nineteenth-century outings for families, craftsmen, and workmen, the memories that Irish ex-laborers who had become foremen retained of militant excursions to the countryside around Waterbury organized by the Knights of Labor.

Was all of this successful? Judging by the incomplete figures regarding membership and attendance, the answer would seem to be, yes, it was. This at least is what the managers of the company thought. The 130–150 people who gathered together for the first outings, or the 180 foremen, clerks, and old people who revolved around the SFA, organizing a growing number of initiatives throughout the year, gave Goss the impression of a "nucleus," as he called it at the end of 1914—precisely at the moment he signed the agreement with Bethlehem Steel for the enormous British order. Necessarily limited, this was, however, a force around which it was possible to form an organization capable of containing the centrifugal thrusts and to meet yet another unexpected challenge thrown down by the market.[59]

I I

Fuses and Profits

1. A DIFFICULT ORDER

Scovill's prospects at the beginning of 1914 were far from bright. At the annual general meeting in early February, Edward Goss presented a balance sheet that, as he anticipated in a letter to his father, compared badly with the "magnificent results" achieved by American Brass, a copy of whose final balance the general manager had just received from the president of that company. The difference between the profits obtained by the two companies corresponded in no way to the difference in capital: whereas the ratio in terms of capital stood at one to three ($5 million for Scovill compared to $15 million for American Brass), in terms of profits it was one to five ($402,000 for Scovill compared to $1.9 million for the holding). As a matter of fact, Scovill's profits for the financial year that had just concluded were the lowest that Goss's company had recorded in the previous seven years. Nor did the forecasts seem to encourage excessive optimism, at least for the immediate future, in view of the overall situation of the national economy. The winter of 1913–14 had witnessed a recession that had led to cries of panic for the fourth time in forty years, starting with the "Great Fear" of 1873. In New York alone the number of unemployed had reached 300,000 in 1914. We have no figures for Waterbury. But what is certain is that Scovill dismissed more than four thousand workers in the space of a few months, between November 1913 and the following spring, reducing personnel by 11 percent. Considering that this figure corresponds almost exactly to the difference between the percentage of female workers in the period prior to the recession (31.2 percent in 1912) and the percentage of women employed in 1914 (21 percent), it is logical to deduce that it was essentially this section of the workforce that was affected by this drastic reduction.[1]

Yet by the spring the company's situation was already beginning to show more comforting signs. Orders started to mount thanks to well-established markets such as gas and electric lamps. Good news was also coming in from a field where the company was less at ease, involving orders that had to be subjected to exhausting technical inspections: For the first time Scovill had managed to deliver three lots of cupronickel to the military arsenal in Frankford, Pennsylvania, without any snags. Despite the small scale of the orders, this was an important test for the company to have passed, because it added an extra chapter to the long history of experience in the military market, which would only a few months later be the reason why Bethlehem turned to Scovill when it received the British war order.

The company had been in contact with the army ever since the first war fought by the newborn republic against its former mother country, the War of 1812. On that occasion Scovill had learned at its own expense that the first and most serious difficulty facing an army or navy supplier was how to obtain payments before any delay proved disastrous for the company's cash flow. In that particular case, at the end of the conflict, instead of the figure agreed upon for the buttons supplied to the government, the brothers who had founded the company had received a message in which an official apologized for temporarily not being able to pay them and urging them to exercise "the mild New England virtue of patience."[2]

Other problems, more directly linked to the distinctive features of the military market—monopsony, the chronic irregularity of demand, the subordination of production needs to highly complex variables such as diplomatic strategies and national defense—had emerged in the 1880s and 1890s. This was the period when the new federal strategy of strengthening its military forces, starting with the fleet and the garrisons in coastal cities, had brought Waterbury its first orders for components of arms and munitions. These orders had led to interminable disputes about the interpretation of contracts and constant revisions in the technical specifications requested by the client. Both arose out of the vicious circle that had been created between the company's limited technical experience in this field and the chaotic decisionmaking processes of the military machine. Called upon to operate in an area that technologically had yet to be firmly established on an international level, and constantly under the threat of sudden cuts in funding, the military multiplied and projected onto the outside— onto the suppliers—technical deficiencies and both long-standing and more recent rivalries between the various departments of a central civil service still in search of its identity. It was indeed difficult for the federal authority (and the military structures) of a growing country like the U.S. to establish its identity, for while it was increasingly projected toward the outside commercially, it was still highly isolationist in its political imprinting.[3]

The other factor was that, despite all these problems (which could lead to small-scale orders dragging on for years), there were undoubtedly positive technical and organizational repercussions that benefited the company and its civil production, thanks to this encounter with such a special market segment. These repercussions were to be felt even in the anomalous case of the United States, where military expansion was extremely limited compared to the formidable arms race underway in Europe. Here, too, the size and the technical tolerances of the orders, the exclusive regime of monopsony and the absolute priority of the operations, their position at the intersection between the most diverse manufacturing processes and techniques—all these factors made the military the point where the most advanced lines of scientific and organizational development converged. As had already happened in the steel industry, which had seen the genesis of some technical solutions that were to dominate civil production from the constant clash between means of offense (artillery) and protection (armor plating) for the war navy, in the quarter century prior to the First World War, Scovill, too, profited greatly from the complicated and often frankly arbitrary procedures of quality control imposed by the military arsenals. It was pressure from army experts and the specific manufacturing needs of grenade fuses and cupronickel that introduced the company to the laboratory analysis of materials and products. The Frankford arsenal not only provided Scovill with the first laboratory on which it relied both for war production and the manufacture of goods designed for the conventional market, but also with specialized personnel trained to closely supervise the company's military production. Sent to Waterbury during the Spanish-American War, some of these engineers established a relationship of such trust with the company that they were still numbered among its consultants in the fall of 1914, when Bethlehem asked Scovill to draw up a feasibility study for the order that the steel company had started to negotiate with the British high command.[4]

The order required an effort that far exceeded the hundred fuses that constituted Scovill's daily production capacity in July 1914 or the five thousand pieces whose manufacture, due to the continual revisions of specifications requested by the Frankford arsenal, had taken four years (from 1905 to 1909). Bethlehem asked for the delivery of two thousand units a day, equally distributed between eighteen-pound cases for pieces of artillery and twenty-one–second time fuses for grenades. Having received assurances from military consultants about the possibility of finding adequate solutions to the technical problems the order entailed, Scovill submitted the terms of its offer to Bethlehem. This was sent back very shortly afterward, complete with the new figures of the agreement that in the meantime the steel company had reached with the British government. The agreement made reference to a daily volume of parts that still had to be settled in detail but that was significantly higher than the amount Scovill had agreed to provide, and with much tighter delivery dates. So when it came to signing the final agreement, the Waterbury company made no attempt to hide its concerns about its ability to fulfill its commitment.

The management's main worry was that, judging by the manufacturing plans, accepting the order would require, in the words of John Goss, "a tremendous and immediate enlargement of the personnel," with "the danger of breaking down the existing good morale of its organization by the acquisition in so short a space of time of such a large group of workers as would be necessary." It was "too great a risk to assume that such a large number of workers could be assimilated without seriously threatening the stability of the organization." However, after much uncertainty and discussion, the management of the Waterbury company reached a compromise with the steel company. Scovill would not accept the order in its entirety, but promised to double the daily load quoted in the provisional tender, in other words to supply two thousand pieces of each of the components requested.[5]

Among the factors that led the Scovill management to make this commitment was its conviction that it could rely on the group of company veterans (at the end of the war it was discovered that there were about 250 workers, including managers, with at least twenty-five years of service in the company) gathered together largely in the SFA: a group of middle managers and workers, many of whom had received their training during the execution of military orders at the time of the Spanish-American War. This meant that they had been part of the technological and organizational development of the company as it had expanded, in the space of fifteen years, from 2,000 to 3,500 workers. For these veterans, too, the extent and pace of the change that came over Scovill from the beginning of 1915 onward was quite remarkable. One need only consider the first sum of money allocated by the board of directors in November 1914 for the construction of new buildings made necessary by the British order. The figure of $200,000 represented almost half the entire sum of investments that had been made for the same reason since the beginning of the century, and in a short space of time more than a thousand square yards of new manufacturing areas had been constructed, ten times the figure for the whole of 1914. As these operations went on, the factory increasingly gave the impression of being a permanent construction site, and in the space of a couple of years (1915–16)—with walls pulled down and buildings hurriedly put up to make room for new departments—more than a million dollars were spent on expansion.[6]

Inside the new factory buildings there was room for a stock of machinery whose construction had required capital that shattered all records in the company's history. From $60,000 in 1912, that figure had increased sixfold by 1914 and two years later had reached $3 million. With the exception of threading machines, gradually used for the production of the smallest fuse components, the machines were, at least initially, not completely automatic. Faced with such a massive, sudden demand, the management decided to avoid "deliberately the use of automatic or special purpose machinery," which would entail excessively onerous costs and preparation times that were too long if they were to meet the deadline for the military orders. It was easier and less costly, as far as the production processes allowed, to take time with fitting out completely automatic machines and in the meantime to assign to more general workers the task of looking after machines that were easier to set up, in the hope of profiting from the relatively favorable situation that had come about on the labor market in the winter of 1914–15 for those few businessmen who had begun to benefit from the war orders.[7]

In general, the initial repercussions of the war in Europe had been anything but positive for an American economy that was trying to come out of a recession. The outbreak of hostilities was followed immediately by the freezing of international financial transactions and the blockade of trade between the two sides of the Atlantic, conducted up to that point primarily by the British and German fleets. This led to severe personnel reductions in all the main New England factories in August and September of 1914. However, by the end of the year the sectors most directly connected to war production, such as factories producing arms and explosives, showed strong signs of recovery, followed gradually by canned-food manufacturers and shoemakers. After falling during the 1913–14 winter recession from 3,600 to 3,200, personnel at Scovill rose again to 3,500 in the fall of 1914, and when the British order became operative, an exponential growth began that brought it up to 5,600 workers in June 1915. By this time the number of pieces to be delivered to Bethlehem every day had reached twelve thousand, exactly triple the amount laid down in the first contract signed with the steel company.[8]

2. HEALTH IS THE MAIN THING

Conditions on the labor market soon became much more problematic for companies than might have been expected in the winter of 1914–15. In a very short space of time the war resulted in an enormous reduction in transatlantic migration, with the number of those arriving at America's ports falling by three-fourths (from 1.2 million to 300,000) between 1914 and 1915. This fact, together with the effects of the war orders, quadrupled the demand for labor over supply. A significant echo of the national scale of the phenomenon even reached those in the Naugatuck Valley, who were not regular readers of *Bradstreet's,* the financial journal for Wall Street brokers from which we have taken the figures just given, but read instead the more modest *New Haven Corriere del Connecticut.* This paper started to publish advertisements in Italian in which, for example, the leading company in the rubber industry, Goodrich of Akron (Ohio), promised "easy, clean, healthy and continuous work all year round. Good pay . . . the most beautiful rooms in the world of work," in Akron, "one of the best cities in the United States."[9]

We do not know whether Scovill, too, published messages like this outside the Naugatuck Valley. Certainly, when it came to hiring, it basically continued to rely, as it had in the past, on the informal mechanisms of matching supply and demand provided by the various ethnic communities, where internal, and no longer transatlantic, migrants ended up. A sizable number of new employees in 1915–16 came from other towns in Connecticut, from the state of New York, and from Pennsylvania, as part of a vast process that in the space of a few months, between the winter of 1915 and the following spring, led to a 20 percent increase in the city's population.[10]

Let us take a look at what happened to one of these newcomers, who had started working at Scovill in February 1916, as he himself testified orally. Pasquale De Cicco was fifteen years old when he arrived in Waterbury at the beginning of that year. He had spent four years in Brooklyn, where all his family (parents and six children) had gone to join Pietro, the eldest child, who had emigrated to the United States some years before from a small town near Pontelandolfo. Pasquale had come to the brass capital at the suggestion of the second-born child Gus, who had moved to Waterbury in the fall of 1915, attracted by "the awakening of our factories,"[11] as the main Italian-language weekly paper had called the boom in orders and jobs that the war in Europe had brought to the brass factories. Gus, who was already working for Scovill, found Pasquale the job thanks to a contact he had with the head of the employment office, whom Gus had known as one of his customers in the barbershop where he worked during his free time, in order to supplement the meager wage he earned in the factory—little more than two dollars a day.[12]

The employment office was a novelty that had been introduced at the time of the war orders, as part of a more ambitious attempt to continue further with the organizational centralization that John Goss had embarked on in the previous decade. It is not easy to reconstruct this process, because the whole series of circulars sent out by the factory super-intendent in the period from 1915 to 1917 is missing. On the basis of later company documentation and material to be found in local history archives, however, it is possible to establish that, shortly after the signing of the agreement with Bethlehem, Goss, in order to integrate their proce-dures and resources, united the cost office and the central time office, set up at the beginning of the 1910s. The new office was called factory accounting and comprised about thirty clerks, who then numbered fifty in the space of a year. It was from within this office that, in the winter of 1914–15, in the face of the first demands for an expansion of the work-force, the employment office was carved, a small structure originally com-posed of a full-time head and some other clerks lent part-time from the accounting department. The employment office performed functions apparently not unlike those that, on a more informal basis and together with many other administrative tasks, were carried out by any given clerk in the old management office at the time when John Goss had started his career as an executive. It is true that this new office could hire workers directly, as we have seen in the case of the young De Cicco; more often, however, for the time being it limited itself to administrative certification. In practice, the process of looking for and selecting personnel was left largely up to chance, that is, in the hands of the foremen. Despite the sim-ilarity in their names, there was a big difference between this office and Ford's employment department, which in 1914, in agreement with the so-called sociological department, administered hiring and the sophisticated pay system—the famous five dollars for an eight-hour working day.[13]

Undoubtedly, Scovill cut a poor figure compared to these avant-garde phenomena. Likewise, apart from some initiatives in the field of health and accident prevention that we shall come to later, the company had none of the welfare programs (work environment and accidents, cafeterias, profit sharing, pension schemes, recreation, lodgings) initiated at the turn of the century in companies that were pioneers in labor policy, such as National Cash Register (NCR). These welfare and social control programs had at times arisen out of the ashes of or as an extension of nineteenth-century paternalism, and progressive attempts were made to fit them in with the production side and the ongoing processes of engineering rationalization. By 1914 they were recorded in at least 2,500 companies.[14]

Before the war there had been very few companies with an employment office. It was the conflict in Europe, with its attendant labor market prob-lems, that persuaded both those companies that already provided some welfare services to their workers and those that had yet to do so to create structures of this kind. The companies with longer traditions of active labor policy started to form departments for the selection, training, and management of personnel, departments that then frequently went on to incorporate welfare under the largely interchangeable names of employment department, industrial relations department, or, for the time being, more rarely, personnel department. In most cases, though, the hiring department was often as rudimentary and limited in form as the department at Scovill. Here, at any rate, as its own personnel gradually increased, the new service introduced and developed the practice of gathering information about the workforce in a way that had no precedents in the company in terms of the information covered or, at least as far as the managers' intentions went, in terms of the systematic nature of the surveys conducted. As is clear from some of the periodic checks of this information carried out by Goss and his direct collaborators, management's objective was to gain a more accurate picture of hiring procedures, the criteria used by the foremen for assigning jobs, and the payroll.

In fact, at times the continual growth in the scale of operations frustrated the expectations of the management, confronting them again with well-known problems. Discrepancies, in some cases substantial discrepancies, emerged between the personnel figures registered in the individual departments and those in the possession of the employment office, whose data bank relied on a rapid interview conducted by the clerks with the newly hired workers. Their answers were copied onto a blue file comprising various sections, each corresponding to a particular piece of information: name, age, address, nationality, marital status, knowledge of English, previous working experience in general and at Scovill in particular, and reasons why the candidate had left his or her previous job or had left Scovill. When called to the employment office, De Cicco duly replied to all these questions, even though he lied about the most important point: his age. Although he was actually fifteen he declared that he was a year older in order to avoid trouble with the law on the employment of children under the age of sixteen. Once the formalities had been completed, he was sent to a foreman who gave him a modest, "boy's" task to perform: assembling small components.[15]

Among the many questions that the newly hired workers were asked, the one about nationality needs to be emphasized. The war had made manufacturers, as well as the majority of institutions in the country, aware of the ethnic problem. Before then, and only in the three- to four-year period immediately prior to the outbreak of the conflict in Europe, only three welfare pioneers—U.S. Steel, International Harvester, and Ford—had taken steps in this direction. The first two had set up English courses as part of a large-scale series of campaigns to inform workers about accident prevention and health care in the work environment launched between 1908 and 1910 to ward off industrial conflict and to parry the accusations leveled by the Progressives against the corporations.

The conviction that too many accidents, attributed in principle to workers' carelessness, could be due to the fact that many foreign workers did not understand English had persuaded International Harvester to introduce into the world of manufacturing a model of accelerated language learning devised by the YMCA, the social welfare body that was acquiring a new role in the efforts to integrate new immigrants. Extended to U.S. Steel three years later, these courses were adopted by Ford in 1914 as part of a package of labor policies that saw the simultaneous appearance of the aforementioned sociological department as well as a department for safety and health and the first statistics on workers' countries of origin. However, it must again be emphasized, these pilot schemes were notable exceptions before 1915; that is, before, under the effect of the war in Europe, militant nativists and social workers who had for some time been pressing for the assimilation or more or less forced "Americanization" of the newcomers stepped up their campaign and urged companies to pay attention to the origin and language of their workers.[16]

The North American Civic League for Immigrants (NACL), an organization that embodied the most deeply entrenched hard-line tendencies in the movement for the assimilation of immigrants, reached Waterbury precisely in the period 1914–15. It is impossible to say whether Scovill's decision in 1915 to start to collect statistics about the ethnic composition of the workforce (see Table 3) was determined by the NACL's propaganda, which at that time was still on a very small scale. At any rate, initially the process of amassing data did not correspond to any systematic company program aimed specifically at this important segment of a workforce that was growing at a remarkable rate. Nevertheless, the problems of these workers slowly

TABLE 3.
Scovill Workforce by Nationality (1915–1918)

Year	Total	USA %	FRA/CAN %	GER %	RUS %	IRL %	ITA %	LITH %	POL %
1915	6,400	38.2	5.0	1.8	1.1	11.6	18.8	7.0	11.8
1916	11,000	36.0	3.8	1.1	8.9	9.7	19.5	6.3	5.4
1917	12,800	40.0	3.4	0.9	9.0	8.5	19.3	5.8	4.3
1918	12,900	45.0	1.4	0.5	8.0	5.9	18.4	4.0	2.7

Source: Annual Report of Accident Statistics 1918, SCII, case 34.

TABLE 4.

Accidents (1914–1918)

Year	1914	1915	1916	1917	1918
Workforce	3,600	6,400	11,000	12,800	12,900
Accidents	4,800	11,300	17,500	15,700	15,800
Average numbers of accidents per employee	1.33	1.78	1.59	1.27	1.22

Source: Annual Report of Accident Statistics, 1918, SCII, case 34.

started to acquire a certain visibility. As had already happened in more illustrious companies, this occurred in the context of a drive to promote health and safety at work that the management had initiated shortly before the arrival of the war orders and which had subsequently been intensified.

The hiring process already involved not only the creation of a file containing personal and work data but also a further one that recorded some elementary health information about each employee under six headings: general health, hernia, epilepsy, heart trouble, convulsions, and varicose veins. When De Cicco was hired, this information was collected by a clerk from the employment office without any medical examination being carried out. However, there was a fully equipped sickroom for workers already employed by the company that was given the official name "plant hospital," with a part-time doctor and three full-time nurses (two women and one man), all paid by the company.[17]

Equipped with a number of beds to be able to attend immediately to victims of accidents or those who had taken ill and were awaiting transfer to the local hospital, the sickroom had been set up at the beginning of 1914, expanding the emergency room that had already been in operation for some years. Anticipating a similar initiative by American Brass, the company management of Scovill had coupled the creation of this structure with a campaign of information and accident prevention based on leaflets gradually introduced by the SFA throughout the factory. By 1915 the expansion of personnel, the first signs of an increase in the already high accident figures (Table 4), and the fear of the possible consequences of dealing with explosives forced the management to reinforce this campaign through a series of short courses for foremen and notices posted around the departments warning about the danger and giving instructions about how to treat certain materials or use particular machines.[18]

What made Scovill take this step? The main reason was the state law on compensation for workers passed in Connecticut in May 1913—as usual much later than other more progressive states. If correctly applied, the law threatened to create numerous problems for the company. Although it was, like most measures on this subject passed in the country, formally "optional," it could in fact force companies, which otherwise risked long and costly legal battles, to reimburse workers in a certain number of cases for accidents and also for some occupational illnesses. The seriousness of these illnesses had leapt to the attention of national public opinion on the pages of an important Progressive magazine two years earlier, before the Connecticut law was passed. A well-documented article had appeared in *Survey*, illustrating the true "secret of the brass caster," as the title announced. The "secret" was not, as had been argued during that same period in reports about the "mysteries" of processes of the foundry in the pages of *Foundry* or *Brass World*, technical in nature. The real secret was the serious health problems that afflicted these workers. On the basis of a detailed study the writer demonstrated how an occupational illness, the so-called "brass founders' ague," explained the low average age of these workers. Of the 1,750 brass casters examined by him in Chicago, only 1 percent were over fifty and 15 percent over forty. The article ended with a question: "What sort of industry is this in which nearly six-sevenths of its followers are too old at the age of forty?"[19]

It is important to emphasize both the name of the author and the date of his article. The author was Emery R. Hayhurst, one of the leading experts on workers' health in the Progressive Era, who fought valiantly side by side with the workers in their battle for health. The date is significant because that same year—1911—the National Safety Council (NSC) was set up, an institution supported by corporations like U.S. Steel and International Harvester to oppose, through the authority of engineers, efficiency experts, social workers, and company doctors, the work of people like Hayhurst. Hayhurst was part of a reform front that included both judges who, since the beginning of the century, had increasingly taken the side of the workers in accident cases against companies heard before state courts, and legislators in the individual states who put forward bills for the compensation of workers involved in accidents such as the law passed in Connecticut.

The objective of the NSC, whose directives Scovill followed in its own accident-prevention policy, was to preempt the reformers and give the initiative back to manufacturers through large-scale information campaigns focusing on prevention and on-the-spot post-accident measures. The collective question of workers' health was in short transformed into an individual problem of safety, where accidents were basically caused by the carelessness and ignorance of the individual worker. The individual had to be educated

to avoid accidents, surrounded by an environment (of machines and systems of ventilation and lighting) that would counteract his or her inborn
tendency to make the wrong gesture or movement, and the worker had to
be cared for as well as possible in plant hospitals in the case of less serious
accidents. When it became absolutely inevitable, he or she would be com-
pensated, but all attempts would be made to exploit any of the numerous
subterfuges that the tangle of laws, often the result of laborious legislative
engineering, soon offered. The result was that in the early 1920s it was discovered that on average workers, in the event of absence due to injury,
received only a quarter of their wage and not the third stipulated in the various state laws.[20]

However, this does not alter the fact that in the period between 1909
and 1913 the sentences issued by the state courts that were partially favorable to the workers and the passing of the laws on accidents generated in
the employers a fear of soaring costs and an increase in industrial conflict
and legal offensives by the reformers compared to the period prior to the
so-called workmen's compensation laws. This fear explains the remarkable nationwide success enjoyed by the NSC and its massive Safety First
Campaign.

The NSC logo stood out on the accident-prevention posters hanging in
the various Scovill departments and in the boxed advertisement that
appeared in the *SFA News,* the four-page monthly bulletin for foremen and
managerial staff whose initial circulation, in May 1915, was 350 copies. At
the time there were only a few dozen company bulletins in the entire country, but they spread remarkably during the war, and at the height of their
popularity there were over four hundred companies publishing bulletins.
In some cases they took the explicit form of a message from the management to all the workers, a message warmly recommended by a managerial
magazine "to offset the reading of the millions of biased labor union and
Socialist periodicals." In other cases, as at Scovill, at least at the outset the
bulletin was designed as a vehicle of communication for managerial staff.
The idea came to one of John Goss's assistants. One day he had come across
a publication of this type by General Electric, and he suggested that the
board of the SFA follow this example to encourage "a broader interchange
of ideas among its members."[21]

In its first year of publication, at the top of the "educational" subjects
that occupied the largest portion (43 percent) of the total space (Table 5),[22]
we find the programs and results of the Safety First Campaign. A year later
they took up 17 percent of the space in the magazine, less than a page an
issue.

TABLE 5.

Space in *SFA News* Devoted to Various Purposes (1915-16)

Purpose	% of space devoted
Education	43
SFA news	22
Inspiration	19
Humor and misc.	15
Specific work advice and orders	2

Source: Jo Ann Yates, *Control Through Communication: The Rise of System in American Management* (Baltimore, Md.: Johns Hopkins University Press, 1990), 193.

So it was no accident when, to illustrate the plant hospital in December 1915, the bulletin made an exception to its iron rule of four pages a month and added an additional two with a packed photographic supplement. Mainly it featured pictures of medical equipment, stretchers, and medicine cabinets. In the only photograph of people at work, against the shining white of the equipment, the beds, and the doctors' and nurses' uniforms, barely broken by the overalls of a worker receiving medication, one can make out Miss Nora O'Brien, social worker and superintendent of the pool of nurses. In the same issue O'Brien told the story of the origin of the Safety First Campaign on a national level and explained its intentions at Scovill. Its origins were varied: "The growing socialistic spirit . . . the efforts of various groups of charity workers who have taken the cause of the dependent working man's family to the legislature . . . wider humanitarianism in the people at large." There were no doubts about the objectives: "the effective prosecution of safety work." First of all, "the plant must be always kept in good physical conditions"; "physical conditions," added O'Brien, meant "everything related to machinery, buildings, and the material conditions under which the work is done." Second, "the human element must be educated, trained and disciplined."[23]

Some months earlier John Goss had dedicated one of his rare articles in the bulletin to this topic, pointing out that,

Safety and haste do not naturally combine. Avoid haste unless the method is well thought out and planned so that it is safe. Safety work, being a study of the right and orderly way of doing things, will increase efficiency and aid economy but will not jeopardize the worker. Remember that while every man is hired to do some particular work, the safety of himself and his fellow-workmen is more important than that work. And if a workman has a *preventable* accident, to that extent is he unsuccessful in his job, and to that extent is his foreman unsuccessful in his foremanship.[24]

That this was not simply rhetoric is demonstrated by the fact that, pragmatic man as he was, Goss agreed to double in one year the personnel costs for the company sickroom, increasing them from $7,600 to $15,000 between 1915 and 1916. In support of this policy he later cited the figures for the number of accidents per employee, which did indeed show that there was a slight but steady decrease during the war period (Table 4).[25]

However important these figures may be, there is a risk that referring only to the number of accidents diverts attention from the impact that this campaign had on day-to-day life in the company and especially on its organizational and communication mechanisms. To appreciate this one needs to read once again the efficiency-oriented statements by O'Brien and Goss in light of what the body in charge of the safety program actually did. It bore the rather pompous name of Permanent Consultative Committee for Safety and was made up of about fifteen people: members of upper management such as Goss, all the department heads, and some foremen. The very fact that it had been set up merits attention because it inaugurated a responsive system of integration between top management and intermediaries, which cut across the hierarchical and functional divisions on the basis of a concrete topic of general interest. This system was later adopted for other problem areas, from research and development to work planning. Of particular importance is the way in which the Committee used the vast amount of data about accidents. The most serious accidents were collated in an annual report that gave a detailed reconstruction of how they occurred, adding a proposal for avoiding a repetition of the event (recommendation) and the results of applying this proposal (action). By way of example, let us take a look at the final report for 1916. In that year the Safety Committee took strict disciplinary measures, for example when it dismissed an Irishman who had been working for the company for only a month in the annealing furnaces, together with a colleague who had thrown a fuse at his head, causing lacerations and contusion and putting him on the danger list for seven days. Sometimes it undertook no action. This was the case with a French Canadian, who had been working in the plant for a year and had lost two-thirds of the phalanx of his right-hand index finger (and had been off work for over a month) because he had "deliberately placed finger between tools while machine was in motion." The same happened regarding the only fatal accident recorded for 1916 out of a total of about seventy serious accidents mentioned in the Committee's annual report. The victim was a Lithuanian, who had been working at Scovill for barely a week when he was hit by a metal bar while he was checking the working of a forge. In the case of the French Canadian, the members of the Committee simply expressed their conviction that "this experience would be a good lesson to this young man." In the case of the Lithuanian it had to acknowledge that it was "unable to solve how the accident happened" and left everything in the hands of the coroner.[26]

In most cases, however, there was a prevalence of detailed recommendations and actions that were then turned into rules and standardized procedures. These ranged from technical measures to repair or reduce the danger of a machine to instructions to foremen about how to use a tool or a material or how to choose the right workers for a particular task. The numerous accidents due to the hasty setup of a machine or the insufficient training of the workers show how the workforce was called upon to make up for technological and especially organizational deficiencies. These were widespread in the factory, where by mid-1916 a personnel of almost eleven thousand people were producing forty thousand pieces a day (and thus the piece/worker ratio had increased by 100 percent since the previous June). To get around the problems of training, a large number of the steps taken by the Safety Committee took the form of written instructions given directly to the workers, when necessary in their own language, or oral instructions, given through an interpreter who repeated how the work was to be done "until foreman is satisfied that they can do the work satisfactorily."[27]

The use of interpreters and written instructions in the language of the immigrants (for whom sometimes even the signs about dangerous work processes were translated) were the only measures adopted at this time that took into account a section of the workforce—those who were foreign-born—who at no point during the war represented less than 50 percent of personnel (Table 3). The main difference between Scovill's safety program and what was being done at U.S. Steel and Ford lay in the absence of any kind of systematic plan aimed at the immigrant workforce. Apart from this, the Waterbury company tried to integrate this initiative as far as possible into its production dynamic. It was driven in this direction by the labor-intensive approach adopted to deal with the war orders. As these mounted, and with the related increase in personnel, Scovill started doing something about workers' health not so much in order to neutralize the state law on accidents but in an attempt to regulate, maintain, and restore the human factor that had always constituted the primary and fundamental driving force behind the company.

This human factor was, however, always subordinated to objectives and instruments that management saw as absolutely essential. These included, for example, working hours, piecework, and overtime. In truth, the arrival of the war orders seemed at first to intensify the limited moves toward a reduction in working hours that had emerged to curb attempts to organize unions in the first decade of the century. At that time Scovill, following the example of other companies in the area, had made an average reduction of three hours a year (fifty-five in the summer and fifty-eight in the winter, paid the same as sixty hours) in the working week of sixty hours, a week sanctioned by a state law of 1887. To attract workers and in view of the broad profit margins guaranteed by the British orders, the management decided in 1915 to extend the summer working week to the rest of the year, which meant closure on Saturday afternoon and equal wages for sixty hours. Soon, however, Saturday afternoon closing was done away with and, by introducing compulsory overtime, the effective working week of at least fifty-eight hours was reintroduced, although with increased wages as a result of overtime.[28]

When one looks again at the statistics for accidents in light of the data about the working week, what strikes one particularly is the haste with which the company bulletins dismissed the relevance of the timing of accidents, a factor that scientifically more qualified occupational doctors considered crucial. The bulletin reported on this question in summary fashion in May 1915, pointing out how the data were by no means clear-cut and how the limited available documentation pointed to a concentration of accidents between 9:00 and 10:00 A.M. According to the bulletin, the cause of this was presumably the fact that "the operators reach their highest speed at that hour," that is, after a couple of hours of working, "slowing up more or less from then on until the day's end."[29]

In fact, more careful surveys made in the following years would indeed confirm the correlation between speed and accidents, but would also show that the fatal hours for accidents were in the latter half of the day and in particular toward the end of the day. What counted was the interaction between speed and effort, which pushed up the accident curve at the same moment as production levels fell. As was shown by a comparative analysis between Scovill and a factory with eight-hour shifts started in July 1917, the decisive factor determining tiredness in workers was the number of working hours, which the Waterbury management considered an element that could not be changed significantly—and if so only increased.[30]

In view of these constraints and prejudices, the health problem became for the Scovill management a means of investigating the production structure not unlike longer established operating tools such as disciplinary and technical-organizational circulars. There were, however, two important differences: first, on an apparently neutral terrain that was of prime importance for all levels of organization, heads of department and foremen received, with the backing of some of their representatives, detailed instructions about how to use and train operators; second, on the same terrain, management started to address the workforce as a whole, at the same time taking care not to undermine the foremen.

Safety initiatives were indeed targeted at everyone: they involved the thousands of injured workers, the growing numbers of workers (4,600 in 1915, 11,000 the following year) given free health care by the company for ailments not connected to accidents, but whose treatment was now considered a determining factor in prevention, and the workers from the most varied areas who saw their departments plastered with notices. In the spring of 1916 the SFA and the management decided to introduce on these notices the cartoon figure of a typical worker, designed to point out mistaken or dangerous behavior, or more often to refer to the most serious accidents that had occurred over a given period (six months, a year). The name chosen for this graphic representation of the average worker, who bore the stylistic features of a skilled nineteenth-century worker complete with apron and hammer in hand, was John Scovill. This combined the last name of the founder, which was still the company title, and the most common English first name, which also happened to be the name of the omnipresent factory superintendent. To make it absolutely clear at whom the message was aimed, the caption under the drawing added that he was any company "laborer, machine operator, mechanic, etc." This figure was given the ungrateful task of showing in a lighthearted way how many accidents occurred to the various parts of a worker's body. Thus the drawings that appeared in the company bulletin and were reproduced on posters hung up in the departments indicated the numbers of accidents recorded in 1915: a thousand to hands, eight thousand to eyes, two hundred and fifty to the head, each number connected by an arrow to the various parts of John Scovill's body.[31]

Some workers seemed to be convinced that Scovill was a real person. This is reflected in messages sent, in the period between the fall of 1914 and the following spring, to the management by the "new" immigrants to ask for work or to complain about some injustice or other suffered at the hands of the foremen. The addressee of their broken English was at the beginning Mr. President Scovill, who then during the course of the letter became simply "Mr. Scovill." On the accident prevention posters that name was no longer only associated with a physical locus, and possibly a boss, but also with a small, old-fashioned, and stylized double of the worker who was there to remind them what they should not do and what would happen if they failed to comply with the safety regulations (without, of course, explaining how to reconcile these rules with the work rate imposed by piecework). It probably barely attracted the attention of workers whose first concern was to cope in an environment that struck the outside observer for the "stale smell of gas and metal . . . the darkness . . . the noise," amidst machines crammed into narrow spaces. This was, however, the first, embryonic element in a series of tools that personified the company and more or less consciously invited those working there to identify with it. And more were to come. They grew in number parallel to the circulation of the company bulletin, which increased almost tenfold (three thousand copies) in 1916 compared to the first issue (whereas the workforce had only doubled), confirming that the change in title in June that year was not simply a question of form. Although the abbreviation SFA was still clearly visible, the original name of *SFA News* was replaced by *Scovill Bulletin*, a magazine that was open to and targeted at all company workers.[32]

3. THE SCOVILL GIRLS

The spring of 1916 did not only signal the appearance on the scene of John Scovill. One of the assembly departments where the majority of workers were women (where men represented under a sixth of the workforce) also saw the founding of the first company association made up of ordinary employees. It was named the Scovill Girls' Club and was composed of about thirty young female workers.[33]

Unlike the situation in numerous other arms factories throughout the country and in particular those in Bridgeport, a city close to the Brass Valley, the presence of women was no war-induced novelty for the Waterbury company. And in fact, although the war saw a gradual upward trend in levels of women's employment (Table 6), it never brought Scovill back to the figures registered in the nineteenth century (31 percent in 1859, 32 percent in 1887, 34 percent in 1892) or shortly before the conflict.

However, these figures were considerably higher than those found in the rest of the metal manufacturing industry involved in producing war goods: the figure of 26.3 percent women employed at Scovill in 1918 was exactly double the average for the metal manufacturing industry in the country as a whole, and in Bridgeport, the level of female employment in the metal

TABLE 6.
Female Workforce (1914–18)

Year	1914	1915	1916	1917	1918
Female workforce (%)	21	24	25	26.9	26.3

Source: SCII, vol. 254 and case 36.

sector with the highest percentage of women—small arms—did not exceed 19.7 percent. This confirmed that brass was high up on the list of women's industrial jobs, and this position had earned the sector a fixed place in manuals on women's jobs.[34]

Before the war, brass factories had been no exception to the established gender stigmas common throughout other industries, both in terms of occupational content and working conditions. Women found posts at the lowest levels in that "other" expanding factory (assembly, work on semiautomatic machines, packaging of products) that coexisted with the highly skilled workers in the tooling departments and with the "thinking machines" in the foundry. What it meant in the years immediately preceding the war to do piecework, which had always been the means of payment most commonly used for women's work, is explained in the words of Modestina De Angelis, an Italian girl who worked for Scovill between 1906 and 1911. The department she started working in as a fifteen-year-old girl, surrounded by girls who had emigrated from small towns in the area around Benevento close to her own town, "was like a family." Less familial but certainly very common was the way payment was handled by an Irish foreman: "The boss would come over with a watch and put a price, a piecework. They made it so that they lowered wages when you produced more."[35]

If one looks at the 1910 federal census (which only covered people over the age of sixteen), one can only deduce that this department made up of Italian girls was an exception, unless one assumes that a large amount of underage work was going on that has left no trace in any other source. For in that year only 10 percent of women who were born in Italy and immigrated to Waterbury at over sixteen years of age were registered as part of the official workforce. In line with a more general tendency in the country that was linked to the traditional forms of control exercised by Italian families on their female members, this was the lowest figure among the various ethnic groups. The share rises to 33 percent in the case of Lithuanian women, 37.5 percent for Irish women and French Canadians, and 50 percent for women born in the United States of mixed parents (an immigrant and a native-born American) or native-born parents.

It is impossible to say how many of these immigrants worked for Scovill. The first (incomplete) surviving statistics about the ethnic composition (and marital status) of the female workforce concern 1920–21. It is, however, possible to draw a profile of the age of the women working in the company during the war period. The 1918 company census shows that almost 68 percent of employed women were under thirty, 27.1 percent under twenty, and the rest (40.7 percent) between twenty and thirty. The same census also shows how during the war, besides occupying almost all the semiskilled or unskilled positions, women, at Scovill as elsewhere, continued significantly the process of the feminization of office work to which we have already referred as being in its early stages at the beginning of the 1910s. Out of 489 clerks in the central offices (3.9 percent of the overall workforce), there were 246 women as compared to 243 men.[36]

However, there are no systematic figures that might allow us to clarify two crucial points. The first is whether the percentage increase in the female component between 1914 and 1918 (Table 6) was made up of newly hired workers or whether at least some of the third of the women (approximately 10 percent of the company total) who disappeared from the payroll between 1912 and 1914 came back to work in the factory. The second point is whether the majority of the newly hired were workers with some experience of wage earning in the prewar period or not; in other words, whether Scovill can confirm the hypothesis put forward by Maurine Greenwald and Alice Kessler-Harris, suggesting that the war led not so much to a massive influx of female workers as a shift by women toward better-paid men's work. What is certain is that the number of women hired by the company greatly exceeded the figures given in Table 6. One must not forget the high levels of turnover, which in 1916–17, for example, was at a monthly average of 10 percent for women. Undoubtedly there are examples here of women with factory experience prior to the war, which in some cases must mean experience working for Scovill. However, both in the company documentation and in the oral records collected between 1979 and 1980 by a team led by Jeremy Brecher and kept at the Mattatuck Museum in Waterbury, there seems to be a prevalence of cases of young women workers for whom the war period was their first wage-earning experience, perhaps after some experience of working at home as dressmakers. Dressmaking was seen as good training for the dexterity required in the use of small machines operated by handles or pedals with which the operations of pressing and finishing fuses were carried out. For example, Caroline Nardello was the daughter of a dressmaker and a dressmaker herself who ended up in the factory as an eighteen-year-old during the war, doing the job of checking and assembling fuse components.[37]

It would be wrong to undervalue the transition to wage earning from a type of domestic work more specifically linked to the brass sector: the assembly of buttons, brooches, and thimbles. Very common among immigrant women workers, especially those who were married, this form of "black" work experienced a downturn during the war, falling by almost four-fifths between 1912 and 1918. Someone who did this kind of work was Fenka Szyncltanscha, a nineteen-year-old Pole who, when she was hired in October 1915, explained that she was tired of doing this kind of work at home and that she preferred the factory where she hoped to earn more. According to the Lithuanian worker Hap Laski, it was the war that brought the girls and married women who belonged to his ethnic group to Scovill for the first time. This is also what happened to unmarried girls like Rowena Peck, Sarah Cappella, and numerous others interviewed by Brecher and his colleagues.[38]

There is no evidence that Scovill experienced the problems about the type of uniform the women had to wear that were recorded in a Bridgeport factory. In that case only after a long tug-of-war was an agreement reached between the management—who wanted to extend the customs established for the men to all workers—and the women workers. The Bridgeport women refused to give up at their workplace any distinctive signs (of gender and generation) or the taste for fashion and the consumer patterns that, within the limits imposed by their wages, the flapper vogue was beginning to encourage even in proletarian quarters. At least in the less dirty or heavy departments or working positions, few were willing to yield on the question of shoes: most refused to wear on the shop floor a pair older than those they came to work in. As for uniforms, made fun of by the men when they first appeared wrapped up in overalls, the female workers forced a compromise from the head of personnel. What they had to wear was "a large apron . . . something after the sort that is worn in laundries."[39] Such aprons are clearly visible in the photographs of women workers at Scovill. But the affinities with their colleagues in Bridgeport obviously did not stop at their uniforms. All of them had to live with the system of piecework, which, as before the war, was the most widespread form of payment at Scovill for women's tasks.

Exactly what Modestina De Angelis reported—the cut in the rate applied to simple piecework—proved to be a normal practice. In September 1915 the company bulletin stepped in against this practice, urging the foremen not to reduce the rate, but rather to fix it more "reasonably" from the beginning, so as not to have to speed up the work rate or reduce the basic pay. Here one can see the efforts of the recently established Piecework and Planning Committee to advise the foremen, whom the company formally allowed full discretion in running piecework, to adopt methods of remuneration that would be less open to manipulation (or, basically, less understandable to the worker) than simple piecework. Already familiar features in the metal manufacturing industry since the end of the nineteenth century, these incentive schemes involved remuneration that decreased automatically in proportion to growth in productivity.

Incidentally it should be recalled that the Piecework and Planning Committee was created in Scovill's best empirical and "co-optive" tradition, without engineers or grand proclamations, as the term "planning," with its clear Taylorian stamp, might imply. What John Goss did was to remove from direct production a forty-year-old foreman whom he trusted, who had been among the founders of the SFA and who had in the course of over twenty years of working for the firm seen most parts of the factory. He made him a kind of "jack-of-all-trades" who, with the help of an assistant foreman and a skilled worker from the tool room, examined remuneration and planning systems and "suggested" to the foremen how to improve them.[40]

The changes in the system of piecework, the first women assigned to skilled work, the very different type of components that had to be dealt with and tasks that had to be performed, the much greater size of the orders, and the structure and the manufacturing spaces—all these were new elements in the women's departments that had not been seen before the war; however, they should not divert attention from the many continuities in women's duties and working conditions. The new piecework reproduced and continued the "normal" speeding up of working rhythms already present in the old system. Even at the moment of their greatest expansion, skilled women workers amounted to less than 1 percent of total women workers; the rest were semiskilled and unskilled operators who checked the pieces to be assembled, mounted them by pressing and finishing, manually and by machine, and packaged the finished products. These were the tasks that the women had to concentrate their attention on if they wanted to get up to the $2.80 that was the average pay for piecework in 1917 (a rate of pay that brought them closer than ever before—and herein lies the real difference from the prewar period—to the male workers, who only earned forty cents more). The word "attention" is used deliberately, because the idea comes up constantly in the oral testimony of women remembering how at the small presses "you had to watch for your fingers . . . a lot of people had their fingers cut off; you had to watch it." This applied especially, for example, to the women responsible for cleaning fuse covers. The cover reached the women worker on a conveyor belt, and she took it off and put it into a machine that she operated manually with a handle: five turns in one direction, five in the other. Then she took the piece out of the machine and placed it in a container: four thousand pieces a day, adding up to a total of forty thousand turns on the handle.[41]

When faced with such an image it is very tempting to label these women workers as simple machines, always prepared to give up their lunch break and capable of stopping only at the sounding of the siren. This was the view taken by the Connecticut Department of Labor in its portrait of the typical woman worker. But this picture proves to be very reductive when one looks more closely. For one thing, the women workers were able to defend themselves, both individually and collectively, against their bosses and against the obsession with producing more at all costs. This eagerness took hold, for example, of one of the many social workers and intellectuals who at that time put on overalls (or an apron) to see how what one of them called the "underbrush" lived. Her curiosity led her to a brass factory and one day she decided to hit the pedal of her press 8,500 times in a morning "to see what could be done if I went to the limit"; Cornelia Stratton Parker described how "I ached body and soul . . . by that time I had been on that one job several days and was sick to death of it." Her work companions told her, "You're a fool to work the way you do. . . . Where d'ya think ya goin' to land? In a coffin, that's where," and Stratton Parker gave up her career as a brass worker after only a few days. The large numbers of women workers (some months it was almost all of them) who left Scovill, in a monthly turnover rate of 10 percent in 1917, did so of their own accord, but presumably not for the same reason as their more illustrious colleague. They left because they wanted to look for better employment, where they could earn more, as can be shown by the first company surveys on this point carried out between the end of 1917 and the beginning of 1918. From 1916 those who remained, like their male colleagues and the clerical workforce, benefited from the fixed monthly bonus, which amounted to 10 percent of the individual wage, paid by the company in the hope of preventing the continual drain of the workforce. This measure landed Scovill in the pages of the *New York Times;* an article, which was duly repeated a year later, praised its extraordinary profits for the financial year and the rich dividends paid out by the company (Table 7).[42]

No less important than the "individualistic strike"—the expression used by a federal government report to refer to leaving one's job in search of better fortune elsewhere—was the capacity women showed to conserve their forces collectively. Women used mechanisms that a federal report by ergonomists who visited Scovill in 1917 called "stereotyping of output."

TABLE 7.
Capital, Turnover, and Profits in Millions of Dollars (1914–1918)

Year	Capital	Sales	Profits
1914	5.0	7.1	0.5
1915	5.0	24.2	6.0
1916	5.0	56.2	13.4
1917	5.0	58.5	9.2
1918	5.0	43.5	2.1

Source: Bishop, "History of Scovill," pp.137–59, and the company balance sheets in SCII, vol. 254.

The department where fuses were drilled gave a "notable" example of this, to use the words of the experts, which was worthy of the techniques of self-reduction of production that had always been attributed to skilled workers. During the whole of the week when they were being tested, each female operator on the night shift produced exactly the same number of holes as her colleagues, either speeding up, to catch up with unexpected pauses caused by machines or conveyor belts breaking down, or slowing down; they timed everything with such precision that the federal observers described it as "unnatural."[43]

Departments like this not only created social relations in the factory that above all took the form of tacit agreements between the women workers to self-regulate energy expenditure, but they also came up with the initiative for founding a company club for women. Behind this idea was the need the women felt to extend to the small amount of free time they had available the forms of exchange and communication that had evolved inside a group made up of peers or even slightly older women in the same department. It began on a small scale, as an exclusive arrangement involving a dozen or so working companions who started to meet in each other's houses in their spare time, organizing parties and outings together. All (or at least almost all) of these pastimes were organized under the aegis of the Irish community. The majority of the girls belonged to this community, and some were daughters of Scovill workers. One such Irishwoman was Miss O'Brien, the sickroom matron to whom the young women turned for advice about how to organize their first party that was to be more than a family meeting. O'Brien helped them find the local hall of the Knights of Columbus, a national Catholic organization engaged in mutual aid and religious and civil propaganda, founded in nearby New Haven almost forty years earlier by Irishmen, who still largely ran it.[44]

Given the success of the initiative, the matron, in the typical spirit of the world of social work from which she came before starting work at Scovill, suggested to the girls that they enlarge their horizons. They should be "having in mind several hundred Scovill girls who, due to congested living conditions, were deprived of wholesome diversions." As in other centers of military production, and in fact even more so, in Waterbury difficult living conditions and a lack of opportunities for socializing awaited the considerable number of young women who came from outside the town in search of work.[45]

When O'Brien suggested that the girls in the assembly department look around, she was probably thinking of the example of companies such as NCR, where at the beginning of the century there was already an association of women workers with five hundred members, or Westinghouse, where the person in charge of welfare activities had helped some women workers to set up a women's club in the early 1910s. So she got their foreman interested in the cause of the women's free time. He too was Irish and had been a founding member of the SFA. He helped the women workers to find premises and possibly also a small financial contribution. The result was a formal body, the Scovill Girls' Club (SGC), which, following in the footsteps of the SFA and with its encouragement, aimed to "establish better acquaintance among the Scovill girls" and "to promote mutual service" in the company and the community.

Only a few months later, after a broadly based campaign in the various departments, the SGC was able to boast hundreds of members of various nationalities, although first- and second-generation Irish continued to make up the majority. Their calendar of events for the fall of 1916 was packed. Among many others, there were plans for a series of monthly dances, culminating the following February in a St. Valentine's Day grand ball; projects for fund-raising; sewing clothes for the children of deceased workers or those unable to work because of accident; and a play entitled "The Triumph of Rebecca" directed by the foreman's wife.[46]

The most important immediate commitment, however, was to make the SGC, only a few months after its foundation, the center of the most important company social event of the year 1916, the first open-air party that extended to all workers what had been up to that time the simple foremen's picnic.

4. A FAMILY

The scene that presented itself to the local reporter who went along to the city park in Reidville one sultry Saturday afternoon in August 1916 was, at least judging by the account that he submitted to Waterbury's main newspaper, quite unusual. For years the park had been the setting for the noisy festivities and fireworks in celebration of Independence Day. For some time, at least for the latter half of the nineteenth century, among the general populace this event had lost any residual sacred aura it might have had and had become, in Waterbury as in the rest of the country, "more a carnival than a somber ceremony." It was therefore not surprising that with the encumbering memory of such precedents in mind, the reporter could not believe his eyes when he saw a crowd of 7,500 people that "never carried itself so decorously, whether in the games or at the various amusing diversion, in word, speech and act." Amid this impressive gathering of Scovill workers (half the entire workforce, it was estimated) and their relatives, gathered together for their first annual "get together day," "not a word was spoken there which mother, or sister or little brother might not have heard safely," in other words without endangering their moral integrity.[47]

At that time, gatherings of this type were a phenomenon limited to those few industrial companies that were precursors of welfare policies, such as, for example, Procter and Gamble in Cincinnati (Ohio). Since the end of the nineteenth century, Procter's annual picnic had coincided with the ceremony of the public handing over of dividends to those who had joined the company's share program for workers. Another company with strong paternalistic traditions, Norton of Worcester (Massachusetts), introduced this measure only a couple of years before Scovill. There was a multiplication of similar initiatives after America's entry into the war as part of a more general Americanization drive. Numerous companies followed suit, making the get together day another typical product of mobilization.[48]

At Scovill the project arose out of the ever more frequent discussions inside management and the SFA about how to hold together what Goss and his most loyal collaborators called the "army of men who have not had the opportunity to learn to be first-class mechanics, and others who could never possibly become first-class mechanics," a contingent whose growth within the company structure seemed to be unlimited. Hence the decision to project onto the company as a whole the model of the foremen's picnic, giving an industrial scale to the organization of games and the field kitchen with snacks and drinks, which until then the SFA and those surrounding it had run by themselves, in an amateurish way, with the help of their families. A crucial factor here was the willingness of the SGC girls to work in the kitchen and also to help prepare the "athletics carnival" where their colleagues were the leading figures.[49]

The contests included tugs-of-war, sack races, and skeet. The spirit of intense competition was often soon dispelled when one of the contestants committed some involuntary gaffe, and the general festive atmosphere that pervaded the crowd would take over. This seemed to sum up the ideal mixture of individual commitment and cooperation, personal initiative and ordered hierarchy, that John Goss held so dear. He had expressed this idea a few months earlier when commenting on an "efficiency course" to which he had financially contributed and which was open to managers, foremen, engineers, and anyone who wished to apply. Goss was extremely impressed by the "thirteen principles of efficiency" expounded by the consultant running the course, which was designed to mold a successful, modern personality in a world of technology and business marked by a high degree of division of labor. However, he urged his collaborators not to become too obsessed with specialization, lest they lose the sense of "service" and mutual respect within the community to which they belonged. For Goss,

teamwork and cooperation were no less important than individual efficiency, and for this reason he saw the course as effective in terms of the
image it created, with "executives rubbing elbows with assistant foremen
and time clerks, all dipping into the same fund of knowledge and truly
exemplifying the spirit of the New Century, in which old standards give
place to new and the same does for all."[50]

The fact that the headline carried by the leading local newspaper above
its account of the Reidville gathering was identical to the one used for the
company bulletin's description of the event suggests that it met with the
approval of both the SFA and Goss. The headline ran: "The Big Family Picnic of Scovill Company Employees," and here for the first time we find the
name of the company allied to the classic metaphor of traditional paternalism and modern company welfare. And indeed both in the park in Reidville and in everyday life on the shop floor the metaphor was taking on
bodily form at Scovill. Even without any explicit directives to this effect
from management (this was, however, the case in various companies,
including the textile giant Amoskeag Company), the foremen and their
assistants had brought numerous family groups into the various departments. Leaving aside the numerous oral testimonies on this question, even
a cursory examination of employment files for the period from 1916 to
1918 reveals the substantial presence of coresident family groups. This is
even reflected in the starting lineups for the various contests held at Reidville, where the same family names recur time and again. And after all, this
was not only the situation among the rank and file; at the head of the company stood another family, whose two generations of managers now
looked down on the athletic progress of their employees from the bleachers erected in the park.[51]

But even here, at least judging by the local reporter's description of the
event, the Gosses were true to their well-known reputation for reserve,
almost as if to emphasize that, if Scovill was a "family," this particular family was still not the product of the explicit paternalism of its executives. The
only note of "human interest" that involved them, albeit indirectly, was a
special mention of the old President Chauncey P., Sr. The paper recalled
how it had been Chauncey who, more than sixty years previously, had hired
Jarvis E. Ellis, "the acknowledged grandfather now of all the employees
there," who, as far as his age permitted, still occupied his post as factotum in
the warehouse and in the main factory yard. At Reidville Ellis sat "in a cosy
seat on the bleachers," "the picture of good health and mental power," living
testimony to the company's surprising continuity. Together with this "best
behaved throng," he was, concluded the newspaper, "the most forceful
argument against industrial unrest."[52]

5. SUGGESTION BOX

The expression "big family" was used again some months later in a brief document that the members of the Safety Committee discussed during a meeting in February 1917. The document was the first report on a recently launched project on the model of other companies as part of a campaign promoted by the National Safety Council. A month earlier a safety suggestion box had been placed near one of the factory gates; it was a kind of mailbox above which hung posters urging employees to submit "safety suggestions and any other ideas that will promote the welfare of workmen and the efficiency of the shop." Each message, said the posters, had to be written on a form available from the foremen and would be given "due recognition" by the Committee and the company management. The first collection produced only thirteen suggestions from the workers, but the Committee considered more than gratifying the information about problems caused in the departments by defective toilets or inadequate regulations about staff entering and leaving at the end of shifts. So it was decided to expand the scheme and to multiply the number of boxes placed at strategic points throughout the plant. "After all," observed the Committee, "we are just one great big family here, inside the gate and out, and every member of the family has the right—and a duty—to speak up on these things."[53]

The suggestion box was the result of various attempts made by John Goss over the previous two years to set up a network of information from below that involved the workers directly and made it possible to judge whether the language of his circulars was being translated into real action. For, in his own words, this language "had . . . many . . . different meanings . . . it could be easily misunderstood . . . by the junior executives down the line, and then maladministered." For this reason, in 1915 Goss had asked the person in charge of the accounting department to train some young clerks "*not* to audit figures but to audit conditions in the operating of the plant in its various sub-divisions and rooms." Spot checks carried out by these technicians during the various phases of the manufacturing process had been useful, although less than the manager had expected, and above all had roused some suspicions, especially at lower levels of the company's control structure. Then Goss had tried to "publicize very broadly more or less in writing, and verbally when we were talking to groups of employees the fact that they had the privilege to 'challenge' any condition in the plant which they did not like which affected them . . . or which they did not think was to the best interest of the business." The word "challenge," he added, was not meant "in its militant sense, but in its inspirational sense." The idea of "challenge" was at the basis of what other businessmen at the time called "personal contact": the attempt, by giving the workers the impression that they had access to the top management, to lend new life and importance to the bureaucratic regulations issued by those top managers. Here, too, there had been some positive results, but, according to the company executives, the plan had met with reticence and hesitation on the part of the workers, who were concerned about possible reprisals by their direct superiors if they came out openly with their complaints. Few showed the determination of an Italian immigrant, Tony Calabrese, who, in a letter addressed to the management, had protested his innocence with regard to production problems that had caused him difficulties with his foreman: "Cristoforo Colomb! Please Mr. Scovill, you speek Mis Parsons [the foreman], and tol him I gooda workaman, I no ticka wop . . . Mr. Gones truckman he missa da work."[54]

The system of the suggestion box, brought to the attention of the company by the National Safety Council at the end of 1916, seemed to be a way of opening an upward channel of communication for workers (but in this case within the framework of an overall plan in which the intermediaries were also firmly involved) at the same time as safeguarding the anonymity of those who had something to say but were unwilling to expose themselves. As the notice above the box made clear, signing the form was, although warmly recommended, not compulsory. The suggestions received in the first year of the program were, as a matter of fact, mostly signed. They contained notes on various aspects of production: safety in the strict sense of the word, as well as technical and managerial questions.

Once again, however, despite some undoubtedly positive features that persuaded the Safety Committee to keep the scheme alive and even expand it, involving the mass of the workers in an initiative of this type proved to be a much more arduous and less gratifying task than mobilizing workers in a public park during their free time. The positive elements of the scheme were, on the one hand, the fact that it provided information—even of apparently minor importance—that might give management a clearer idea about some of the most disparate aspects of the production system, and on the other hand, the signal it gave, in the form of some of the messages left by some of the immigrant workers, that even among the mass of semi-skilled workers there were those who wanted to exercise their talent for coming up with small technical or managerial measures and were anxious to make themselves known to management. Both these factors, however, need to be weighed against the number—and content—of the messages. There were not very many in 1917: a little over a hundred in the first half of the year, almost double that in the second half. In terms of content, most suggestions, even those that had the honor of being published in the bulletin and were rewarded with a letter of thanks from John Goss, concerned matters of only secondary importance and tended very often to be vague, even though they may have encouraged management to take a look at some of the more forgotten corners of the factory. The overall impression is that the few workers who bothered to fill out the forms did so in a context that, in spite of the plans Goss had to involve the employees, left no other real opportunities for "challenging" (in all senses) different from the silent stereotyping of output practiced in virtually all departments. Exemplary in this sense were the "ideas" that came from the foundry. They concerned minor safety regulations and had little or nothing to say about what was really happening in that section—the section that underwent the greatest degree of technological change during the war.

Indeed, in the foundry the demands imposed by the orders, and especially the opportunities for experimenting with new technologies protected by the profits of war and with the assistance of personnel with international technical experience sent by the British military arsenals, created the right conditions for rapid progress in the process of transformation that had been started in the first decade of the twentieth century. The qualitative and quantitative characteristics of the orders for fuses led Scovill and other companies to invest decisively in two areas of innovation in which they had until then operated with uncertainty due to the vicious circle of prohibitive costs, the limited opportunities for application, and the difficulty of designing plants. The processes of hot forging with hydraulic presses made it possible to eliminate one of the essential parts of the old system of pit furnaces—casting—and enormous oil furnaces (which then became electric) radically modified the role of the operator compared to the small traditional furnaces, reducing his discretion and autonomy.

The broad profit margins afforded by the war orders made it possible for the first time to absorb the initial difficulties and inefficiency attendant on experimentation with new systems (which immediately guaranteed not only unimaginably high quality levels using the old furnaces—even ten or twelve times better—but also gradually falling reject rates). Things were made less traumatic by the situation on the labor market, which was for the moment relatively favorable to supply. This gave the casters who were most resolutely attached to their craft, and who refused to work for lower wages with the new equipment, the chance to leave Scovill with reasonable prospects of finding work with smaller companies that could not afford anything other than the traditional pit furnaces. The postwar period suddenly exposed the irreversible character of the crisis affecting the craft, as proved by the increasing number of old-style skilled casters to be found among the ranks of those in search of employment and by their unemployment rates, which, for example, in Massachusetts, more than tripled between 1917 and 1919 (from 4 to 13 percent).[55]

In the brutally direct language of a promotional brochure published by one of Scovill's competitors, the sector had finally started to overcome the key problem of the old furnaces: "the human element." Or rather, as can be seen in the technical trade journals during the war, a new type of "human element," apparently more integral to the company management and to its need for control and legitimization, was beginning to assert itself: the "brass chemist." In the words of the Scovill company bulletin in the spring of 1917, the old type of manufacturing process "based on guess-work . . . is daily receiving a death blow" from the internal laboratory. These blows came in the form of the 2,500 controls carried out every day by a research and analysis department that had grown in size almost four times (from 39 to 146 employees) in the space of a couple of years. A third of these were graduate chemists, and two-thirds were men and women with lower qualifications whose job it was to carry out routine tests.[56]

After years of lagging behind, the brass industry had finally caught up with the steel industry, in time to take part in the general dilution of the casters' craft, which was probably the most significant consequence of the war, from a technological point of view, for the entire American metal manufacturing industry.

Likewise, the brass chemists, just like the casters, found themselves participating, more or less consciously, in a process of displacement of professional fortunes that went beyond the confines of the department. This process, which moved in exactly the opposite direction of that which affected the casters, consisted in the great opportunity of sudden technical indispensability and public profile that the events going on in the European trenches gave to American chemists, irrespective of whether or not they were directly involved in the most cruel aspects of that "total war."[57]

III

The Last War

1. A QUIET STATE?

In its first editorial the company bulletin promised its readers a menu of information, some science and technology, and the occasional article to boost "company morale"; and during its first two years this was precisely what it delivered. This continuity in subject matter was broken only when it started to publish more news items about the social life of the company and gave over more and more space first to health and technical innovation and then also to organizational change and rationalization as applied to all aspects of factory life, as well as life outside the factory. Thus flow charts showing a model company organization appeared side by side with personnel efficiency tests or announcements of prize contests for girls who could prove that they were able to reconcile decorum and economy in running a home.

Against this background, where little or nothing was said about political events in the country, what was happening in the Old World was mentioned only rarely and then in rather cryptic tones during the whole period from the launching of the bulletin (May 1915) to the entry of the United States into the war (April 1917). The dominant tone may have been ironic and allusive, but underlying it was a certain sympathy for the Allied cause. "Allies" was the term used to refer to the foremen who during a social dinner had unleashed an "attack" on a turkey, as reported in an article that played on the double meaning of the word "turkey." The writer jokingly described the offensives of the Central Powers in terms of "a regiment of uhlans" reduced to an inglorious fate: stuck to a glue factory near Reims and removed only after a great deal of effort. In another instance, the "call to arms" issued by "General Pinochle," with its stern injunction to all "patriots" to "enlist," turned out to be none other than the announcement of a cards tournament.[1]

The war was either repressed or made the object of rather grotesque allusion; but this was merely the extreme expression of the attitude taken by the elite of Waterbury and Connecticut. Jolted only by the sinking of the *Lusitania* and later the *Arabic,* throughout the whole period prior to the spring of 1917 the WASP ruling classes that set the political and cultural tone in the state seemed to have chosen a life of calm and caution. Their newspapers did occasionally contain correspondents' reports from the trenches and in some cases they came out in favor of the Allies (for one thing because of the powerful economic interests associated with the war orders), but this did not mean that they gave up their traditional isolationism. This feeling was also reinforced by the scant enthusiasm with which the Irish—the longest-established ethnic group and the one that was second only to the WASPs in terms of being firmly rooted in the local political apparatus—viewed the prospect of American intervention on the side of Great Britain.[2]

During the first thirty months of the war in Europe, the Connecticut establishment showed no signs of any substantial change in its approach to the ethnic problem, although in other states this question was beginning to be the focus of growing attention. Connecticut was true to its reputation of being, among the seven states of the Union with the highest density of immigrants, one of those where the YMCAs held the fewest number of language courses. Nor was there a particularly marked increase in the power of organizations such as the North American Civic League for Immigrants (NACL). In its first ten years (1908 to 1917) the NACL's promises of industrial peace for those who adopted its methods of "taming" immigrants won it the financial support of no more than five businessmen in the whole of Connecticut.[3]

Waterbury was no exception to this picture: only two English courses were available (by 1915 these were attracting about 550 people—150, all Italians, attended the course put on by the YMCA, while another 400, Italians and Lithuanians, frequented the evening classes organized by the Federal Bureau of Naturalization). There was one section of the NACL that opened in the city in 1914–15, and it was still trying to find its feet a year later. It is true that the city responded to the appeal of the Federal Commission on Immigration to make 4 July 1915 Americanization Day, and both in 1915 and the following year the Independence Day celebrations were certainly much livelier. Newspapers ran articles reporting from the European battlefields side by side with articles about the tradition of 4 July and the history of the American flag and the American national anthem. Teachers from the local high schools gave talks on the main square about "citizenship" and "patriotism." A new monument to war veterans was unveiled in the nearby town of Wolcott. Nevertheless, there were none of the exaggerated manifestations of fervent patriotism and "Americanization" recorded elsewhere. The orators who spoke in Wolcott went no further than displaying their profound but contained respect for the national historical traditions typical of local historical societies, which were very strong in the state; they made it clear that their thoughts were focused more on the Connecticut infantry battalion stationed in Arizona, ready when necessary to go to the aid of General Pershing in Mexican territory, than on any possible participation in the conflict in Europe. For their part, Waterbury's businessmen hardly distinguished themselves in this respect, as happened, for example, in Worcester (Massachusetts), where Norton and other companies took a direct and leading role in the 4 July celebrations in 1916. The spirit of the summer outing and the worries about the effects of the fireworks continued to be matters of prime concern in the newspapers.[4]

Is there any way of explaining the attitude adopted by the ruling class? According to the author of the most important study on propaganda in Connecticut during the First World War, the conduct of the establishment was due both to its deeply rooted isolationist convictions and to the extreme sense of security that the political stability and the low level of industrial (and social) conflict that had characterized the state in the prewar period allowed the elite to feel. After all, why should the Republican WASPs have any doubts about political stability, since they had exercised uninterrupted control over both houses of the state assembly (with the exception of the Senate in 1912) for more than twenty years (1894–1917)? This phenomenon was founded, as we know, on the state's peculiar electoral system, which meant that, in the words of a contemporary observer, "a small town of 200 population has the same number of representatives as a city like New Haven with 150,000."[5]

In turn, the general political climate, together with the intransigence of the employers' front and the relative prosperity that the state had enjoyed for the fifteen years preceding the war, explained why there was relatively little industrial conflict. It also explained the serious problems that beset the workers' efforts to organize unions and the lower profile of social and ethnic issues in Connecticut compared to other areas. One need only recall that in March 1915 even the businessmen of Bridgeport, a town that during the war was to become an arena for some of the most intense industrial conflict in the country, thought that as there had been only three strikes the previous year, it was "hardly likely that any serious trouble may occur." And although the fifty-five strikes recorded in that town by the end of the year proved how wrong the local employers' predictions had been, they still did not shake the confidence of the state establishment in the basic solidity of Connecticut's institutions and social fabric. It was argued that the war orders, which had strained social peace because of the consequent sudden and uncontrolled broadening of the production base, would bring such prosperity as to dispel the specters of conflict and to silence any voices concerned about the loyalty of the immigrants.[6]

Nevertheless, at the beginning of February 1917, immediately after America's declaration that it was breaking off diplomatic relations with Germany, Waterbury was to experience an unexpected foretaste of the anxieties that lay beneath this superficial overconfidence. Two days after the announcement of Wilson's decision to break off relations with the Germans, in this city, where German-born immigrants represented about a tenth of those born in Italy and a fifth of those born in Ireland and who had never shown any signs of hostility toward the institutions, rumors of possible attacks by agents of the Kaiser suddenly started to spread. The writer of a book that had come out a few years earlier, which envisioned a German invasion of the country, saw his fantasies unexpectedly taking on concrete shape: in particular, Connecticut was considered a prime target for a possible aggressor because of the high concentration of military production in the area. While the Democratic mayor, the Irishman Scully, was secretly asking the Republican governor Holcomb for protection for "the safety of our factories, public buildings, and water works," John Goss recognized in an interview that "there is a good deal of hysteria in the air just now."[7]

As a good old-line Yankee, the governor preferred to keep to the path of caution followed thus far and left the city to dispel its fears by itself. In the space of little more than a month, however, a series of fires broke out in several factories in New Britain, which were immediately seen as acts of sabotage by foreign (or immigrant) agents, rekindling this "hysteria" and forcing the governor to change his tune. Holcomb took sides with those who now openly raised the question of the dangers facing Connecticut, populated as it was with potential "enemy aliens." This term was applied by the most intransigent to all those born abroad, whether or not they came from the Central Powers, and in particular to the so-called "new" immigrants. Among those who took this line were two executives of American Brass who had been among the very few businessmen to belong to the NACL in the period before the war.[8]

In the brief space of time that still separated the country from entry into the war, sudden outbursts of tension and fear combined with the activist fervor with which the state establishment prepared for possible intervention in the conflict. In these circumstances one particular feature emerged that, although with some radical differences in the tone and scale of the initiatives taken, was to mark the entire mobilization campaign in the area. At the moment when the emergency facing them called for action, the conservatism and provincial pride shown thus far by local public and private institutions proved to be precious assets. Indeed, these qualities produced cohesiveness and an ability to decide and act rapidly that grew out of the conviction that it would be possible to reduce the complex (and unprecedented) situation in which the establishment found itself to simple and familiar issues of order and social control.

By the end of March 1917, Connecticut, along with the state of New York, but with more zeal and discipline, had completed a vast census of its industrial resources. Called by Governor Holcomb in agreement with the state's leading businessmen and politicians, it represented the first occasion since the 1910 federal census for a detailed survey of the number of immigrants and the composition of the various immigrant communities. The excitement of the previous few weeks, of course, was also reflected in this exercise: in the forms that the census officers took around the companies and private houses, those born abroad were hastily termed "enemy aliens." City by city, Connecticut was covered by a blanket survey that laid down a dense network over its territory. Very few could not be traced and in Waterbury only about twenty out of a population of sixty thousand escaped the combing of the town by the local committee engaged to carry out the census.[9]

2. FLAGS AND UNIFORMS

The Goss family was involved in the census in two guises: one, so to speak, civic, the other more directly corporate, embodied respectively by John and his brother Edward. John was called upon to be a member of the small committee set up in the city to conduct the census. It was made up of several local politicians and two brass industrialists. The majority of the 1,250 volunteers who actually carried out the survey were middle-class WASPs, with the exception of about a hundred Irishmen and about thirty Italians, who also came mostly from the middle classes of their respective ethnic groups. Although on a small scale, this participation in the census, albeit in lowly positions, of non–Anglo-Saxon groups in fact anticipated the gradual and difficult process of testing and co-optation to which the ethnic elite, especially of the "new" immigrants, would be subjected during war mobilization.[10]

For his part, Edward Goss, in his position as general manager, signed the forms with which Scovill made its contribution to the census. In answer to the question whether, in case of war, he thought it would be right to exempt some of the nine thousand male workers from military service and, if so, how many should be exempted, the general manager replied that "practically the entire organization could be assigned to duty in connection with the manufacture of ammunitions or supplies if required."[11]

Barely a month later this is precisely what happened. Upon the announcement of the declaration of war, walls, desks, and equipment in Scovill's various departments were immediately festooned with stars and stripes made by the workers. In the words of an eyewitness, in the press department, "the colors on each machine [were] so arranged that they rode up and down with the motion of the machine." Unfortunately for the management, in this case patriotism and safety in the workplace did not go completely hand in hand; the danger of fires forced them to remove some "mammoth flags hanging on the side walls or draping from the ceilings." They did this, however, in such a way that "their motive in making such a rule be clearly understood" by the workers, so as not to offend the sensibility of those who had sewn and hung up those signs of a "spirit of reverence" toward the nation.[12]

A major role in the preparation of the decorations had been played by the company's women's club. Mobilization for the war gave it an immediate incentive to multiply its initiatives and lent a new, unifying purpose to ongoing projects. This was the case, for example, with the club's first annual outing. Scheduled as an event on the SGC program from the beginning of the year, when it was finally held in July, it became an occasion for the girls to show that they were, as the company management noted with some satisfaction, "interested in other things than play." Not that play was missing; indeed, the outing was the occasion for the first exhibition of women engaged in sports (running, baseball) and contests of skill (tug-of-war, sack race). This was a kind of dress rehearsal for the get together day due to be held a month later. Everything took place amidst a riot of American flags. Moreover, between one competition and another and before the final grand ball, the girls earned the appreciation of the management and the Red Cross. John Goss, who was a member of the state board of the international charity organization, praised the collection that the girls organized in favor of the Red Cross and the enthusiastic reaction they gave to the appeal for a course for operating theater assistants: with only twenty posts available there were 150 applications.[13]

In the months immediately following, as the first contingents of American troops reached France, the SGC gave full confirmation of its willingness to support mobilization. The operators and clerks from the women's club were particularly active in fund-raising, writing letters, and sending food packages to enlisted Scovill employees. Between the end of 1917 and the beginning of the following year the number of those enlisted from Scovill had reached five hundred.[14]

Already featured on the cover of the August issue of the company bulletin, which in the meantime had doubled the number of its pages to eight, from the fall on "our boys on the front" occupied a regular and ever more important slot in the publication. The latest list of enlisted soldiers and information about fund-raising and sending gift packages were juxtaposed with numerous photographs showing soldiers about to leave for the front or during a break in the encampments of the American Expeditionary Force, and their letters from Europe.

The rigid morality of the YMCA and the precepts of "food efficiency" that the bulletin dispensed periodically to the workers did not seem to apply to them. Tobacco and cigarettes, which were normally stigmatized in the company diet as "things you can get along without" (together with Coca-Cola, coffee, and tea), turned in the messages from the front and in the replies from the SGC girls into absolute necessities, welcomed on their arrival in the trenches as the most important items in the gift packages.[15]

The soldiers became the company's outpost on the field of battle and at one point were even able to endorse the excellence of Scovill's products, as can be seen in two letters from the front in which enlisted workers talked proudly of the fuses that they had either personally seen in operation or had heard talked about favorably by their superiors. At the same time, almost imperceptibly, the "boys in khaki" became for the management— who now had even fewer qualms about using the bulletin directly as their own instrument—a way of entering into closer relations with the employees. Among the ever more insistent invitations to their readers to apply to the SFA or the SGC to contact their relatives and colleagues in Europe, they slid in messages designed to suggest a sense of closeness between those at the top and those at the bottom of the company, a closeness cemented by the problems and dangers they both faced. This could take the form of a photograph from the front of the youngest offspring of the Goss family or letters in which some employee, addressing the head of the plant directly, illustrated similarities and differences between the French landscape and the countryside of New England, and in particular asked to be kept abreast of how things were going in this or that department, what his colleagues were up to, and how the manufacturing processes were proceeding.[16]

Communicating with the other side of the Atlantic was an early, efficient means that workers were encouraged to use to demonstrate their patriotism. Another way, according to the dictates of federal and state propaganda, was to take out Liberty Bonds, which were issued in four successive campaigns throughout the plants and districts of Waterbury starting from the summer of 1917.

Raising funds and stressing to the nation the value of savings and personal sacrifice were the declared objectives of the public institutions that promoted these campaigns. Soon, however, the most convinced supporters of

"Americanization" at all costs interpreted Liberty Bonds as a test of new immigrants' loyalty to their new homeland to which they had to be subjected, if necessary with force. In various parts of the country cases were recorded where the collection of funds for bonds was transformed into an occasion for using coercion and discrimination against the newcomers.[17]

At Scovill, at least officially, no pressure was needed to produce the response the immigrants gave to the second campaign for national war loans between October and November. In the words of the company bulletin, the "foreign-born employees" had "come through nobly," standing out among the 50 percent of the workforce who had contributed $71 a head to the collection, amounting to a total of $465,000, about 10 percent of the overall sum raised in the city.[18]

In urging the workers to take out Liberty Bonds, the company had been at pains to make it clear that "the Scovill Manufacturing Company gains nothing financially whether you buy a Bond or not, but it does feel keenly a pride in seeing its employees every one of them buying a Bond." In fact, judging by the posters hanging up in the plant and on street corners, it was the workers themselves who stood to gain. This was the main argument in the appeals: almost two-thirds of the space on any given poster was taken up with a detailed explanation of the opportunities that the bond offered in terms of "investment" and "savings." Then in the last lines, in a section entitled "patriotic duty," the floodgates of idealism were opened. "If you count yourself American, if you are one of us, then Uncle Sam is you, me and one hundred million more like us. What do you say? Buy another Liberty Bond today."[19]

The spirit in which the Treasury Department had launched these campaigns was, after all, in line with the more general intention that dominated all war propaganda during the first phase of the American intervention, up to the beginning of 1918. Responsible for this was George Creel, a former muckraker, whom Wilson had asked to head the Committee on Public Information, the federally coordinated organ of propaganda activities. Convinced that "patriotism is in no sense an instinct," Creel had started off with the firm intention to combine the idealistic impulse to engage in a "war to end all wars" in the name of democracy with the only rhetoric—itself the product of the Progressive Era—that he thought was equal to such ideals: a pragmatic, transparent rhetoric based rigorously on the facts.[20]

Contributing to reinforce this decision was the strong fear of spectacular failure that had marked the first uncertain stages of mobilization, inducing Washington, especially when it came to asking people for money, to use simple, effective arguments that would be certain of having an immediate impact on all. These arguments also contained traces of that mixture of prejudice, resentment, and projection vis-à-vis immigrants, which in the preceding decade had often led to seeing Italians or Poles as mere items in the national economy: they were seen variously as production factors avidly accumulating savings for the day when they would return home from whence they had come, or perhaps as potential consumers.

After all, it should not be forgotten that such echoes could be heard in those very same government posters inviting people to enlist voluntarily, which circulated in 1917, also in Waterbury, in the different languages of the immigrants. For example, the block letters of the heading on one of these notices in Italian ("Fight for Your Country" and "Be Brave") could not completely divert attention from the list of personal advantages and economic benefits ("Full pay in case of illness and while you are on leave. Free medical service, full pension in case of disability"), a list that ended with a final condition that seemed to come straight out of a job offer ("No Lazybones Need Apply").[21]

The picture of the first phase of propaganda for Liberty Bonds would not be complete without mentioning the third type of approach being used in the campaign alongside the flag and the wallet: the sentimental nature of the appeal to the worker's (patriotic) heart was also transferred onto an object closer to the interests of the addressee of the message than any abstract national ideal, especially if he was an immigrant. It can be embodied in a poster that was making the rounds in the company in October 1917. The poster appeared to enshrine the spirit that drove the SFA and the five hundred girls of the company's women's club to mobilize for their colleagues on the front. It depicted a woman and a soldier in a tight embrace that, one could guess, would be their last before the man set off for the war. The caption said: "Will He Come Back? The Probability is vastly greater if he is properly equipped and trained. . . . Have an Honored Place among your neighbors by doing the next thing to going, loan your money to the Government." Public propaganda suggested that immigrants should think of their family members, colleagues, and neighbors when it asked them to make a sacrifice and urged them to give their savings in exchange not for a dull receipt from the usual ethnic banker (who could even run off with the money), but for one with a picture of the Statue of Liberty and countersigned by a foreman or a government official.[22]

3. HIRING, TRANSFERRING, FIRING

Among the many statistics that piled up on John Goss's desk in the last few months of 1917, next to those about the sales of Liberty Bonds were others that were decidedly less comforting. These were the figures about the annual turnover rate, which in the period 1916–17 reached 176 percent. Of course, Scovill was not a particularly anomalous case on the manufacturing scene at the time. Turnover had been a chronic problem in American industry practically from its origins, a matter of specific concern for manufacturers and social engineers since the beginning of the twentieth century, and now during the war, levels had begun to skyrocket. Investigations by the Federal Department of Labor showed that levels of turnover of 440 percent among laborers and 150 percent among skilled workers were by no means exceptional in various industrial centers in the country. In nearby Bridgeport annual averages fluctuated between 200 and 400 percent. It was not, however, as the result of a comparison between Scovill and other companies with similar turnover rates that another government body, the Bureau of Public Health, was to provide Goss with the data about his company. In fact, the figures were part of a comparative analysis carried out the previous summer in Waterbury and in a Detroit company whose turnover was only 30 percent. The official report of the commission kept the name of the company rigorously secret, although it was not difficult to recognize it as Ford.[23]

There had been talk of the automobile company in the SFA at the end of 1916 in relation to the successful methods it had adopted to combat turnover. In particular, there had been the proposal, which had appeared anonymously in the bulletin (and which had in effect come to nothing), to test the applicability to Scovill of Ford's practice of concentrating all dismissals (voluntary or decided by the foremen) in the employment department, so as to change them, where possible, into transfers to other departments and thus to avoid having to "keep on hiring and firing thousands of people."[24]

The question of labor turnover, then, was not unknown to the Scovill management. Once again, without John Goss's circulars for this period it is impossible to follow management directives in detail. Nevertheless, we do know from other contemporary documents and from company material from a later period that by spring 1916 the first surveys on this subject had been carried out. These had been behind the decision to introduce a 10 percent monthly bonus for all employees. This survey had been followed by another in September of the same year, which had shown peaks of monthly turnover of 25 percent in some departments. By the explicit admission of those who had carried out the survey, this one, too, like the one before it, had been conducted using very approximate statistical means, and the only proposal it had made was contained in the brief note that was to remain a dead letter, saying that they should follow Ford's lead.

A very different analysis was submitted to Goss by federal experts at some point between October and December 1917: a vast array of comparative data with a series of explanatory hypotheses and some possible concrete solutions.[25]

What were the variables that according to the government experts explained such divergent figures between the two companies not only in turnover, but also, as we shall see, in what was in effect the main focus of the investigation, namely "industrial fatigue"? According to the ergonomists of the Bureau of Public Health, this phenomenon could be explained neither by any significant technological differences, nor by factors such as the level of centralized authority, the accounting system, or the methods of work planning. In terms of control, administration, and work planning, the Scovill management came out of the comparison with their more eminent colleagues very well. As a matter of fact, only a few years earlier even Ford, despite and indeed precisely because of the new technologies, had still had acute problems with turnover, which in one year had reached levels of 370 percent. To remedy this problem the company had devised policies on wages, working hours, hiring, and firing, which the federal ergonomists, who thought that managing the work factor was the most important variable, took as their term of comparison in their report.

Ford's $5.00 daily wage was certainly a major difference if compared to the $3.20 and $2.80 earned, respectively, by male and female pieceworkers at Scovill. While acknowledging the part played by wage differentials, the ergonomists placed more emphasis on Scovill's policy of cutting down production times and use of piece rates that decreased proportionately to yield. In their view, these were the main reasons for the workers' tendency to regulate their working pace and a possible reason for high turnover (in November and December of 1917 almost two-thirds of the workers who left quit voluntarily). Restriction of output and turnover were seen in this study as two ways in which the workers—whose absentee rates were double those at Ford (3 percent as compared to 1.5 percent)—reacted to the lack of recognition given to their efforts.

Working hours were considered a decisive factor by the Bureau of Public Health in explaining the number of accidents. As we know, at that time Scovill, although it had an official working week of fifty-five hours, in actual fact worked for an average of at least fifty-eight hours, and some weeks even exceeded sixty hours, as attested by numerous former employees. As part of their criticism of the ten-hour day, the ergonomics experts pointed out the difference between the accident rate in the last of the eight hours at Ford (which at the time was exceptional even in the automobile industry) and the tenth hour at Scovill: 157 for Scovill against 117.4 in the automobile company. At the same time they were keen to point to the possibility of introducing periodic short breaks to relieve the pressure of working for ten hours.

On the question of turnover, the report stressed the problems caused by the mechanisms used by the company to hire and fire human resources. Without a method of selection of workers "different from the choice made by the foremen" and even including medical examinations to identify those physically incapable of coping with certain speeds (thus reducing the danger of accidents), it was very unlikely that Scovill would be able to resolve the problem of turnover. If it wanted to remedy this problem, it would have to review all dismissals, either voluntary or decided by the same foremen, and change them into transfers to other departments.

Basically what the experts had in mind and what they were suggesting between the lines of their report was a modern personnel office, similar to those that were spreading in various parts of the country, thanks partly to training courses organized by federal mobilization units to groom the emerging professional figure that would run these services. Whether they were called employment managers, industrial relations managers, or, more rarely at this early stage, personnel managers, these new experts offered themselves as people who, in the field of human resources, would perform a function analogous to that carried out by the most innovative engineers on the factory floor. Proof of this were the specialized skills with which they were supposed to conduct the selection procedure (if necessary through the use of tests), the training and transfer of labor, as well as incorporating into this new function the old tasks typical of welfare work. On the subject of welfare, the federal experts did not fail to point out to Scovill the absence of a cafeteria and the city's poor housing conditions.[26]

What had the Washington ergonomists found in lieu of any such welfare services when they entered the Waterbury plant in July 1917? To illustrate the situation it is necessary to step back some months to the spring of that year. At that time the employment office had been detached from the administration and made part of a new unit called the industrial service department. This term, which was later to become one of the ways of referring to a modern personnel office, was used at the time as a synonym for welfare department, especially when the company wanted to dispel the impression of paternalism or lack of connection with production needs, which the other term seemed to suggest according to some (and certainly John Goss was one of them).

This new staff, made up of about fifteen employees, shared some tasks with the social service units, albeit in a rudimentary and rough manner. As can be seen from the few documents available about its first few months, it dealt not only with registering newly hired workers, but also had to subject them, upon entering the company, to a longer interview, introducing the person to the company, its objectives, and internal structure. In addition, it looked after the administration of the numerous files related to worker compensation (in 1916 Scovill made payments for accidents and illness of over \$14,700, a figure that rose to \$23,800 the following year). Furthermore, they sought to iron out any possible difficulties that arose between foremen for reasons such as the transfer of personnel from one part of the factory to another. Lastly, especially to employees who were newcomers to the city, they offered advice and material support in the case of particularly grievous examples of hardship caused by growing housing congestion and in general by the deficiencies in local services (hygiene, transport, catering) pointed out by numerous sources.[27]

At the beginning of the year a loud alarm bell had resounded about the limitations of the city's infrastructure, which can perhaps help us to understand, in the absence of direct documentation, the decision made to set up a new service and especially the choice of the person to put in charge of it. His name was Rev. H. D. Gallaudet, and he was a minister known to the Gosses because he was an associate of their church, the First Congregational Church. For a company to take on a minister for an activity that involved welfare and in general dealing with people was by no means unusual. After all, Ford himself had done something similar, although as part of a much more sophisticated policy, when he put the sociological department in the hands of an Episcopalian pastor. There was, however, a specific reason why the company decided to give Gallaudet a full-time post. In January and February 1917 he had been the person who, together with the local charitable institutions, had endeavored to deal with a case that had caused quite a stir in local public opinion. The Kennedys were a family of Scovill workers whose tragedy was reported in the local papers, where for once the name of the company was mentioned not in the usual tones of praise for its success, but in the context of accusations of property speculation.

Newly arrived in Waterbury, the seven Kennedys (the parents, who both worked at Scovill, and their five young children) lived together in a small room for which they paid a rent that as a result of the housing shortage had tripled in the space of three months, and which took away about a fourth of the father's pay. Moreover, the father suffered from rheumatism, was probably an alcoholic, and was consequently only able to work off and on. Due to the terrible hygiene conditions in which they lived, two of the five children came down with diphtheria. Gallaudet, who was actively involved in charity work for some local religious institutions, was one of the people who discovered the case and brought it to the attention of doctors and social workers. Their attempts to help the family were, however, in vain;

despite the treatment given by the company itself when the problem became common knowledge, the two little Kennedys died.[28]

Gallaudet did not have to deal with such dramatic situations as this after he was taken on by Scovill to run the industrial service in the spring of 1917. The main problem he had to face was rather that of balancing the need to help those in hardship with the constant pressure from Goss not to create precedents by being too helpful toward the workers. So generally he provided initial help, when necessary advancing money but, once it became possible, handing the cases on to the care of the local private charitable organizations, which operated on a small scale and had only modest funds at their disposal.[29]

When the Commission of the Bureau of Public Health came to Waterbury, Gallaudet and his men registered the newly hired workers, prepared them for their entry into the factory, and looked after the cases of compensation and help for the very poor using their common sense and discretion. A further task had just been added with the start of mass enlistment, namely helping workers engaged at the recruiting office to deal with exemptions for reasons of work. In the view of the federal ergonomists, none of this defined the work of an employment department able to cope adequately with the problems of the company.

Ironically, while the experts were depicting Fordian neopaternalism as the quintessence of modernity and enlightened managerial practice, the war was about to inflict several death blows on that experiment at the same time as revealing its innermost nature. Contributing to this were the erosive effects that galloping inflation was having on the five-dollar wage, the climate of suspicion and oppression that soon turned every immigrant into a potential subversive for the innumerable spies circulating in the various departments of the Detroit company, and the growing and unscrupulous use of convicts and handicapped people. For all these reasons the Ford policy emerged from the war tarnished in its image as a "progressive" company offering transparency and affluence for all its workers (an image that had also appealed to some fringes of the labor movement and to left-wing intellectuals). This change was then confirmed by the speed with which the company rid itself of all these features at the beginning of the next decade.[30]

There is no direct testimony of Goss's reactions to the first report he received from the federal commission. Clearly he did not appreciate the leaks about the report that appeared in the leading local paper in early October 1917, if it is true that the company executives sent out a note criticizing the paper for publishing information about the company without its consent. What within the article did not go toward Scovill's good public image? Judging by the headline and the main body of the article, it appeared relatively harmless. The headline read: "Experts Find a Model Plant at Scovill." This was followed by a long discussion of the company's health facilities that justified the words of the headline. Perhaps Goss's note to the paper was meant to defend the right to secrecy and to the absolute anonymity that ought to have surrounded the investigation. More probably, what he didn't like was the last part of the article, which pointed out that there was still much to be done in the city on the question of excessively heavy working shifts, the lack of cafeterias, the difficult housing conditions, and the poor state of the local transportation system: "Living conditions in Waterbury," concluded the paper, "tend to defeat the purposes of those who want to better munition-workers' health and help Uncle Sam into the fight."[31]

As to the study itself, Goss gave the experts permission to continue their investigations until the end of 1920. Subsequently, however, he commented that it was a biased investigation because basically it was too favorable toward labor. This verdict reflects the mistrust, if not outright hostility, felt by manufacturers toward Progressive intellectuals, who were perfectly embodied in the ergonomists who had supported Wilson's mobilization, because they were convinced that it was also, and above all, an occasion for internal reforms (and would lend further legitimacy to their expertise).[32]

All these reservations did not, however, prevent the manager from acknowledging, although with significant qualifications, many of the points (and indeed even the most important points) made by the federal report. Or at least this is the impression one gets when one looks at the measures adopted by the company management over the next few months.

These measures, introduced from the end of 1917 onward, included some very significant changes in labor policies. However, Rev. Gallaudet was not the person who put these new projects into effect; he had in the meantime left for the front as a volunteer, leaving his assistant Robert Platt in charge of the industrial service department. Platt was also a familiar figure to the Gosses because he had for years been a teacher in local technical schools and, in particular, had distinguished himself as a journalist and a prime force behind some of the educational and recreational programs offered at the YMCA.

When he was still Gallaudet's assistant, Platt had been put in charge of the activities of the employment office while Gallaudet himself looked after what was more strictly speaking the welfare side of things. During this period Platt had joined the SFA and become a member of the Safety Committee. When he took over the industrial service he tried to make use of this familiarity with the foremen to win the approval of at least some of the middle managers for initiatives that his service (whose staff in the first half of 1918 had increased from fifteen to fifty workers) structured along three main lines of development.

The first was the ever more pressing problem of finding workers, especially unskilled workers. In this respect, although Platt was well aware of the need to assert the authority of the management, to avoid confusion on the payroll, and to ward off the dangers of abuses by the foremen at the expense of the workforce, he saw that working alongside or even replacing the foremen in the search for hands was a much more immediate need. The initiative was rather a response to certain objective limits placed on the ability of the intermediaries to find new employees: the contraction in the local labor supply and the breakdown of the usual informal mechanisms that fed it (both the result of accelerating mass enlistment). These difficulties are reflected in the messages Edward Goss sent to the military authorities who requested the urgent delivery of their orders. All sent within the space of a few days, they seem almost to be carbon copies of one original letter. One of the most typical ones said: "Working conditions in Waterbury with respect to a supply of common labor are nothing short of alarming. . . . This is no wolf cry . . . we need 200 able-bodied laborers to even approach what has been scheduled." Even John Goss's private correspondence, when he touched on the subject of work, was dominated by his obsession with the "shortage of hands."[33]

In order to systematically broaden the recruitment area, Platt tried to intervene in the "natural" dynamics of supply by affixing posters in the various departments urging employees to write to friends and relatives inviting them to come to Waterbury. A more profitable method was, however, to establish firm relations with officers from the Department of Labor, which by the end of 1917 had started to move workers from big cities such as New York to the North Atlantic. In the case of women, for example, after reaching an agreement with the New York government officials about the need to carefully avoid "the woman of loose morals, of uncertain health, of superficial intention, of bad disposition, or who is too poor to accept the wage and from it send home a certain sum," the head of the industrial service successfully set in motion a considerable flow of new arrivals. There were, it is true, occasional mishaps, such as the middle-aged woman whose eyesight was so bad that she was unable to see the fuse components she had to assemble, or the pair of unemployed ex-ballet dancers who, when they discovered what kind of a place Waterbury was and the sort of work they had left New York to do, were enraged. On the whole, however, this activity earned Platt the trust of the management and some respect among the foremen, as it resolved the problems they were having as a result of sudden defections by laborers.[34]

On this basis, but not without meeting with some resistance among the foremen, Platt instituted some measures in a sphere thought up until then to be their exclusive prerogative and responsibility: the firing and quitting

of workers. Toward the end of 1917 and in the spring of 1918 Platt interviewed some workers who were picking up their last pay envelope and
asked them why they were leaving the factory. The following summer the
first systematic exit interviews were introduced, and these became an
essential tool in the monitoring of resignations and, if possible, in transforming them into internal transfers. Two intervening events were decisive
in producing this result. One was an internal technical-managerial innovation, which redefined, at least formally, the powers of the foremen on the
question of piece rates and offered the workforce a chance to become better integrated into the overall structure of the company, and the other was
an external factor, which helped impose controls on the final departure of
the workforce from the company.

The technical innovation consisted of a measure designed to eliminate
what, as we have seen, were considered some of the main reasons for the
high turnover rate: time cutting and the incentive based on an inverse proportion between pay and productivity. Introduced throughout the company in the fall of 1915 on the initiative of the Piece Rate and Planning
Committee with the aim of reducing friction between foremen and workers, this incentive was not proportional to productivity and in the end had
only increased those difficulties, as the federal ergonomists had discovered. Based on their recommendations, in the spring of 1918 John Goss
eliminated this system of bonus payments and centralized the control of
piecework by transforming the Piece Rate and Planning Committee into
a permanent planning department. With a staff of ex-toolmakers, whose
numbers grew within the space of a year from three to eleven workers, the
new department took on tasks that made it more similar to Taylor's
departments of the same name, services that the war and the need for
standardization dictated by the enormous military orders were spreading
throughout the metal manufacturing industry. The planning department
was meant to concentrate the examination of all the piecework manufacturing processes being carried out in the company. By studying manufacturing techniques it was to provide foremen with suggestions about
"reasonable" times to assign to the various tasks paid at piece rates.

In this case the personnel service run by Platt agreed to work together
with the planning department in filing the individual time cards (to be
kept in the planning department) with hourly attendance and performance written down by the timekeepers (who, in turn, in order to be put
more directly under the control of the management, were removed from
the sphere of competence of the foreman and assigned to factory accounting). Moreover, the personnel office filled in the workers' individual time
sheets with performance data, which were completed at the moment of

hiring; these files then became a kind of résumé of the individual's career inside the company.[35]

The external initiative that helped the company to overcome the inertia of the foremen, who saw every attempt by the management to interfere on the question of piece rates, or even more so with regard to firing practices, as threats to the basis of their power in the company, was a project developed jointly by Waterbury businessmen in June 1918. They were concerned about the collective, class implications of the turnover phenomenon: the fact, that is, that, in the words of the main Italian-language weekly, "with the present request for hands, a large number of lighthearted young men and women have been walking around the factories, conducting themselves in a rather arrogant and harmful way. . . . The minute they set foot in another factory they talk glowingly about their pay and in this way instigate their fellow workers to quit working." To avoid such situations the manufacturers put forward the idea that, at the local office of the U.S. Employment Service, the most important of the federal agencies created to assist companies in finding laborers, information about all workers who either quit or were dismissed be collected and filed, together with information about their reasons for leaving the factory and a short note on their conduct while they had been working.[36]

Even cited in a major nationwide manufacturers' journal, *Iron Age,* as a model of cooperation in the business world that the whole country ought to imitate, this plan—known as the "Waterbury Plan"—was then disseminated through other parts of the country by the U.S. Employment Service. One of its effects was to favor the adoption of exit interviews at Scovill, which presented them to the foremen as an inalienable undertaking in comparison with other companies. Ahead of this new measure there was a vast campaign organized by the industrial service making it compulsory for all workers about to leave the factory to pass through the employment office for an exit interview.[37]

As a natural corollary of this measure came the procedures—introduced in the fall—for workers to be transferred from one department to another. This involved the delicate questions of changing dismissals into internal transfers, as well as normal transfers of workers, requested by foremen, by management, and by individual workers. Internal transfers in particular tended to be rather complicated, because they involved interviews with both workers and foremen. However, in terms of procedure, they had the positive effect of forcing the company to attempt the first job descriptions in order to draw up maps of compatibility between the various jobs. This practice was inspired by experiments being carried out by some electrical manufacturing companies since the beginning of the century and introduced into the company by the Yale engineering school, which worked together with Scovill on several training schemes. As for the effects on turnover, these new measures—exit interviews and internal transfers—had only recently been brought in when the Armistice was signed, which once again changed the production and employment situation, forcing the company, as we shall see later, to readjust and revise its plans. As was pointed out in 1918 by E. H. Davis, a young economist from Brown University hired by Goss the previous summer to put some order into the company's statistics, the managerial innovations had been too recent to expect immediate results in the battle against turnover. The turnover rates in the year just finished were very high, with a decrease of only ten percentage points (166 percent as compared to 176 percent) since 1917.[38]

In addition to the changes made at the two extremes of the life cycle of the workforce inside the company through the centralization of hiring and firing, the industrial service also introduced initiatives that corresponded more closely to the interests of the new man in charge of the department: the training and education of personnel. Taking inspiration from a Dayton (Ohio) company, referred to by the leading national management magazines as a model case, Scovill introduced a short course in technical instructions for machine tenders. Moreover, with the help of the planning department, which included a large number of ex-toolmakers, and under the guidance of the Yale engineering school, Platt reworked some experiments conducted in a fragmentary fashion during the previous years in refresher courses for skilled workers in the toolmaking department, one of the departments that had expanded most during the war (from four hundred to almost seven hundred workers), and added an apprenticeship project for electricians. Lastly, again in accord with the planning department and with some members of the Yale engineering school, which was pushing its courses in the direction of managerial studies, the industrial service organized short periodic sessions for foremen and technicians, which were a cross between training and education (that is to say, the educational activities were not directly linked to the technical side of a job). They were designed to encourage foremen to become interested in organizational questions and in the development of their role first and foremost as "builders of men," who were meant, on the basis of rules and "personal contact," to express on the shop floor the managerial style that management wished to see adopted.[39]

Scovill's most ambitious educational plan for its unskilled workforce was to introduce English courses for immigrants. The first impulse in this direction came from the Connecticut Council of Defense, the state mobilization body created by the governor, as in the rest of the country, at the end of April 1917. Both in its central section in Hartford, the state capital, and in the outlying counties and cities, it was made up mainly of business-men, politicians, and merchants whose roots were firmly in the WASP community. At the end of 1917 the Council created a Department of Americanization, which used its bulletin, *The Americanizer,* to persistently remind Connecticut's businessmen of the need to adopt measures aimed at those "elements in the pot of Connecticut" who, to use Governor Hol-comb's words, "had not yet melted."[40]

Influenced by this kind of discourse and exchanges of views with other businessmen and politicians on the board of the committee for mobiliza-tion in the county, to which he belonged, John Goss commissioned a first survey that showed that as many as 45 percent of the company's employees did not speak English. This statistic was not too distant from the figures that had persuaded Ford (35.5 percent) and the great slaughterhouses of Chicago (around 50 percent) to start language courses. Later, more careful surveys showed that the earlier figures referred to the numbers of those who had difficulty with English, while those who were unable to speak it at all were about 15 percent. Goss and Platt still thought that the figure was sufficiently high to justify launching courses. The belief that this measure could substantially improve communications on the shop floor, force immigrants to try to integrate better into American society, and preempt the danger of subversive demonstrations overcame all reservations about the expenditure of time and money that the plan entailed.[41]

Thus by January 1918 the Naugatuck Valley, too, had its first company course in Americanization. Using premises and teachers supplied initially by the city's schools, a twelve-week language course was started for what was at first a small group of workers (a few dozen). Following a directive from Goss, the foremen had chosen them from among "our most intelli-gent and loyal foreign-born employees." The course consisted of five hours a week (one hour of lessons a day, the tenth of a daily shift paid with a token figure by the company, Monday through Friday), and it followed what had become the classic YMCA method for companies (language, arithmetic, and a little civics).

The war had led to an expansion of the civics course and its patriotic ele-ment; more pressure was put on the students to apply to the authorities for American citizenship, and they were also reminded of the crucial connec-tion between language and work. Accordingly, the first lesson opened with the expression: "We manufacture arms." Then the students went on to learn how to say "I need," complementing it with the word "work," and were taught the meaning of the word "because" through the phrase "I have found this job because I was a good workman."[42]

The course started off on a small scale with just a few male students but then became more firmly established, expanding to include women by the following summer. From fall 1918 onward its potentially positive effects on manufacturing performance were to become fully evident. It also had the effect of enlarging the company's radius of action to include ever more spheres of the lives of its employees, as well as influencing their ways of thinking and behaving. We shall come back to this question later, when we try to draw up a balance of the situation at Scovill in the immediate post-war period.

4. PATRIOTS AND SPIES

After the introduction of the English courses at the beginning of 1918, Robert Platt started devoting more and more of his spare time to his participation in the new forms of propaganda that had now gotten as far as Waterbury. For a middle-class Yankee like himself, it was not difficult to obtain the three letters of introduction from businessmen or local politicians that at least initially (later the procedures became less rigid) were a prerequisite for those wanting to become members of the so-called Four Minute Men (FMM). Started in Chicago on private initiative and recognized officially by the federal Committee on Public Information (CPI) at the end of the summer of 1917, this organization began to spread throughout the country only in the winter of 1917–18 and exemplified better than any other the information offensive launched across the country at the beginning of the new year.[43]

The FMM owed their name to the attempt to renew the spirit of the militia—the minutemen—active at the time of the American Revolution and especially to the ability of their members to make a speech about any subject concerning the war effort within the time limit of four minutes. The length and the format of each performance were adapted to the place it was held and the public at which it was targeted. In the words of a contemporary writer, "In this vastly busy country of ours thousands of men dash into their day's work without being able to even glance hurriedly at the daily papers. These same myriads of men go out to the movies at night for rest and relaxation." The number of Americans who daily attended the cinema was certainly no less than ten million and, according to some estimates, was even as high as thirteen million. And the FMM saw cinemas as the best places to reach this vast mass of people using "the greatest swaying force in the world—human speech."[44]

The immediacy of oral communication, the possibility of accompanying it with gestures whose universality had been established in the eyes of the spectator by long exposure to the practices of the politicians, actors, and hucksters from which the FMM took inspiration, and the surprise effect the speaker's sudden appearance on the platform could have on a movie theater or vaudeville auditorium during the brief interval between one number and another seemed to be the best guarantee of success for the formula. And it was indeed highly successful, judging by the number of mobile orators active in the country (35,000) and in Connecticut (over 500), the number of rapid-fire speeches they made and the number of people the FMM managed to reach with their performances. In Waterbury alone, in less than a month (between April and May 1918) no fewer than 440 minirallies were held, reaching an average of 50,000 people a week (out of a population of just over 90,000). The movement spread at a dizzying pace: in November of that year the number of speeches given by the FMM and other similar organizations went up to 257 over a period of ten days, reaching a total audience of almost 180,000 people.[45]

These figures introduce us to the prime characteristic that clearly shows the difference between the wave of propaganda that swept the country in the early months of 1918 and what had been done thus far: the breadth of the effort and the amplitude of the energies unleashed. An impressive mass of varied means of communication were deployed: the cinema, with a fourfold increase (from five to twenty) in the average monthly number of films about the war in the period between 1917 and the following September; and mass education, involving the enlistment of 150,000 collaborators of the CPI. These included whole teams of historians, headed by one of the most prominent historical scholars of the time, James Franklin Jameson, whose task it was to make sure that schoolbooks and government publications highlighted the deep-seated roots of America's relations of cooperation and friendship with Great Britain and France.[46]

Unprecedented numbers (of pages and circulation) and the "invention of tradition" could also be found in the modest company bulletin published by Scovill. Between January and April 1918, although there had been no dramatic changes in the numbers of company personnel, the circulation of the bulletin almost tripled, leaping up from three thousand to eight thousand copies, while the number of pages went up to twelve and in some issues even sixteen. Scovill was in a particularly favorable position to "invent a tradition." It could boast some gold coins minted in 1824 to commemorate the visit of the Marquis de Lafayette to America. These had already been reproduced in 1876 to be presented to the French commission at the World Fair in Philadelphia, and during the most heated phase of the mobilization Scovill had made a new copy, which it donated to the federal government to give to the French ambassador. The bulletin gave this event broad coverage, inaugurating the custom of publishing photographs of company mementos accompanied by notes explaining and underscoring the sense of solidity that these relics embodied. The caption beside one of these mementos, the copy of a contract signed in 1816, read: "It is not every concern that possesses a copy of an order received and filled . . . in the year 1816. . . . Today we are planning and building and acting with the purpose of filling orders on this same spot in the year 2016."[47]

What possible explanation is there for this explosion of propaganda activity? First of all, it can be seen in connection with the growing conviction held by various federal agencies that, as the war undertaking became more pressing, it became increasingly necessary to add more "enthusiasm" on the part of an active minority to the power of "facts," to make up for the fact that America—a nation with deeply rooted isolationist sentiments that was also riven by deep ethnic and racial divisions—did not face any immediate danger of invasion. Then there was the second, decisive peculiarity of this phase of mobilization: the diverse nature of the messages, expressed through mechanisms of dissemination that highlighted the cultural armory accumulated in the organization of emotions and the creation of "channels of desire" through the pages of newspapers, which at the turn of the century were all "blood and lingerie," or by means of "privacy in public," and the new perception of the relationship between space and time that cut through the darkness of the movie theater. This background became the engine powering an apparatus that soon saw the "battle for the minds of men" undergoing radical transformation. This changed into a plan that was designed not so much to touch the minds as to provoke its addressees into more visceral and immediate reactions. In line with the catchphrase "visualize the war," figures and symbols such as the "invading Hun," the "mother of war," and the "atrocities of the enemy" crowded around "our boys on the front" as part of civil rituals that—and this can be seen also in the 1918 Liberty Bond campaigns—became increasingly impassioned.[48]

These rituals centered on a term that the First World War made the focus of systematic attention in the United States: morale. The term had started to be used in the American army at least as early as the 1870s and had later made its way into the industrial world (John Goss talked about it in one of his circulars at the beginning of the century). It was not until its use in war propaganda, however, that this quality was made an explicit focus, becoming a collective, largely unconscious sphere that remained difficult to define but was amenable to ever more sophisticated managerial strategies as it moved beyond the army to enter industry and society as a whole. "Morale is an intangible which cannot be reduced to a concrete definition," wrote the author of one of the first manuals on the "systematic development of morale" in the immediate postwar period. He could rely on his experience with the Morale Branch, a body created by the American army on the occasion of the war. For this reason he was able to add that, although "no two conceptions of it are alike," because "its qualities vary with conditions," it was also true that "it can be felt, described, stimulated and guided."[49]

Among the examples of actions that could be taken to influence collective feeling, the manual mentioned meetings like the one Platt organized for the Scovill employees in one of the main cinemas in the city in February 1918. It was part of a tightly structured schedule of twelve meetings (nine in the evening and three matinees) in the space of a month. The program itself followed the classic pattern laid down in detail for the state. Opening with a religious address by a pastor from the First Congregational Church, it then went on to a series of patriotic songs sung by a local choir, the Liberty Chorus, which also included some company workers in its ranks. Apart from the national anthem, the program also included "America the Beautiful" and "The Little Soldier." The choir then made way for a women's dance number ("The Nymph in the Wood") followed by the recitation of a poem entitled "Our Flag" and extracts from speeches by Wilson, Lincoln, and Washington on the theme of America's mission in this war and in history.[50]

The highlight of the evening, however, was the projection of slides from the front accompanied by comments from a veteran Canadian infantryman, Arthur Gibbons. An undisputed star in this field, both in Connecticut and in other states, Gibbons told with vibrant rhetorical skill of the "atrocities of the Germans," drawing on his own experience and the writings of people like Dr. Newell Dwight Hillis, minister of the Plymouth Church of Brooklyn, who after serving for several months in France and Belgium had compiled a veritable apparatus of pamphlets and speech outlines on this subject, backed up by particularly effective photographs. The subjects he dealt with were "the cold-blooded murder of babies, little girls and boys and their mothers, by German soldiers and officers . . . the mutilation of dead bodies . . . the devilish ingenuity of the German War Staff in directing the complete devastation of whole districts . . . the torture of French soldiers and Red Cross workers." The pictures of bodies were accompanied by comments such as the following: "This man defended his home and the honor of his young wife against two German officers. They literally carved his limbs into bits, and mutilated his body in ways that men only speak of, and then in whispers." In the words of one eyewitness, the theaters at these events were always packed with enthusiastic audiences, and "everybody took home a vivid impression of the war."[51]

Investigations carried out after the war into all the propaganda services of both sides demonstrated that behind these "atrocities" put on display with such force, there were often specific mechanisms at work: news stories were exaggerated, their emotional effect was intensified, and the war was reduced to single episodes taken arbitrarily out of context; and on occasion stories were even completely fabricated. And it is significant that in the internal correspondence inside the Connecticut Council of Defense about the preparation of these programs, the CPI's original intention to make a distinction between the image of the German people and the image of the German government was termed a "waste of time and energy." This is how, in the spring of 1918, some members of the Council expressed themselves in their comments on programs such as the one described above, going on to suggest that the ferocity of the "Huns" and the "uhlans" should be depicted with ever more emphasis.[52]

Letters like this are important because they shed light on the third key element—besides the scale of the programs and the nature of the message—in this new phase of the propaganda drive: its center of gravity. The structural characteristics of diversification and fragmentation of American society, together with the great excitement that drove private agencies, permanent federal public structures, and mobilization bodies that had been specially created through a combination of public and private resources, soon had the effect of showing that the decisive level in mobilization and in particular in propaganda was not federal power but the power of the individual states. This was especially evident in states like Connecticut, which were blessed with great political stability (and basic uniformity) and a dense and efficient network of middle-class or upper-middle-class private agencies for the protection and development of the best Yankee traditions (Sons of Liberty, Daughters of the American Revolution), and which had considerable financial resources at their disposal.[53]

The centrality of the state and local dimension of propaganda had two consequences. One was, as has already been hinted, a selective interpretation of the messages that came from Washington. This meant not only accentuating their rising emotional temperature, but also reinforcing their authoritarian components and toning down the promises of more internal democracy, which, in the eyes of some, Wilson's internationalist rhetoric implied.

Second, in the interaction between the conditions of emergency and the margins of autonomy wrested by individual states from the federal government, in areas such as Connecticut mobilization came to resemble a projection onto an absolutely unimaginable scale of a phenomenon that could already be seen at work in the activities of the Anglo-Saxon establishment before the war; namely, the circulation (with a multiplied effect that also reinforced the power structure as a whole) of people, ideas, and resources among the worlds of production, public opinion, and public (especially state) institutions. The war had the effect of revealing this process of integration, consolidation, and standardization between the various spheres on the most disparate levels of public life: from the institutional centers of mobilization to the municipal councils (where, against the background of mounting nativist resurgence that marked the November 1917 elections, the Republican Yankees won back the position of mayor even in Waterbury, where they had lost three times), to an FMM or Red Cross rally run by any Scovill manager (Platt and Goss were soon joined by other colleagues).

Of particular importance in relation to this phenomenon of parallel functions between mobilization and the world of production was the part played by Alfred J. Wolff, the veteran toolmaker who, as we saw, was one of the founders of the SFA. His long experience as a captain in the Connecticut National Guard made him an automatic candidate for the position of manager on the local draft committee. And in this role he was able to exercise a function of social control, build up relationships of psychological subjugation, and enter the privacy of individual workers and their families. It was his job to go to the county or state authorities to vouch for the good intentions of the Syrian or Italian worker who had not responded to the first call to arms because he could not understand English, but who had promised to do his duty in the factory. He saved a Russian worker who was in trouble because, after changing his job and residence four times in five months, he had not replied to his call-up papers. After all, who else could a woman worker turn to if not Wolff to report that her husband, who also worked at Scovill, in actual fact lived with another woman and therefore was not supporting his children despite having been exempted from the draft for family reasons? Again, it was this veteran of French origin, whose service in the war had led to his promotion to the rank of colonel, who reported to a company foreman the case of an employee of his who wanted to avail himself of the right to neutrality that he felt was due to him as a Swiss citizen. Wolff spoke to his colleague about this after threatening the Swiss employee using an approach typical of propaganda: the news would spread around the town, his "life would be made miserable for him" and

> . . . when the war was over all the papers would be kept as historical records at Washington and that when his children and grandchildren in years to come would look up the history of his case in the books about the greatest war the world had ever known their feelings could be imagined when they found he was considered a coward.[54]

The role Wolff was playing in his spare time was perfectly in line with the new position that he had been given in the company as a result of the war.

He had been put in charge of the department that between 1915 and 1918 had seen the biggest percentage growth, moving from 16 to 179 workers (in other words, from 0.25 percent to 2.2 percent of the total workforce). This department was called plant protection and in theory was meant to deal with all aspects of company "security," ranging from the basic defense of its perimeters and buildings against any attempt at theft or damage, to the need, reinforced by the launching of the Safety First Campaign, to guarantee the plant against dangers such as fire or damage, accidental or not. In reality, as noted by the War Department officials sent by Washington to oversee the working of the service, it was primarily a formidable spying machine. From this point of view it had no need of "improvement" by the federal structures, who instead urged that more attention be paid to the enforcement of fire regulations.[55]

Reading the meticulously drawn-up list of people that Wolff had on his payroll, one might consider superfluous the CPI posters headed "Spies and Lies" that were hanging up all over the plant urging every worker to "become a detective" and to "report the man who spreads pessimistic stories . . . cries for peace or belittles our efforts to win the war." The plant protection department of Scovill, as in the other main companies in the city, paid directly about fifty members of the municipal police, hired specially during the war period to work for the company. In addition, there were at least 125 guards who patrolled the factory, plus various informers among the workers and Pinkerton agents hired full-time to "do nothing but hang out in the saloons around the plant where workers meet after work."[56]

Naturally, as with every other large-scale spying activity, the files resulting from this thorough activity of vigilance and militarization of the plant have to be read taking into account the misunderstandings to which amateur informers fall victim, as well as the zealous excesses that the Pinkerton professionals committed in order to justify their pay. Unfortunately, only a small fraction of these files have survived. But even the limited sample available seems to offer ample confirmation of the view that Goss and Wolff repeated proudly in the correspondence they conducted with the authorities and with private individuals; namely, that the company remained true to its reputation as an "open shop" plant with everything under control.[57]

The employees whose names landed in these files were, for example, workers reported for spending "most of their time sleeping" or "walking around the factory instead of working," and also foremen and assistant foremen who extorted gifts or favors from their workers in return for turning a blind eye to poor performance, German workers with a "suspicious"

air about them, and the occasional Italian or Russian worker with a reputation for revolutionary union activity or Bolshevism. In the case of one of
these men, a certain Boyko, the plant protection department, in its typically
terse language, reconstructed his every movement—whether he was buying a Liberty Bond or attending a friend's funeral.[58]

Besides otherwise unknown figures like Boyko, the company also had on
its files people such as the veteran militant of American radicalism, Joseph
Ettor, the national leader of the Industrial Workers of the World (IWW)
and a hero of the 1912 Lawrence textile strike. The brief note about him in
the Scovill archive shows how company intelligence targeted not only the
workers but also any activity surrounding the factory. It offers the only
remaining trace of a whirlwind visit to Waterbury by Ettor in February
1917. Ettor had already been to Waterbury in July 1915 to hold a speech in
Italian before a crowd of 150 of his countrymen and to make an initial
attempt to organize the working class in a city where, except for the brick-
layers' and cigar makers' unions, everything else was open shop and there
was no room even for the moderate American Federation of Labor (AFL).
At its conference that year, the state federation of the AFL had criticized the
attempts by the revolutionary union to make inroads into the city. About
his second visit to Waterbury, in February 1917, we know only that Ettor
was arrested by the police and then immediately released on bail.[59]

The following June, at the first signs of agitation in the factory—in a
city that in the years 1917 and 1918 had seen only four strikes (compared
to twenty-three in Bridgeport and eighteen in Hartford), all in the building sector and only one of which had ended successfully for the workers—
a militant Italian by the name of Ferri was immediately fired. One of his
colleagues, who was perhaps also a member of the same small group
(around twenty) of Italian syndicalists, including Vincenzo Pasquandrea
and Giovanni Burgnis, all or almost all of whom had left from the same
part of Italy (the area around Foggia and Benevento, where most of the
Italians living in Waterbury and working for Scovill came from) had to leave
the city. His name was Mario Pasquale De Ciampis and he had arrived in
Waterbury in 1916, where he had found a job at Scovill working in internal
transportation, which made it easy for him to get around the whole of the
factory, and, as far as he could, to engage in political activity. In his words,
in the climate of espionage that was felt throughout the factory and the
city, he was given a tip-off that "they were looking for me. As soon as they
spotted us, we were thrown out, they would arrest us. That is why I had to
leave Waterbury."[60]

His comrade Burgnis, who worked in another brass factory in the area,
also avoided arrest. However, he still left traces of his presence in the plant

protection department at Scovill in a file that, in a note dated February 1917, opened with the words: "Dangerous Italian—I.W.W.," and then grew bigger over the years.[61]

What happened to these radicals offers a Brass Valley microcosm of a more general process that was going on across the country: the destruction of any form of dissent, a process that was the reverse side of the attempts at sometimes forced integration that accompanied wartime mobilization. It is obviously impossible to ignore this atmosphere of intimidation and preventive repression when examining the effective influence of these figures within their respective communities and in the life of the city as a whole.

The impression that one gains from accounts such as that given by De Ciampis and when looking through ethnic and WASP newspapers is that these are voices that had little opportunity to express themselves within a local social system that left very few avenues open for dissent either within or outside the several ethnic groups that comprised the city. Externally, they were exposed to government and company propaganda and managerial and public repression; internally, within each national grouping, the left-wing working-class militants had to contend with the maneuvers of the elite of these various colonies, especially within the groups of so-called "new" immigrants. As in many other cities, these elite sought to transform the pressing demand for loyalty to their adopted country coming from the Anglo-Saxon establishment into a means of renegotiating their group role within the wider balance of local politics, as well as reinforcing the position of each respective elite inside its community of origin.[62]

An in-depth analysis of the space that the nationalist leaders of the various immigrant communities managed to carve out for themselves in the public arena of Waterbury would require a separate study. The amount of space varied according to factors such as the size of the colony, its "seniority of service" in local society, how it had been formed, and the political and institutional reality of the mother country in the old continent. To gain an idea of the complexity of the forces at work and of the intricate tangles of lines of affiliation that ran through the individual ethnic groups, let us take a look at two communities considered even before the war the most important among the "new" immigrants present in the city, communities that also happened to live largely in the same part of town: the Italians and the Lithuanians.

According to some unofficial estimates, the Italian colony comprised some twenty thousand people, both first and second generation, most of them coming from the same part of Italy, an area concentrated between Sannio and Irpinia. The so-called *prominenti* of this community had already shown in the prewar period that they were capable of overcoming the parochial nature of mutual aid organizations tied to individual villages and small towns of origin and could present themselves as leaders of a relatively compact group in the eyes of the WASPs and the Irish who controlled the city. This was demonstrated by the existence of a couple of Italian-language weekly newspapers, an independent national parish, early signs of involvement in the local political scene (at first their loyalties were divided between Democrats and Republicans, but later they leaned more clearly toward the latter), and a permanent city committee for the organization of Columbus Day celebrations.

With the entry of the United States into the war these *prominenti* tried, both personally and as representatives of nationwide organizations such as the Sons of Italy, to exploit the ties between the two countries in the name of the Allied cause: on the one hand they threw themselves into campaigns for the Italian Red Cross, and on the other they responded to the appeal by the FMM, who, in the spring of 1918, opened their ranks to "ethnics" so that they could address their fellow countrymen in their own language in support of the Liberty Bond campaign. They did this with such intensity that at one point in May 1918 a rally had to be cancelled because, in the words of one of the coordinators of the events, "the Italian people seem to be tired and do not show the interest they ought to."[63] Furthermore, some of these *prominenti* supported the program organized by the NACL to create sections for various groups, each under a reliable person, often a social worker, belonging to the same ethnic group.

De Ciampis's testimony with regard to the NACL and its Italian secretary, Mary Besozzi, is important because it shows not only the difficulties but also the objective ambiguities of the relations between left-wing militants and nationalists inside the Italian community. While repeatedly emphasizing that there was an absolute ideological gap between the two camps, De Ciampis could not deny the role played by the nationalistic mutual aid associations and their members co-opted by the NACL to resolve the everyday difficulties of the immigrants ("Mrs. Besozzi . . . she was honest, a very honest person, and she treated everybody well, she was never on the side of the bosses, she treated good, in a nationalistic way, of course"). Nor did De Ciampis make a secret of the respectful relationship that for similar reasons bound the small radical collective to the conservative Catholic journalist, Luigi Scalmana ("we were his best friends, he respected us, we respected him"), who, according to De Ciampis, was one of Scovill's spies.[64]

The situation in the Lithuanian community was more complicated, as can be inferred from the fact that, given the subjugation they had suffered in their land of origin under the czarist empire, the Lithuanians were officially registered as Russians during the 1910 federal census. Roughly half the size of the Italian colony, with its own independent church and nationalist association, the Sons of Lithuania, this group suffered the disruptive repercussions of events in Europe more intensely. The Wilsonian principle of self-determination gave them a strong focus around which to uphold the cause of both the mother country and America. This was proved by demonstrations where the stars and stripes were hung up next to a quotation from the Lithuanian hero, the Grand Duke Vytautus, who had put the Germans to rout in the fifteenth century—precisely what the Sons of Lithuania now wanted to do with "the Huns." Inevitably, however, there was at the same time a sharpening of tension in relations with the Poles, who drew strength from the explicit reference to their situation contained in the Fourteen Points, and with the Russians resident in the city.

Things were complicated even further by the October Revolution. This brought together some of the Russians and some of the Lithuanians, at the same time, however, as deepening the already existing divisions inside the Lithuanian community. The section of the community made up of the longest-standing immigrants, mostly merchants and professionals, hastened to offer their loyalty to the United States in a spirit of anti-Bolshevism. Groups of brass workers who had immigrated in the decade before the war to escape conscription under the czar, on the other hand, saw Lenin's promises of self-determination to the nations that had been subject to czarism as offering an effective opportunity for reconciling an attachment to the Lithuanian national cause with a socialist faith renewed by sympathy for the revolutionary experiment launched by the seizing of the Winter Palace.[65]

In Waterbury, as in the rest of the country, this experiment drew a new dividing line between that which was American and that which was not, and after the Armistice, "Bolshevik" and "Russian" took the place of "socialist" and "German" as targets for the authorities and "hundred-percenters."

By 1918, while the war was still raging, the word Bolshevik had made its appearance in the Scovill plant protection department files, next to "socialist," "radical," and "IWW." It is difficult to say what these terms really meant to men like Goss and Wolff. Perhaps they summoned up specters and threats that, as had already happened with the entries about German spies in February 1917, must have seemed very distant but still capable of taking on concrete form at any moment. They appeared remote if one looked at the history of the factory and the city and was lulled by the feeling of security that a simple glance at the payroll with all its guards and informers would suffice to encourage. They came closer, however, if one tried to make a mental connection between the anonymous masses that streamed through the gates and the terrible housing conditions they lived in and the foreignness of their languages. They approached even more ominously close if one saw a connection between the image of that confused mass of people entering the gates and the tensions and conflicting hopes that both the news arriving from Russia and from the collapsing Central Powers and the Wilsonian catchphrases of freedom, liberty, and independence (which the authoritarian spirit behind those patriotic rallies could not completely obscure) brought to the surface even in a "militarized" city like Waterbury.[66]

5. THE OTHER ARMY

It is perhaps no accident, then, that at Scovill as in many other companies at the time, the growth of the spying machine was part of an explosion of welfare initiatives aimed at cushioning the impact of problems such as housing, cafeterias, language, and the different cultures of the employees.

The first person to bring up the problem of a cafeteria had been a worker at the beginning of 1917. The very first suggestion placed in the suggestion box concerned this point, but the relevant company committee had dismissed it with a certain haughtiness because, as a purely "gastronomical" problem, it had nothing to do with the technical side of the factory or with the work environment. The industrial service had been less supercilious when discussing this issue at a meeting held in December 1917 on the advice of the federal ergonomists. But it still took the concrete example of other Connecticut companies, which, in the spring of 1918, had started to run catering services with apparently positive effects on turnover and morale, to persuade Scovill to set up its own cafeteria. In this way the Waterbury company joined more than 220 companies nationwide that, according to a 1916–17 survey, provided a similar service to their employees. Initially designed for two thousand people, the cafeteria was soon enlarged, and in its first year it served more than 114,000 hot meals each costing about 50 cents, roughly equivalent to a sixth of a laborer's daily wage (at a time when a dozen eggs cost 85 to 90 cents, butter from 66 to 75 cents a pound, and a leg of veal 28 cents, and a girl earning $14 a week who had no cafeteria to go to used to spend on average more than half her wage on what were usually hastily prepared cold meals).[67]

For the running of the cafeteria the company requested the cooperation of the local branch of the YMCA, which made available one of its officers to hire and manage cooks, waiters, and waitresses, and to supervise operations. When it came to the much more difficult question of housing, Scovill worked together with the state officials Governor Holcomb had asked in the spring of 1918 to shed light on what was now considered—even at the federal level—one of the most dramatic cases of urban overcrowding in the entire country. As we know, in the spring of 1917 Scovill had introduced the practice of giving small-scale ad hoc aid to some of the homeless poor. Moreover, it had made available to foremen and skilled workers about a hundred houses that they could buy at cost on an installment plan. Faced with alarming evidence amassed by the state officials in 1918 about average rent increases of 80 percent in the course of the previous two years, and with Progressive journals such as *Survey* dedicating articles to Waterbury entitled "Where the real estate sharks prosper and why," the company realized that what it had done thus far was clearly insufficient. They needed to follow the example of Bridgeport, another classic example of a war-driven boomtown whose two leading metal manufacturing companies had invested about $2 million in housing for workers. So after consulting with some state officials, in record time Scovill built some barracks and cheap housing to accommodate several hundred workers and dormitories for young female workers and clerks that in their first year housed about 2,300 women employees.[68]

At the same time, in collaboration with the Food Administration, the federal agency for food supplies, the company provided employees with free market gardens and everything necessary to grow potatoes and other staple foods for family use. Of the many highly organized campaigns run by the Food Administration to rationalize food resources along the line that ran "from the house door to the trash can," this proved to be the only one that met with any degree of success among the lower classes. All other pleas— the incessant messages about the need to change diet by giving up the traditional foods of the various ethnic communities, considered lacking in protein and carbohydrates, or by reducing meat consumption—fell on deaf ears. The appearance of meat on the tables of working-class families—the result of the wage increases produced by the war—had been too recent to persuade the workers to follow the advice of middle-class experts. With market gardens it was different, because here the patriotic impulse and the echoes of rational "new food" from the beginning of the century that inspired the federal experts chimed in with the traditional aspirations of immigrant families to have their own small strip of land behind their house.[69]

Propaganda, the drive toward efficiency, and the partial satisfaction of a specific working-class need were behind another measure that Scovill adopted in October 1918, in this case explicitly following the dictates of the federal work studies report. The company introduced so-called rest periods, in other words ten-minute breaks after the third and the ninth hour to allow workers to relax by singing in choirs organized by foremen and by members of the Liberty Chorus—the choir that had played such an active role at the patriotic rallies.

The use of breaks to have a chat or for physical exercise had already been seen at National Cash Register at the beginning of the century. During that same period the singing break had been recommended by trade and managerial journals as an essential means of increasing cigar production. Basically, all this did was to sanction and adapt for production purposes a practice widely adopted on the job by cigar makers or women doing assembly work. Indeed, once the necessary skill had been acquired in these occupations, it could become such an automatic movement that those doing it felt the desire to do something else at the same time: singing or listening to someone read out of books or newspapers who was specially paid to do so by the workers themselves. In the cigar industry the fear of political works being read out loud during work led some company managers to introduce the musical interval instead.

Frank Gilbreth, a disciple of Taylor who had a strong interest in psychological problems and human engineering, suggested introducing these short pauses in a manual published during the war years. But it was the war itself, with its parallel impulses toward patriotism and efficiency, that permanently added this new element to the "soundtrack" of industrial life: out of a sample of seventy-two companies that used breaks in 1919, only twenty-three (about a third) had introduced them before 1914, while the rest had done so during the war.

What did workers sing at Scovill during these rest periods? Popular songs, love songs, and patriotic songs—songs with lines like: "But there's one rose that dies not in Picardy / 'Tis the rose that I keep in my heart," or "A cheery smile is as good as a mile on the road to victory," or again, "When the great dawn is shining/back to home, back to love, and you."[70]

The singing breaks were only one feature of a packed recreational program that, every day during the lunch break and after dinner, involved sporting contests, dances, and department dinners. Volleyball, bowling, and baseball tournaments between the various departments were organized, and on the basis of these competitions, teams were selected that went on to represent the company in intercompany championships in the Naugatuck Valley and on a state level.

Thus Scovill participated fully in the massive wartime spread of free-time activities in the most varied industrial sectors and in particular in the metal manufacturing and automobile industries, sectors where the manufacturing processes had previously been considered so tiring as to discourage any investment in recreation or breaks. Scovill's program was rich and varied, and to run it yet another committee made up of upper and middle management was created, and a social worker was hired to help the women's company club better organize its resources for these programs.

In the spring of 1918, on the occasion of the third Liberty Bond campaign, the SGC was asked to run a project that reflected a decisive shift in the tone and content of propaganda; now the front was coming ever closer to the factory gates, and the factory itself was turning into a kind of front. The SGC represented the company at the parade of floats that passed through the streets of the city at the conclusion of the campaign. Before describing the floats, we should first, however, take a look at the posters plastered around the city and inside the plant and consider the fund-raising speeches of the FMM and other orators to encourage people to take out Liberty Bonds (which at Scovill met with a positive response from 83 percent of the workers, raising a total of $550,000).

On these posters the war was no longer seen as taking place elsewhere, something conjured up by the embrace exchanged between a soldier leaving for the front and his bride, but rather as a past future, a nightmare that had already become reality, something that was already having tragic consequences for American workers. "How much of your pay do you think you can keep if Germany wins this war?" read the caption to a picture of a German foot soldier with his typical pointed helmet urging the workers who were leaving the factory at the end of their shift to put money in the helmet. Against the backdrop of walls covered with such messages, orators talked of the bonds in speeches that no longer used the term "investment," and the words that replaced it ("interest" or "enjoying the fruits") only came at the end of a rapid sequence of rather vague but very effective quotations from Washington, Lincoln, and Wilson about the virtues of "democracy" as opposed to "Kaiserism." Everything culminated in the clinching observation that "we have the finest government in the world and should do all in our power to maintain that government and support the war."[71]

And what about the floats? Some reproduced the classic scenes of the soldier at the front, the invading Hun or the mother of war. Scovill's women workers were responsible for three of these floats, and not only did they build the floats themselves, they also appeared on them in person, embodying the figures portrayed. One was a scene of women farmworkers ("soldiers of the land"), who exemplified the market garden campaign organized by the Food Administration; another showed Miss Liberty, who illustrated the deepest spirit of American mobilization and recalled the long-standing ties between France and the United States; the third depicted a group of employees in their working uniforms, dubbed the "industrial army," next to a threading machine and a typewriter.[72]

Thus here for the first time the worker-soldier, who was becoming a crucial figure in federal and state propaganda that was aimed ever more openly at the factories, also reached Waterbury. Soon he would appear again in the photograph of the "army at home," in the words of the caption

under the photograph showing workers entering the factory at the beginning of their shift, a photograph that took up the entire front page of the
company bulletin. The caption went on: "The important thing is, they are
on the job, on something which is essential to the winning of Liberty, and
the continuation of Peace . . . either in a military company or at the
munition plant, they will realize that their manhood has reached a higher
standard of usefulness for the nation."[73]

The idea of the industrial army was in fact not an absolute novelty introduced by the war. It had been a pet idea of William James, who wanted to
send the younger generations to be educated in mines or factories, and it
was taken up again by Frederick Winslow Taylor, who had used it as a
metaphor for the battle against what seemed to him to be the waste and
parasitism of the workshops of the past. In the spring and summer of 1918
it became a classic of the propaganda arsenal, and during the rallies organized in factories in Connecticut in July, it metamorphosed into the figure
of the employee-citizen, whose pledge of loyalty to the company was considered inseparable from his pledge to his new country. Observing the large
rally held for a similar pledge by workers at Scovill, a writer was struck by
the scene that presented itself:

> The vast throng hurried from their various places of labor to listen to elo
> quent addresses by English, Italian, and Russian speakers. . . . An inspiring
> sight was the thousands of uplifted hands, repeating the pledge of solidarity
> to the nation and the Scovill . . . this pledge, representing as it does over
> 13,000 people, promises the speeding up of production for all material.[74]

6. A RESPONSIBLE COMPANY

Only four months later, around the time of the Armistice, the "13,000 people" became, in the terminology of the company bulletin, "13,000 souls."
According to the management and the SFA, "the future of this company"
depended upon their "faith and support" no less than upon the ability of
the foremen and managers. This literal application of the spiritual
approach that increasingly characterized the state and federal propaganda
campaign to the economic entity of Scovill comes across as highly incongruous, especially if one thinks of the circulars with which John Goss at the
time of the great July rally reminded the middle managers to "impress
upon their employees that the factory is closed simply for the purpose of
allowing them to attend the Rally and not to go elsewhere."

And yet this article, in which much use is made of terms such as "soul"
and "faith," reflected in its headline ("The Responsibility of Management")
the same phenomenon that some local papers and the observers from the

Connecticut Department of Labor registered: the war had produced a new relationship between company and workers. This relationship was defined in terms of the "responsibility" and "duties" of the company toward workers who, it was said, were no longer the "birds of passage" they had been at the beginning of the century. The new figure that was emerging was that of the employee-citizen, real or potential, who had been asked, and who had agreed, to swear loyalty to Scovill and to the country and who was now the target of systematic interest and a series of welfare and control measures that kicked in the moment the worker entered the factory and went on to include his free time; these measures applied to everyone, irrespective of their seniority or professional level. Of course, the company had not forgotten its established internal hierarchical dividing lines: the SFA continued to hold its separate dinners and annual outings, and in fact, in 1918 the older workers with more than twenty-five years of service received their first official recognition: each was awarded a medal, and his photograph appeared in the company bulletin. All of this, however, became part of a new and more general attitude of sensitivity on the part of the company toward the needs of the whole labor force.[75]

For a start, hiring new workers was no longer an anonymous administrative process, the hasty rubber-stamping of a choice already made by the foremen. Foremen still took part in the interviews, but they did so in tandem with the employment office staff. Besides interviewing the candidates about their working experience, the clerks supervised the medical test, carried out by the company health service; by the summer of 1918 this test was an integral part of the selection procedure. The test, noted the officials of the State Department of Labor, emphasized the criterion for assigning a candidate to "jobs for which the working-man or working-girl is especially fit," also with the "appropriate" use of handicapped people or those with some health problem. These last candidates, if they got through the selection procedure (in November 1918, out of a sample of 190 candidates, about 10 percent were turned down on the basis of the medical check-up), were then later subjected to periodic tests and therapies.[76]

Again from the summer of 1918, each newly hired worker was given a manual on conduct in the factory. These employees' manuals had appeared in the first decade of the century and were considered by engineers and experts on work problems as a much more personalized and therefore effective way of getting organizational and disciplinary messages across than rules hanging up on walls in the various departments. They had been introduced in the Brass Valley at the beginning of the 1910s in the form of the four pages of "information to workers" provided by American Brass. Five times bigger, the Scovill manual outlined much more complicated instructions, which we can sum up under two headings: rights and duties. Among the duties the most important were: strict observance of working hours (marked by sirens and time clocks); the obligation to follow the instructions of the foremen, the safety regulations (whose detailed explanation took up a third of the manual), and the rules (halfway between technical and safety) about the use of cranes and in general about the functioning of production equipment and services; and the absolute ban on smoking, spitting on the ground, gambling, leaving paper or any other objects lying around, and leaving the department without a pass signed by a foreman.

The section on rights opened with a description of the rules about accident compensation, where again emphasis was placed on the need to learn and comply with the safety rules to avoid the danger of accidents. It then went on to point out the existence of the cafeteria and the possibility of participating in recreational activities, recommending that those who did not speak English or were not American citizens enroll in the language courses run by the company and study civics, and recalling that there was a personal welfare office in the industrial service, which was there to help those in need of advice and support about any kind of family, legal, or economic problem.[77]

Of course, the employee-citizen that John Goss and his associates envisioned only enjoyed rights that had been gracefully conceded by the management. They were in fact capable of selling as largesse even provisions such as the introduction of the payment of overtime (in other words, over the basic eight hours) by the National War Labor Board (NWLB) in the early summer of 1918. In line with a decision taken jointly with the state Manufacturers' Association, Scovill partly gave in to pressure from the federal body to grant wage supplements at least when government orders were involved. It did so, however, without referring in any way to the NWLB, and, by incorporating the increase into the fixed monthly bonus that was carried to 15 percent of all workers' wages, it gave the impression that it was a company plan.[78]

And yet there can be no doubt that, however manipulative it might have been, the company did take it upon itself to meet some of the needs expressed by workers in a wide range of spheres, needs that for various reasons other institutions, public or private, were unable to satisfy. This can be demonstrated by the 3,107 cases of personal assistance registered between the end of 1918 and the beginning of the following year or by its broad involvement in recreational programs, in the "war gardens" project, and in plans for a cafeteria: as a result almost 327,500 people used Scovill's services between September 1918 and September 1919.[79]

If we then go on to look more closely at the company's role in the individual schemes, we cannot help noticing its ability to arouse in its workers at times latent impulses and energies that corresponded to crucial emotional and material needs. The English-language courses are a case in point. The enrollment figures for 1918 (about 300 students, with an average attendance of about 140 men and 65 women) are not easy to interpret because we lack the figures that would allow us to compare them with the rest of the country. To give an idea, however, companies with much more deeply rooted welfare traditions, such as Solvay and Westinghouse, could boast enrollments of 159 and 162, respectively, over the same period of time.

These lessons are important not so much because of the numbers involved (see Table 8) as for the way in which they reflect, even through the somewhat distorted perspective of teachers' accounts, not only the process of integration but also the employees' self-directed motivation and personal involvement. Equally they also illustrate the principle of workers acquiring social and survival skills as well as expanding their "life worlds." Numerous cases bear witness to this: the immigrant who was stimulated by the lessons to go to pick up the first document he had filled out in order to obtain his naturalization (almost seven years earlier) shortly before it was due to expire; the students in the courses who saw the command of the language as a resource that might win them promotion to a less tiring job or a pay raise (in December 1919 a total of 155 out of the 200 workers enrolled in the various courses got "individual raises in great measure due to the increasing knowledge of English"); the married women who went along "to keep up to the standard which their children are setting for them" and so as not to be "called 'Wops,' 'Dagoes,' and 'Polacks' by children sometimes their own"; the girls from one class whose teacher took them to a public park to do a lesson, and who thus discovered that they could use such spaces ("They had never visited it, or realized that it belonged to them for recreational purposes," said a teacher). Similar experiences resulted from guided visits (made as part of the civics course) to public institutions like the library, the post office, "and even the police station." The effect was, the teacher said, to improve their "attitude

TABLE 8.

Students Enrolled at Scovill Courses (July 1, 1918 – August 1, 1919)

	Students Enrolled	Successful Candidates
Males	364	105
Females	62	35
Total	426	119

Source: SCII, case 33.

. . . toward the institutions," which became something "real to them" and were "no longer a source of wonder or fear." The story of the young Italian woman who, unknown to her husband and in constant fear of being found out, regularly attended classes in an attempt "to become an American like the women about her," is testimony to the fact that the encounter with American society, thanks in part to corporate mediation, enabled women to carve niches for themselves within the patriarchal and sexist structure of the ethnic family. One should not think, however, that the immigrants completely gave up the other parts of their identity while they were redefining themselves as Americans. As the instructors noted, the coming of the fine weather led to a drop in attendance because the temptation was too great "now that so many employees have gardens and want to rush home to them as soon as they finish work." Obviously there were also times when the workers preferred recreational activities connected to some religious or nonreligious celebration from their country of origin to English lessons.[80]

Even though the industrial service explicitly used in its internal documents the formula "welfare work" to designate some of these activities, shortly after the Armistice John Goss maintained in public that he did not like the expression because it carried with it a "connotation of charity," whereas the idea at Scovill was to "help [the employees] and encourage them to help themselves." At any rate the Waterbury company ended up in the Connecticut Department of Labor report, together with the textile company Cheney Brothers, which with its largely female workforce had a long tradition of paternalism, as one of the companies in the state that was most engaged in welfare activities. The following year its industrial hospital even earned a mention by the welfare department of the National Civic Federation, which had become one of the most prestigious national centers of debate on the subject of corporate neopaternalism.[81]

Thus the war had not only given Goss's company profit levels that allowed it to temporarily reverse its position with regard to American Brass ($13.4 for Scovill compared to $11 million for American Brass in 1916, and $9.2 million compared to $7.1 million the following year); the conflict had also spurred it on to become a leading player in labor policy. Although, in 1915, American Brass had a slightly smaller health department than Scovill, it could boast a pension scheme, the use of manuals for employees, and a library for workers to visit in their spare time. Three years later the situation was very different—to the advantage of the Waterbury company. As some local observers noted, Scovill was now an institution "with a broadened conception of its duty toward them [the workers]"; an institution capable of identifying and working in ever wider areas where it could act, both inside and outside the factory, for the "welfare" of all its employees.[82]

IV

The Roaring
Twenties

1. THE GREAT EPIDEMIC

The story of the work done by one great manufactory in the city of
Waterbury is here given because Waterbury was the manufacturing
town most stricken and because it conveys a lesson that all may con
[*sic*]. . . . This apparent digression is made for the purpose of showing how systematically this concern takes care of its help and how well
equipped it was to do the work which it did and which undoubtedly
was the means of saving Waterbury from a terrible calamity.

In this excerpt from the Connecticut Department of Labor's annual report
published at the beginning of 1919, the Department's officials focused
attention on the assistance that Scovill had started to provide in the previous fall and continued to provide to its employees and, more generally, to
the citizens of Waterbury during the influenza and pneumonia epidemic
that ravaged the brass capital, as it had the rest of the country and the Western world, between the summer of 1918 and the following spring.[1]

In the United States, this epidemic, which has gone down in history as
the "Spanish influenza," caused the death of almost 550,000 people in the
space of ten months. In the last quarter of 1918 the mortality rate from
pulmonary infections was almost three times its natural level, leaping suddenly to 4.6 per thousand, compared to 1.7 in 1917 and 1916 and 1.5 in the
previous year. When contagion was at its height, Waterbury, on account of
its very poor hygiene conditions, held the negative record in Connecticut,
with a death rate of 7.5 per thousand, compared to figures of 6.4 and 6.2 in
Hartford and New Britain, respectively.

Scovill's health-care service played a key role in the aid provided in the
city: it enlarged its ranks, doubling its staff to fifteen, and set up various
groups of volunteers among the workers. Working long hours of unpaid
overtime, these volunteers helped hundreds of families throughout the
city, both company employees and people unconnected to the company.
Most of the volunteers were technicians and white-collar workers, but also

simple immigrant workers, especially Italians, did their part, according to a division of labor that reproduced the organizational hierarchy that applied in the plant, meaning that the laborers had to do the least agreeable, menial tasks, including grave digging. For their part, the company's trained nurses visited 7,200 families and gave constant assistance to over 870 people.[2]

The illness manifested itself in three different ways, each with its own peculiar course. In the first type, the onset of the illness was mild and the patient appeared to recover rapidly within a few days, only to incur a relapse two or three days later of fulminating pneumonia that proved fatal. The second form also started mildly, with minor pulmonary complications that generally cleared up. It took only a short time—thirty-six, or at the most forty-eight hours—for the third group of patients to meet their fate; they immediately ran a fever and came down with a pulmonary infection whose only outcome was death.[3]

Pasquale De Cicco, the young worker we saw being hired by Scovill in February 1916, fell into the second category. In the two years and more that he had spent in the factory, he had become a "young" veteran; he had overcome the embarrassment of having to confess his real age to avoid the draft and had managed to persuade the foreman to transfer him to slightly more demanding jobs. In this way his pay had risen gradually from an initial 93 cents a day to $1.66, then to $2.25 and finally, at the time of the Armistice, to $3.30, with his working day at one point starting as early as seven in the morning and finishing as late as nine in the evening. He had clearly and openly explained to his foreman that he needed to earn more money because he had to help support his family, who in the meantime had moved en bloc from Brooklyn to Waterbury, and to enlarge the small, popular library for correspondence that he had started to set up with the help of the monthly incentive of 10 percent that his mother allowed him to keep for himself.[4]

The occasion to read these books, which included a course on jurisprudence and a collection of European poetry that aroused in him a passion for the law and the poetry of Leopardi he was never to lose, came a few days after the end of the war when he was forced to bed with influenza. He thought that he had probably caught it because of an act of foolishness during the grand city parade held on 18 November to celebrate victory. On that occasion a group of Italians had driven a cart carrying the carcass of a pig wearing a spiked helmet and a sign saying "Kaiser William" from their church to the graveyard. When it came to taking it off the cart, the people following the coffin were reluctant to touch the dead pig for fear of the Spanish influenza. At this point Pasquale and his brother came forward, put the carcass on their shoulders, and took it away to the place where it was to be buried.[5]

2. EVERYBODY GO HOME

For the youngest of the De Ciccos this moment of glory, immortalized in a photograph of the procession that appeared in the company bulletin, was followed by three days of high temperature. The worst thing was, though, when he was better, Pasquale discovered to his sorrow that he had lost his job at Scovill. He was another victim of what was happening to many other workers in the 1918–19 winter who were hit by the decrease in the demand for labor that followed the end of the war. The situation was particularly serious in Bridgeport, New Haven, and Waterbury. In the first two cities, the new year saw an increase in the unemployment rate of between five hundred and one thousand people a week, while in Waterbury in March 1919 there were eight thousand unemployed. Scovill alone got rid of seven thousand people in a four-month period of massive layoffs.[6]

In the words of the company's management, this was a necessity dictated by the irresistible return of the "eternal law of supply and demand." In the face of this law, the promises about the future that that same management had made to the workers in the company bulletin only a few months earlier—where they declared that the company aimed "to run its factory on the level . . . that there will be jobs for all its employees for years to come"—were to prove hollow.[7]

Many people such as De Cicco or Sarah Cappella, a twenty-one-year-old who had started working in the factory during the war as an operator on the pedal press, found that their jobs disappeared with the Armistice. "I worked there till after the war, then we got laid off," Sarah was later to recall. Like many others, she went back to working "black" at home, a type of work that enjoyed renewed popularity in Waterbury after the steep fall it had experienced during the war. As for De Cicco, once he had got over his dismay at losing his first job, he followed the example of thousands of workers and left the city (which lost 15 percent of its population in a few months). His two elder brothers, who were both barbers, had found him a position as an apprentice in a shop owned by a colleague of theirs in New York. He came back to Waterbury in the fall of 1919 and, with some financial help from his family, alternated working as a barber with studying at the local high school.[8]

Clearly, the situation of those whose wage was not a supplement, however necessary, but was in fact the cornerstone of the family economy was much more serious. The winter of 1918–19 saw the inflationary pressure that had marked the wartime period intensify to the point of wiping out much of the real increase in pay that the war had afforded the average worker. According to manufacturers' estimates, these increases fell nationwide from 22 percent to 15 percent in only a few months. In Connecticut, between the winter of 1917–18 and the following winter, nominal wages rose by 41 percent while the cost of living went up by about 55 to 60 percent.

Up until the Armistice inflation had been tolerable for the workers, because it had not yet manifested itself in all its disruptive force, and because the labor market was still relatively favorable to supply. An altogether more serious problem was having to cope with the relentless rise in the prices of foodstuffs (which rose by 60 percent between 1917 and the beginning of 1919), with jobs that were becoming highly precarious (even more so than in the years immediately prior to the war), and with wages that were considerably lower due to the reduction in overtime and the loss of production bonuses.[9]

In formulating its policy on dismissals the Scovill management showed a certain degree of sensitivity toward the problems of working families. Platt and his assistants divided the workforce into three categories, ranked in descending order according to the worker's right to keep his job. At the top came the employees with large families and with the most seniority. Then came those workers who had stood out by virtue of their performance and who had fewer dependents than those in the first group. Lastly, there were the laborers with little seniority and no family members to support.[10]

By May 1919, five months after they had been decided on, these regulations, according to a personnel office internal memo, had been fully implemented: of the eight thousand employees made redundant, 75 percent fell into the third category, 17 percent into the second, and the rest belonged to the first. The note does not say, however, how these dismissals were carried out, since the factory gates were being besieged by war veterans who claimed the right to be immediately rehired, as Goss had promised, and the unusual to and fro of dismissed workers was putting a strain on the exit procedures that the personnel office had put in place in the summer of 1918. There were even cases of people who, in the confusion caused by such a rapid and massive intensification of dismissals, managed to receive severance pay twice: first they were paid by the foremen, who at one point were authorized to hand over the money directly so as to speed up the procedure; then they rushed to the personnel office to be paid a second time by the administrative services before the receipts countersigned by the foremen got that far.[11]

Clearly, this vast phenomenon of "breaking lines" affected the various strata in the company hierarchy differently. Among the laborers, the areas hardest hit (with numbers more than halved) were, predictably enough, the foundry, the rolled brass section, and internal transportation, where there was an abundance of hands (who made up 35 percent of the total workforce in 1918). There was more continuity, however, in the toolmaking department, where skilled workers predominated (making up 12 percent of the total workforce). The skimming process that took place in the spring of 1919 reduced this department by 10 percent, while the personnel involved in manufacturing processes—mostly semiskilled machine tenders, who accounted for slightly more than half the entire workforce—was reduced by a third.

Between 1918 and 1919 the number of female workers fell from 26.3 percent to 20 percent, but then went back up again a couple of years later to a fourth of the total.[12]

3. A SEA OF PAPER

The foremen and the white-collar workers deserve separate treatment. By the time of the Armistice there were 50 percent more foremen than in 1913. Two years later, the supervisor/worker ratio was $^1/_{13}$, well above the prewar company levels ($^1/_{24}$) and the averages for the entire industry ($^1/_{14}$ in 1920).[13]

It is more difficult to talk about the white-collar workers because of the shortage and imprecision of the figures, especially for the period immediately prior to the war. At the end of the war, "office clerks" (a term that probably referred to the central office and did not include the white-collar workers in the various manufacturing departments) were 489 in number, accounting for 3.9 percent of the workforce, but in absolute terms this was at least three times the total number of white-collar workers employed in 1914 that can be deduced from the most reliable estimates. The layoffs in 1919 reduced their number to 369, with a contraction of a fourth (compared to the cuts of a third and of a half that affected the semiskilled and unskilled workers, respectively). Two years later, in February 1921, by which time we at last have an overall figure, the white-collar workers were over 11 percent of the total workforce (compared to the presumed average levels of 4–5 percent in the prewar period).

The war and the subsequent reconversion, then, led to the consolidation of the command structure and a better coordination of intermediary clerical staff. In line with the nationwide trend, the war also sealed the process of feminization of white-collar workers at Scovill. Women were more than 50 percent of the 489 "office clerks" registered at the moment of the Armistice, and by February 1921 they had even reached 58 percent.[14]

What technical and organizational mechanisms and needs produced and accompanied the expansion of white-collar work and supervision? It hardly needs to be recalled that during the war there had been a marked increase in the spread of written communications, continuing a process we had already seen in the ten years leading up to the war. The difference was that now the phenomenon also manifested itself independently of the largely one-way vertical relationship between the management and the foremen, a relationship that was reinforced in 1918 by the distribution of a manual for middle managers. The prime aim of the manual was to set down guidelines of conduct the foremen had to follow in their relations with the various staffs, making it clear that they had to submit to the rules laid down by the personnel and accounting departments on questions of administration. It also reaffirmed their role as figures of authority who were also to be seen as disciplined representatives of management vis-à-vis the workforce.

Other aspects of the flow of information that had developed during the mobilization were equally important. First, there was the growth in the number of periodical reports that the foremen submitted to the company management in compliance with John Goss's circulars. Within a month the manager's archive filled up with no fewer than two hundred reports about production levels, payrolls, costs, production times, and other variables. Second, there were the important direct communications with the work-force, which the management encouraged through committees such as the safety committee, posters hanging up in the departments, the company bulletin, and the workers' manual. Finally, there was also an enormous increase in "horizontal" written messages, in other words, messages exchanged between sections or departments.[15]

The explosion in formal communications and the ever growing attendant demand for the supervision, coordination, and manipulation of information were the result of the new scale of operations and the need for certification (technical and accounting), which arose out of the contact with military command structures and the expansion of the company's areas of activity beyond simple production. Consequently, the circulation of paper and the added demand for clerical and supervisory personnel came to drive each other on in a circle of cause and effect.

To understand the effects of reconversion, we need to go back to the summer of 1918. At the time the many initiatives taken in response to the most immediate emergencies did not prevent John Goss from keeping his eye on the future. He asked a team of experts in accounting and company administration to carry out a preliminary survey into the overall state of health of the company and the critical problems it would have to contend with when it embarked on reconversion. Familiar with the innovative currents of systematic management that focused especially on the problem of disaggregated costs, these experts seemed to be exactly the right people to carry out a rigorous examination that cut across the entire organization.

After the Armistice, this same group of people were assigned the task of supporting the management in a process of restructuring that threatened to be extremely difficult for the industry. The first to pay the price were the small companies set up during the war to benefit from the military orders. These companies were immediately crushed as they tried to convert to conventional production in a market where even the best-established companies had to pay the price of the excessive productive capacity (on average it had been doubled) accumulated during the war. Proof of this can be seen in the fact that in early 1920 even American Brass was only able to resolve its serious financial problems by sacrificing its independence: through a process of backward vertical integration, it ended up being taken over by America's most important copper manufacturer, Anaconda Copper.[16]

Scovill emerged from the war with its production capacity increased fivefold and a plant two and a half times the size it had been in 1914; it now extended in length for more than a mile inside the city. The first essential thing to do in order to balance the books was to get rid of a substantial section of the workforce as rapidly as possible. But obviously that was not enough. It was necessary to go back to conventional production and thus to the "jobber" approach, which embodied the quintessential spirit of the company. Being a "jobber" meant having some basic product lines (buttons, screws, and hinges) that Scovill under John Goss's administration had tried to standardize; but it also meant putting the company's fortunes essentially in the hands of medium- or small-to-medium-sized orders that involved a significant element of personalization of the goods (lamps, electrical material, valves, all types of components for watches and bicycles, automobile accessories) upon the request of clients.

According to the plant manager and his consultants, the important thing was to match the mentality and the technical and organizational skills acquired during the course of the war to the demands of a market that—because of the company's excess of production capacity and the shadows that the serious uncertainty about the European economic and political situation cast on the international scene and thus also on the United States, who was now an irreplaceable linchpin in that scene—was much more problematic than in the period prior to the war.[17]

In terms of its overall management, the war had taken the company several important steps forward along the path of rationalization; it had brought with it the final elimination of all residual forms of contracting in the foundry; it had forced the introduction of procedures to standardize piecework, favored by the massive scale of the orders; and in general, it had allowed the management to use its administrative structure to exercise more control over trends in payroll and production.

The extraordinary size of the war orders, the profit margins they guaranteed, and the need to carry them out urgently and on the basis of absolute priority were all factors that could cause problems, however, if certain organizational practices that had been worked out during the war to deal with these orders were mechanically transferred to the reconversion phase. Certainly the work of the planning and accounting departments, for example, was more arduous; they now had to contend with orders whose technical tolerances were less demanding but which were also more fragmented and less predictable; what is more, they could not guarantee such high profit margins.

The accounting experts hired by Goss took a three-tiered approach. The first level involved a preliminary check on the reliability of all the statistical data collected in the company. The idea was also to cut down as much as possible on the mass of information from below, which Goss had requested over the years but which now threatened to suffocate him. On this point, the work carried out by the experts with the help of E. H. Davis had immediately positive results. By carefully selecting and redistributing the documentary material, the 200 periodical reports prepared in 1919 became 150 a year later, and then fell to 50 between 1921 and 1922.[18]

Some dreadful mistakes were discovered. Reexamining the data about workers' nationality, for example, it emerged that the sudden increase in the number of Russians in 1915–16 (Table 3) had been largely due to an inexplicable error whereby, in 1915, in a reversal of U.S. census practice, the Russians had been registered as Poles. There were any number of mangled names of employees; this produced discrepancies, in some cases thousands of discrepancies, between the figures in the departments and in the personnel office. This phenomenon once again cast serious doubts on the efficiency of the system of time cards and passes for the workforce.

Not surprisingly, then, this system was the second area where the accounting team decided to intervene. First of all, they introduced time clocks throughout the plant. Every morning, the timekeepers, who for the first time were given a special training course, were meant to note down who was on site and to inform the foremen and the personnel office. This office, in turn, was supposed to carry out spot checks at the homes of the absentees. At the end of the day the timekeepers had to fill out an individual time card recording the attendance of each worker, which orders they had worked on, and manufacturing times (whether piecework or other types of work). Four copies of the time card were distributed: one to the personnel office, one to the planning department, another to the factory administration, and a fourth to the foremen. In this way the personnel office was able to monitor attendance and performance, the planners could define piece rates and working practices, and the accounting department could pay out wages and severance pay.

On the other hand, although the accounting experts agreed that it was important to do something about the actual content of work, they were not convinced that the real problems of a company making such a variety of products could be solved using engineering-based "production motion studies." Such studies, argued the accounting experts, "are all very well in a way, but the real big cost item of this company today is its overhead." Overhead grouped together everything that did not fall under the two main categories of traditional company accounting: labor and raw materials. Despite the attempts to work out standard costs, attempts that Scovill's administrative service had been making since the beginning of the 1910s, overhead remained—at Scovill but also in many other companies—a "black hole." According to the accounting team, the crucial problem was the method used to distribute costs between the various departments. This was to a large extent still based on broad estimates and, what is more, failed to take into account the rapid organizational changes that had occurred during the war.[19]

In an attempt to put things in order, the company was divided into three administrative areas, known as divisions: production (including direct work, that is, the direct transformation of the product), service (functions auxiliary to production such as the tool room, transportation, and the research laboratory), and nonproduction or expenses (in other words, all the staff and services extraneous to production, from personnel to plant protection). For each phase of the order cycle, from the procurement of the order to delivery, a system of checks and inspections was set up, based on a complicated set of forms that the foremen had to fill in, so as to identify the debit-credit relations between the various departments. The idea was to make it possible to see the effective impact on costs of each individual function and thus to fix reliable estimates.

Despite the various efforts to involve the foremen actively through training courses and the distribution of printed material on questions of accounting, the surveys and measures taken by the team of experts met with some resistance. Some of the strongest resistance came from the foundry. Even for one of Goss's most loyal workers, the ex-molder Monagan, who had been running the department for over five years, the accountants and laboratory workers had no right to look at the cost structure and the system of weighing materials. The undeclared war that then broke out between Monagan and one of the experts persuaded Goss once again to slow down the process of innovation. The expert had probably irked some foremen and technicians, even some who were close to the plant manager, because of his overly systematic approach and the rather hasty and rigid way he had presented it.[20]

At any rate, the project of rationalizing the company, which culminated in 1919 in the drawing up of the first internal organization chart in the history of the company, once again highlighted the absolute necessity for a constant flow of documents and a network of specialist services and functions. Although considered crucial to the success of operations, these services could be—and in fact periodically were—curtailed. However, if one accepted the principle that the increasing trend toward the division and specialist structuring of organizational units was necessary for the rationalization of resources and reduction of costs, they could not be dispensed with completely. It was no accident that during the period of factory reconstruction, the administration almost doubled its numbers; the planning department followed a similar pattern, and the personnel office, although it had lost the employees it had gained to cope with the emergency of the last few months of the war, still had about thirty-five to forty workers in the years 1919–20.[21]

4. THE RED SCARE

In the spring of 1919 the effects of reconversion did not spare even the plant protection department, which was more than halved. Yet, with its more than a hundred employees, it was still nine times bigger than it had been in the period before the war, although the plant it now had to oversee was only two and a half times its previous size and the total workforce in 1919, after postwar restructuring, had not even doubled in the five years since 1914.[22]

The atmosphere in the city seemed, however, to justify the maintenance of a surveillance structure of this size. There were the first signs of a phenomenon that in other parts of the country was becoming increasingly violent. This meant that the focus of emotional energy as well as the instruments of pressure and command that had accumulated in an area somewhere between the public and the private sphere during the war mobilization were being shifted obsessively onto one (partly new) target: the Red Scare. To get an idea of what was happening in Waterbury, one needed only to leaf through a local newspaper or listen to a sermon by Pastor Dinsmore, the most popular Yankee preacher in town, who was active in the church Goss attended, the First Congregational Church. At church, in the press, and in other places where local public opinion was formed, such as the Chamber of Commerce, words such as "Russia," "Russians," and "Bolshevism" evoked both the mythical and disturbing image of a nation where "brute force" had triumphed, and the fear that all this might reach Waterbury, or indeed that it had already arrived in the form of the six thousand inhabitants of the Russian quarter.[23]

According to Dinsmore and the local papers, it was there that "rattlesnakes" and professional troublemakers lurked, who ought to be "treated harshly." This is what the hundred-percent Americans of Waterbury urged the authorities to do in Lawrence, the cradle of New England's cotton industry, which in February 1919 had been hit by a general strike against dismissals and the high cost of living, a strike that was seen as a "challenge to civilization." If Waterbury was to be spared such eventualities, added the local politicians, the state legislature would have to authorize the setting up and manning of a city military arsenal worthy of the name, to replace the one that had been standing derelict for years.[24]

These opinions contributed to a spiral of events made up of moves by the authorities and widespread provocative actions apparently staged deliberately to foment anxiety and suspicion in public opinion. An example of this was a police raid on premises where two hundred Russian workers, all members of the Union of Russian Citizens, an ethnic organization responsible for mutual aid and vocational training, were holding a meeting. This roundup caused an enormous outcry, although, despite the banner headlines, the newspapers had to admit that no arms had been discovered in that supposed revolutionary den, simply an enormous red flag and a large quantity of IWW pamphlets, which the policemen had not been able to read because of the Cyrillic script. The very same newspapers put great emphasis on a couple of anonymous letters that the self-styled Bolshevist "bombers" had addressed to Scovill. These were used by the fanatical supporters of conservation against the moderate voices who suggested that, instead of taking a hard line, the companies and the schools should put on more English-language and civics courses.[25]

Already at the time of mobilization, Scovill had shown that in its view the two approaches (the use of persuasion and the ability to fall back on more forceful means if necessary) were not mutually exclusive. While the plant protection department continued to gather information about employees and workers' attempts to organize themselves, the company kept its educational structure, now in the hands of full-time teachers who were part of the personnel office. It maintained and perfected its procedures and rituals.

One of these rituals was, for example, the ceremony where workers were awarded their diplomas. Although it lacked the sophisticated mass stage management of similar events put on by Ford and other companies, this ceremony always produced a certain effect on the workers. According to the accounts by those awarded the diplomas and their colleagues reported in the company bulletin, both the department dinner and the awarding of an imitation parchment where, under the heading "For a Greater America," the student received congratulations signed by the teachers, Platt, and John Goss, were met with great enthusiasm.[26]

Naturally, those who attended the courses hoped that the diploma would be a passport to better, more secure employment, either at Scovill or elsewhere. A good command of English promised to be a decisive trump card in a more competitive labor market, where many manufacturers, worried by events such as the strike in Lawrence, proclaimed their intention to stop hiring foreigners. At least some of these expectations were met in the form of praise from the foremen and the wage increases (and sometimes also the promotions) that accompanied them. Promotions and pay increases linked to the awarding of a diploma had become permanent institutions in the rolling mill. In the foundry there were cases of people such as Joe Kalavuitis and Mike Zalecki who, in the space of three years, moved from being newly hired anonymous immigrants who did not know a word of English to becoming foremen, and much of the credit for this, according to their superior, went to the English course.[27]

The teachers' weekly reports, on which this information is based, were suddenly discontinued at the end of June. The courses were temporarily suspended because of the sudden outbreak of a strike that shattered twenty years of social peace in the main industry in the area. Significant levels of conflict in the brass industry had not been seen in Waterbury since the beginning of the century, when the International Association of Machinists (IAM) had tried unsuccessfully to involve the Naugatuck Valley, a major stronghold of the open shop, in its great national drive among machinists. The June 1919 strike, on the other hand, was a mass event: in Waterbury alone some six to eight thousand workers took part, at least 45 percent of the workforce, mostly immigrant laborers and semiskilled workers.

The conflict spread to the city from nearby Ansonia. There the employees of American Brass had downed tools in protest against the cost of living at the beginning of June, flaunting slogans about the abolition of piece rates, equal increases for all, and recognition of the strike committee that had been spread around the factory gates by a varied array of workers including IWW militants, among whom was their national leader Joseph Ettor.[28]

At the first signs of agitation the Scovill management distributed a flyer inviting workers not to join what it called the work of a small minority of "IWWs and anarchists." They replied to the arguments of the Ansonia strikers—their "lies"—with "real facts": they reminded people of the bonuses paid out during the mobilization, the federal taxes that had deprived them of much of their profits, and the company's efforts to carry out the separations made necessary by reconversion gradually and painlessly.[29]

Infuriated by job cuts, reductions in wages due to the loss of the 15 percent bonus immediately after the Armistice, and the constant increase in the cost of living (15 percent in one year), a large number of workers decided to ignore the manufacturers and followed the example of their fellow workers in Ansonia. This decision was made during a mass assembly that took place in a hall in the Lithuanian quarter, where speeches were held in various languages (Lithuanian, Italian, Russian, and Polish).

The assembly had been convened by the so-called Waterbury Workers' Association (WWA), which was not a union in the strict sense of the word, nor did it have links with any national union, either moderate or revolutionary. It was more of a federation, very fluid and informal, made up of two ethnic groups—one Lithuanian and the other, more numerous, Italian—that were "nationalist" in inspiration and included workers and ethnic "brokers" (lawyers, journalists). Strengthened by links with the NACL, these groups sought to exploit the hardship and growing dissatisfaction among workers hit by reconversion, channeling their feelings in a moderate direction that continued the traditional forms of vertical solidarity typical of ethnic mutual aid societies.

The polemical target of the founders of the WWA was the active presence of Wobblies and Bolsheviks in the Lithuanian and Russian communities, a presence whose influence it was feared could extend to the rest of the workers. According to estimates, undoubtedly colored by the spirit of the incipient "red hunt," but certainly with some foundation, in the climate of high hopes and profound discontent that the Armistice and then later reconversion had created among the workers, the Lithuanian socialists could count on 40 percent of their fellow nationals (an estimated ten thousand people), while as many as three-fourths of the six thousand Russian residents were Bolshevik sympathizers.[30]

As during the war, the impact of the radicals inside the Italian community—there were twenty thousand Italians, making them the largest group, bigger than the Lithuanian and the Russian communities together—was on a much smaller scale. Even among the Italians, however, the news of the strikes coming in from the rest of the country in the spring of 1919 and the tangible impact of reconversion had caused some ferment. With the return to the city of Giovanni Burgnis—a figure familiar to the local authorities—picnics had been organized to raise money for the (mostly Italian) strikers in Lawrence, secret meetings, a painstaking process of establishing relations between left-wing militants and nonpolitical workers. These efforts had gradually won over small groups of Italian workers at Scovill and other companies (also making inroads into the local world of crafts and retail trade) to the class message and the invitation to "do what they are doing in Russia."[31]

The effects of these efforts and of the considerable radical presence among the Lithuanians and the Russians could be seen at the meeting called by the WWA. Despite the repeated calls for moderation among the nationalist forces, the workers made demands that echoed those put forward by the Ansonia strikers and, with their strong egalitarian thrust (eight hours, abolition of piecework, equal raises for all, recognition of workers' organizations), betrayed the influence of the forces of the left.

Subsequent events seemed at first to confirm and reinforce that influence on the decisions made by the workers' front. Even more resolute than the hard-line pickets were the workmen's wives in the working-class districts around the plants. They took to hurling stones to stop scabs from leaving their homes to get to work. Not even the batons and the hydrants of the forces of order, which intervened in support of those workers who remained loyal to the various companies, managed to get them to stop. "The female of the species is more deadly than the male": Kipling's remark was used by Waterbury reporters in their description of scenes that a decade of Wobbly strikes had made familiar to the rest of the country.[32]

Then, as events rapidly unfolded, in the space of only a few days the situation seemed to come to a head. The police (made up mostly of Irishmen) tried to quell the disorders by making indiscriminate arrests of strikers and women. During the clashes a policeman was seriously injured. The arrival in the city of the Connecticut National Guard, backed by small contingents of native workers and war veterans, led to the imposition of a curfew, while the Republican mayor placed severe restrictions on the right to hold meetings (which were permitted only at certain times and only in the open air). At the same time, under pressure from the NACL, local merchants, and Irish Democratic politicians (who hoped to regain control of the local administration by putting themselves forward as guarantors of stability in the city), and concerned about the effects that such a continued deep rupture in the civil fabric might have on the elections due to be held four months later, the mayor persuaded the manufacturers and the strike committee to accept the mediation of a negotiator. However, he imposed the condition on the workers' representatives that no extremists would be allowed to sit at the negotiating table. Therefore, in an atmosphere of great tension created by the tumults and the arrest of a Lithuanian socialist leader who was accused of the attempted murder of the injured policeman, the moderate founding group of the WWA was easily able to deny the radicals access to the small negotiating committee. The committee met at the NACL headquarters.[33]

The exclusion of the left did not occur completely without any discussion or disagreement; and at the same time a new voice was urging the strikers who had met together to beware of the extremists in their midst and not to accept a compromise with the manufacturers. The voice was that of an official of the moderate union, the AFL, who had rushed to Waterbury in the hope of finally carving out some space for his organization among the striking brass workers. The AFL organizer worked on two fronts: on the one hand, he met with groups of skilled workers and circulated the news that they were willing to start a battle, so as to exert some psychological pressure on the employers; on the other, with the help of some immigrant workers, he founded a union chapter and tried to urge moderation on the part of the immigrants already on strike.

The majority faction of the WWA exploited both the manufacturers' fears in the face of threats that the skilled mechanics would also stop work, and the isolation of the left and the desire shown by a sizable section of public opinion for a peaceful solution to the problem. Strengthened by the credit acquired in the city as the only legitimate representative of local interests, the WWA managed to keep the AFL official away from the negotiating table. The representatives of the workers went to the table accompanied by NACL officials—both local (the Lithuanian John Genusaitis) and national (the Italian John Spano).[34]

By presenting itself in this toned down and respectable guise, interethnic solidarity managed, ten days after the start of agitation, to gain a partial victory for the workers. Their most ambitious demands (recognition of the strike committee as a permanent contractual party, an eight-hour working day, abolition of piecework) came up against the intransigence of the manufacturers. However, the manufacturers were forced for the first time to come to terms with a collective body representing their employees. They had to compromise even though it was still indirectly through the negotiator chosen by the mayor (the person in question was the secretary of the local Chamber of Commerce, as well as a manager in a machine tool company not involved in the strike). Moreover, although on average the pay raises conceded by the companies were only half of what had been originally demanded by the strike committee, they were unanimously considered a success for the workers.

"The most incredible levels of pay since the day Columbus discovered America," commented *Il Progresso del New England*, the leading Italian periodical, informing its readers that male workers at Scovill would be paid from $5.00 to $6.00 for a ten-hour working day, and the women could, with piecework, receive as much as $4.60, "equal pay for all without distinctions of nationality." The weekly failed to point out that nationality and gender were not the only "distinctions": the skilled workers were rewarded even though they had not gone on strike. They received increases of 25 percent, whereas the others only got 10 percent.[35]

The fear that the agitation could spread to all the skilled workers was, in the view of all the observers, one of the three main factors that led the companies to accept a compromise. No less important was the surprise effect of the totally unexpected show of unity by the immigrant workforce (at Scovill, for example, according to company estimates, more than half the foreign workers took part in the strike). Finally, another crucial factor was the timing of the offensive; indeed, some Scovill workers had a clear awareness of the importance of this factor some weeks before the strike. At their secret meetings they talked about a return to full order books for the company as spring approached and about the opportunity to make advances, winning back with interest that which had been taken away from them during reconversion. Indeed, in view of the first tangible signs of economic recovery and a labor market that was again starting to open up opportunities, the companies were led to give in because they were afraid of finding themselves shortly with too many orders and too few workers.

Apart from management's general sense of relief at having escaped danger, one company official also had a more specific reason to be satisfied now that the strike was over. This was linked to his role in the company, a role that the course of the conflict had made appear absolutely indispensable. The officer in question was the person in charge of the language courses, who noted with satisfaction that, whereas 53 percent of the foreigners had gone on strike, among those whose attended the courses, the percentage dropped to 3.5 percent. This was a sign that, as he wrote in the company bulletin, "Our task seems clearly defined . . . to teach the foreign born to speak, read, and write English. They . . . will in time become valuable citizens and employees."[36]

Certainly, the education officer forgot to add that, however flattering they might be for the company, the figures regarded too small a percentage of the workforce (at the time of the strike, just over 100 compared to a total workforce of 5,700) to justify drawing such a clear dividing line between the strikers and the rest of the workforce. Leaving aside the numbers, however, the words of the official were important because they reflected the way in which the management had put the strike behind it. Although it is true that John Goss expanded the staff of the plant protection department, he was at pains to stress the company's ability to draw on its wartime spirit to counteract the dangers that threatened from outside. This is why there was not only a renewed commitment to the courses but also a decision to continue with the cafeteria, increase recreational activities, and offer more personal assistance to the employees.

The work of the industrial service benefited, again at the discretion of the management and the SFA, various types of people: workers who had had accidents or were in dire financial straits and were considered to be particularly worthy of receiving small loans, bonuses, or gifts of essential foodstuffs; immigrants wanting to return to their home country, who were given assistance in conducting economic negotiations and dealing with consular paperwork and then accompanied by YMCA agents on the long journey to the old continent; in some cases, even, strikers who had been arrested during the agitation and who had been sentenced in summary proceedings held immediately after the conflict. When the company was convinced of their innocence, it endeavored to get them out of trouble, declaring that by doing so it wanted to confirm that "it can go to the limit to see that fair treatment is given to all our employees."[37]

As part of the recreational activities, a club was set up for the younger workers, the so-called Scovill juniors, a colossal annual get together day was organized, and small musical festivals were staged, first for individual ethnic groups, then for different nationalities grouped together according to the department where they worked. These small festivals were an attempt to respond to the insistent requests that the immigrants expressed during the singing break to be able to sing in their own language. Urged on, like the company's women's association, by a group of about fifty workers aged between sixteen and twenty-five, the youth group was vigorously supported by the management, who invested $250 to give them some premises and to help members show films, stage plays, and hold dances. The annual meeting was unanimously adjudged, at the time and in the years to come, to have been the most brilliant and successful in the entire history of the company. For the first time the six thousand participants (almost the entire workforce) were given a brochure that listed the whole program of games for everybody and the professional vaudeville and circus attractions.

The opening page of this richly illustrated sixteen-page booklet reminded the employees that, in the words of the proverb, "all work and no play makes Jack a dull boy." They were guided through the many prize games, trapeze acts, and a wide variety of contests. Eyewitnesses reported that some of these contests seemed to be part of a gradual attempt by the company to follow the example of the women's club in creating an atmosphere suitable to controlled and "healthy" dating. There were, for example, beauty contests for both men and women, and tests of skill that for the first time involved mixed couples helping each other to guzzle down bottles of lemonade or racing to carry lighted cigarettes to the winning line. This was in line with the fact that for some months the company had been organizing talks for its younger employees, accompanied by the projection of films, about venereal diseases, explicitly urging the girls to inform their boyfriends and to take great care.[38]

5. THE PSYCHOLOGY OF "LO SCIOPERO"

After the *cordon sanitaire*—made up of tradition and conservatism—erected in the Naugatuck Valley had proved insufficient protection to keep Waterbury free of the "epidemic" of strikes that made 1919 a record year in the history of factory strife in the country (four million workers, one in five in the entire manufacturing system, went out on strike), in the first six months of the following year, the city even attracted the attention of the national press agencies as it became a leading player in the two largely parallel developments of the Red Scare and industrial conflict. It gained a place in the history of the former when a clerk in a clothing store was sentenced to six months in prison at the beginning of 1920. He had been reported by a customer who claimed to have heard him say that Lenin was "one of the most intelligent" political leaders in the world. Nor did Waterbury manage to escape the avalanche of arrests of real or supposed Bolsheviks ordered by the attorney general throughout the country in the early part of the year. In March FBI agents took into custody, exactly as the local police had done a year before, two hundred militants of the Union of Russian Citizens. Only this time half of these detentions were turned into arrests, with threats of severe sentences or expulsion from the United States.[39]

In April, for the second time in only ten months, conflict broke out at Scovill and in the other leading firms in the area, which at its moments of highest tension was reported on the pages of the *New York Times*. In terms of size, length, and intensity, it figured among the twenty most significant strikes registered in America by the Federal Department of Labor in the first half of 1920. The scale (at times fifteen thousand workers were involved, almost 75 percent of the city's brass workers), length (over three months), and outcome (disastrous for the workers) made this strike clearly different from the previous one. Nevertheless, in terms of objectives and slogans, as well as organizational center of gravity and forms of coordination, there were similarities.[40]

The trigger for the strike was again the unstoppable spiral of the cost of living. Between July 1919 and the following March there had been an increase of 17 percent, which wiped out the wage raises won by the strike and inexorably plunged the budgets of working families into the red. According to a survey carried out in the Italian community, leaving aside expenditure on coal, ice, and clothing, the average earnings of the head of a family, about $27, were about $3 below the probable amount he would need to expend (on the most conservative estimates) to support five people (the average size of a family). In actual fact, state and federal surveys showed that the wage situation was even worse. The pay of a common worker generally did not exceed $23–24 and, in the words of the Connecticut Department of Labor, "the public would undoubtedly fancy scarcely any workers were under the $18.50 class . . . there were many. . . . Some, usually foreigners, worked for as low a wage as $12, $12.50, $14.50 and $16.50, straight 50 and 55 hour time." Many of these men, concluded the report, were married.[41]

In this case, the first body to react was not the WWA, which in the meantime had been renamed the New England Workers Association (NEWA) in order to extend its radius of action to the whole valley. Its official leadership no longer included any of the negotiators from the year before, who according to the local papers had moved away because of the ingratitude shown toward them by the rank and file at the end of the conflict. Through the voice of its largest contingent—the Italians, who numbered about four thousand members, while the Lithuanian and Russian sections each had about two thousand members—the NEWA tried to maintain peaceful relations with the manufacturers, partly through the mediation of the NACL.

The initiative came suddenly from the small local section of the AFL, which had remained as a legacy of the previous year's strike. Its members, about three hundred Italians, Lithuanians, and above all Russians, decided to stop working and put forward a platform of demands (equal raises for all, eight-hour working day, recognition of the union) similar to the one originally presented by the 1919 strike committee.

Faced with this move, which eventually mobilized a contingent of workers that was at least five times higher than the members of the union, the moderate Italian leadership found it impossible to keep the situation under control. The Lithuanian and Russian sections voted unanimously to go out on strike and thus dragged their Italian colleagues into action. Although still very much camouflaged for fear of repression, a significant radical influence continued to make itself felt in the two most militant ethnic communities. The leader of the Russian section of the NEWA was a worker and mathematics teacher for the courses held by the Union of Russian Citizens, the ethnic organization that, as we have seen, was circulating printed IWW material. To defend himself from accusations of subversive activity, when he was detained by the police he called himself a "conservative Socialist," adding that the Communist Party Manifesto, a copy of which was found during a search of his house, was "very conservative." As for the Lithuanian leader, he was a skilled worker who, without embellishing it with explicit ideological references, never deflected from a line of rigorous defense of the demands for economic improvement and more democracy in the factory advanced by the strike committee.[42]

The hundred days of the strike were played out according to this script: the Lithuanians and the Russians of the NEWA led the offensive, trying in vain to unite with the AFL, and the Italians confirmed their involvement, ignoring the repeated calls to order by their leader, the conservative Catholic journalist Luigi Scalmana. We have already encountered him in the oral testimony given by the revolutionary union activist Mario De Ciampis. According to De Ciampis, Scalmana was a spy working for the employers, but also an ethnic leader not insensitive to the needs of the workers, a successful organizer of mutual aid, capable of exploiting for the benefit of his people the connections he had made with the bosses, some local politicians, and the NACL through his activities as a publicist and teacher. He had reinforced these connections through his participation, as orator and coordinator of patriotic demonstrations, in the war mobilization and subsequently through his active involvement in aid work during the Spanish influenza epidemic.

Other reports by workers and some company documents confirm that Scalmana had relations with the Gosses, to whom he presented himself as a *prominente*, an ethnic leader capable of understanding and influencing the mood of his fellow countrymen. The Gosses counted on him, hoping that his oratorical prowess would win out over the zealous supporters of the strike. Scalmana failed on this count on two occasions: First, he failed to keep the Italians away from the pickets completely, and then, once they had followed the appeal by their colleagues, he failed to persuade them to go back home after they had been offered a company store where they would be able to buy essential foodstuffs at cost. This was the only point in Scalmana's plan to help workers fight the cost of living to which the management was willing to concede. John Goss was very surprised when he heard the strike committee reply that what the workers wanted was not "gifts" but a decent wage.[43]

The management was even more taken aback when they discovered a little later that the store, which was operating for those who had not gone out on strike, was also being used by some of the strikers. The strikers were adopting a tactic of taking turns going back to work for short periods of two or three days, just enough time to earn something for themselves and to fill up the depleted coffers of the NEWA; or, when in the same family both the husband and the wife were employed, they took turns between the picket line and the department. This made it difficult for the company to make a realistic assessment of the real percentage of strikers, which, according to official company figures, in the first few weeks was 35 to 40 percent of the common laborers. What was worse, this behavior on the part of the workers seemed to undermine the image of loyalty to Scovill that had been created during the war mobilization.[44]

Goss had confirmation of this when the strike committee reversed the model of the employee-citizen that had emerged during the war in the interaction between welfare and patriotic propaganda. The workers replied to the accusations of the WASP establishment that they represented a fringe of excitable people who were unworthy of the "spirit of 1776," with a militant version of "Americanism," which we often find during this period (for example, among the Slavs who took part in the general strike in the steel industry in Pennsylvania, the Italian, Spanish, and Cuban cigar makers in Florida, and the French-Canadian textile workers in Rhode Island). Some flyers and rally speeches suggest that it was the militant Wobblies linked to the Union of Russian Citizens who brought the phenomenon to Waterbury. The fact is that very soon thousands of workers started flourishing the coupons of the Liberty Bonds they had bought during the war, reminding the manufacturers of the promises of "democracy that our boys gave their lives for" and the "word of honor of our manufacturers who promised everything and gave us nothing," and called the foremen and the manufacturers "Kaisers," "Huns," and "Tsars."[45]

At the same time, speeches were made at rallies branding welfare as "a joke . . . a mask to camouflage the foremen's shortcomings." And when Goss replied that by ignoring the "eternal law of supply and demand," they were behaving like "children who go into tantrums," the NEWA strike committee reacted with polemical references to the singing breaks and in general to the company's recreational schemes. "We don't go into the shops to sing 'ring-around-the-roses.' We produce, and we have a right to demand our price," that is, the right to a wage that covers "a little amusement, of our choosing, in our free time." The committee went on to give a detailed list ("a bombardment" was how it was described by a local paper) of "scores of questions of an intricate economic nature," asking to be given access to the company's balance sheets so as to be able to measure their wage demands against them and against the relationship between prices and costs.[46]

Just as in the previous strike, and in fact even more so, the two parties clashed violently. The most dramatic confrontation occurred toward the end of the agitation and involved the men from Scovill's plant protection department. The head of the company's horse guards killed a young Italian striker after an exchange of fire; precisely what happened was never brought fully to light, and the security guard himself was injured in the incident.

During the impressive funeral that followed, the three sources that went together to make up the identity of the striking workers—use of American democratic rhetoric, class solidarity, and ethnic origin—were highlighted and combined in a truly balanced manner, as had rarely happened during the course of the whole strike. "Deepest sympathy from the people of Waterbury" were the words written on the enormous wreath of flowers, donated by Italians, Lithuanians, and Russians, which lay on top of the coffin—a reiteration of the perfect right of the immigrants to feel that they were an integral part of the city. The Italians had already had occasion to appreciate interethnic support when the Lithuanians and the Russians, who tended to have more money because many of them were bachelors or had no family, had collected money to help out the bigger Italian families when things had been at their most difficult.[47]

Parallel to these acts of solidarity from the outside were similar impulses coming from the entire Italian community. "Innocent victim of an ignorant, brutal and ferocious police force" was the headline reporting the death of the Italian in the paper edited by Scalmana. The same paper had for some time been publishing regularly a long list of donations under the heading, "The heart of the community is with the strikers." Next to mention of $54 donated by a certain Alessandro Guastaferro were written words that Scalmana must have published only after some hesitation: "I beg you to remain united at all costs so that once and for all we can put an end to the slavery that the capitalists are forcing upon the poor workers." Slavery was also the word used by an Italian woman whom the papers dubbed the leader of the strikers and who, together with Scalmana, gave the funeral oration.[48]

Decidedly less inflammatory, but equally sympathetic to the cause, were the statements with which professionals and economic operators accompanied their considerable contributions to the donation fund started by the Italian newspaper. This was the material base that allowed the strike to continue for such a long time. Behind the enthusiasm with which the workers rejected Scalmana's calls for moderation at meetings lay the conviction that they could count on the merchants, landlords, and even bankers in their own community. In a mixture of sincere concern about people who came from the same village on the other side of the Atlantic, national pride, and fear of losing money and customers (a banker who had spoken out against the strike was attacked by a mob of workers who withdrew savings to the value of $50,000), they provided financial help, granted loans, and suspended or deferred payments. No less important for the workers was the awareness that after all Scalmana, however much he was outvoted and forced to threaten resignation (a threat that the assembly turned down each time), would continue to stand by them: he would go on raising funds, running cafeterias, and finding people jobs as laborers for a couple of days, to enable them to support their family and continue the strike in one of the many factories in the surrounding countryside.[49]

"They pay him great homage whether they abide by his judgement or not. Frequently they don't but they shout 'Viva Scalmana' just the same." This was how the complex relationship between the leader and his people was described by an English-language observer whose vivid portrait gives us an insight into the tangle of interests, hopes, and expressive needs that animated any assembly of the Italian section of the NEWA. The article in which this journalist sought to penetrate the "psychology of 'lo sciopero'" as he took a look at the 1,600 workers gathered in the basement of the Italian Catholic church of Nostra Signora di Lourdes, is worth quoting more extensively:

> They are, normally, without any means of self-expression. They work, they sleep, they eat, they read a little, they talk things over with their friends from day to day. . . . Then the strike comes. Here is their opportunity to get together in a mass, to talk out loud and debate . . . have a chance to show they are men . . . shout their defiance to the bosses and to the world, and as they shout they can gesticulate with eight fingers, two thumbs, and both arms. . . . In a thousand˙ ways the strike makes a man feel he is something more than a mere number and that his individuality is something bigger than a brass pay check.[50]

A barber who offered his services for free, a pair of artistes who organized entertainment for the workers, and a confectioner who displayed an enormous cake baked especially for the assembly complete the picture. "A vacation" is what some workers called it. What else could one say about the grand open-air ball organized by the Italians at the beginning of June, attended by four thousand people—Italians, Lithuanians, and Russians—set alight by "the captivating rhythms of the city band and the Caruso band"? Or how else could one describe the workers' processions, with an American flag at the head, which on a sunny day crossed the city and encouraged those watching from the factory windows to leave the building and join them?

Behind those windows at Scovill, foremen were bustling about looking for laborers among the remaining employees capable of filling the gaps that continued to open up in a workforce that had in some parts been more than halved, and where entire units of the production system (manufacturing, transportation, and the new, sophisticated foundry section) were paralyzed. Frequently even those workers who were loyal to the company showed signs of impatience and refused to carry out tasks that they thought were too "difficult" or "heavy." At times the effects were tragicomic, when newcomers or elderly workers made mistakes, or when the management decided to move white-collar workers to manual work, to recall veterans who had been in retirement for years, or to bring students from local schools into the factory.[51]

In the meantime, the work of the plant protection department was very intense. Even before the bloodshed mentioned earlier, the company horse guards had made their presence felt in charges against workers' pickets, and spies had been coordinating with FBI agents, moving around meetings and adding to the personnel files of people like Giovanni Burgnis. At one of the strikers' meetings, Burgnis stood out when he became involved in a violent altercation with a nationalist lawyer close to Scalmana who had tried to turn the discussion about the workers' platform into a long-winded eulogy of the role played by Italy in the First World War. The assembly, which had just voted unanimously for the continuation of the strike, now suddenly found itself divided into two factions, with the majority favorable to the nationalist current, and a smaller, but very fierce, group around Burgnis. In the words of one eyewitness, in a moment "the patriots and antipatriots had it hot and heavy."[52]

Barely a month later, such controversies and in general the atmosphere of the assembly seemed very distant as thousands of workers passed back through the factory gates, this time for good. Not one of their demands had been met by the manufacturers, who indeed after a hundred days of strike had issued an ultimatum, threatening not to rehire anyone who failed to turn up for work by a certain date. To what extent had disputes like the quarrel between "patriots" and "antipatriots," which had broken out in the individual ethnic communities, weakened the unity of the workers' front? The other side of the solidarity shown during most of the strike was in fact the small- and large-scale daily rifts, the recurrent arguments, the difficulty in coordinating the various groups inside the NEWA—on their own and in their interrelations—around a coherent strategy.[53]

Two further factors aggravated these problems. The first was the problem of relations between the NEWA and the AFL. The main point of division between the two organizations— which had a numerical relationship

of five to one in favor of the first—was the difference in the type of workers' representation that they demanded in their respective platforms
(although both made similar wage demands). The AFL wanted the manufacturers to consider the local union chapter as its only contractual
partner. The NEWA, on the other hand, wanted bargaining to be the
responsibility of factory committees elected in the individual plants. Scalmana interpreted this request as a moderate way of thinking about a company union of the type that had come to the fore in various parts of the
country during the war. The Russians and the Lithuanians took a more
radical view, seeing the committees as truly independent factory councils,
united by a coordinating committee between the various companies, as
had been seen during the wartime strikes, for example, at Bridgeport—a
position that put them clearly to the left of the AFL.

Urged to do so by their Russian and Lithuanian members, the two organizations often appeared on the verge of joining forces, but they never
succeeded in overcoming their different approaches to the question of
representation and the shortsighted defense of their respective labels. At
times this defense revealed once again the clash—already evident the year
before—between the logic of a national organization (the AFL) and local
pride (the NEWA).[54]

As if this were not enough—and here we come to the second problem,
namely the stance of the skilled workers—after a month and a half of agitation by the immigrants, a third platform appeared. The skilled workers
now joined in the strike, urged on by an organizer from the machinists'
union, the IAM. Their platform advanced wage demands that differed
sharply from those of the general laborers and, despite official declarations
to the effect that they wanted to contribute to the unified extension of the
strike front, their intervention actually had the sole effect of complicating
the picture and undermining the workers' unity.[55]

In an immediate comment, the syndicalist Italian-language union paper,
Il Proletario, put forward the view that it was the lack of a coherent unified
leadership that thwarted the potential for mobilization inherent in the
NEWA, that "nucleus of a marvelous workers' organization." The newspaper added that among the reasons for the outcome of the conflict was the
different configuration of those external factors—which a year earlier had
contributed so decisively to the partial success of the workers. Most
observers at the time argued for the relevance of this problem, as did most
economists and sociologists who, in the period of the New Deal, reexam-
ined the history of the strike through the filter of oral testimony. In their
interpretation, the workers' mistake had been to undervalue the effect of an
economy where conditions were opposite to those of 1919. The strike had

been called at a moment when the postwar economic cycle, after reaching its highest point in January 1920, was about to wind down into a severe recession that would overshadow the country at least until 1922. This explains the absolute hardening of the manufacturers' position, an attitude that was reinforced by the continuation of workers' mobilization and the concurrent contraction of orders. In this situation, manufacturers such as Goss took the view that not only were there no margins to allow for the distribution of anything at all, but that a production standstill, despite the problems that the underutilization of plants would create, could be beneficial, because it would allow them to dispose of excess products in stock, to absorb the depletion of the portfolio of orders without needing to fire workers, and to save on costs. This is why, despite the difficulties that the strike undoubtedly caused in the day-to-day life of the departments as it went on, the company management appeared less concerned about guaranteeing a return to full production and did not hide its conviction, based on information about a labor market that was daily becoming more difficult for supply, that it could crush the striking workers.[56]

One must also remember that closely interconnected with the structural situation was the stance taken by public opinion and political institutions, a stance conditioned in its turn not only by the state of the economy but also by the atmosphere of the Red Scare. On a terrain where the full effect of the "red hunt" and nativist hysteria could already be felt, the workers' initiative came up against a veritable wall—institutional, cultural, and political. Three months of clashes and provocations also saw the sudden redefinition of patterns of belonging and lines of solidarity between vast segments of the local population, as well as a kind of crystallization of a long history of social contradictions, accumulated and repressed during the course of the profound transformations that had affected the city in the last quarter century and had accelerated during the war. The twofold result was that, on the one hand, there was an alignment of WASPs and "old" immigrants against "new" immigrants and, on the other hand, a coming together of the anti-worker cause and hundred-percent Americanism. So, unlike the year before, there were no voices raised by local public opinion that were in any way supportive of the workers or favorable to an agreement between the parties. Likewise, at all levels of the institutional hierarchy—from the union to the governor and up to the Federal Department of Labor, which at one point the AFL had tried to involve in mediation—the workers, branded as "foreigners" by the establishment, were left to their own destiny.

As had been the case in the major textile centers of the North Atlantic seaboard—decidedly distant from the Brass Valley and from Waterbury in that they could boast a greater militant tradition, but very close in that they were both areas of early industrialization that were feeling the effects of the recession—the combination of internal difficulties within the workers' movement and, in particular, unfavorable external elements frustrated the attempt by the world of labor to speak with a collective voice.[57]

6. RECESSION, VACATIONS, MUSCLE CONSCIOUSNESS

"As far as we are able to judge from our interviews with men . . . the strike has been forgotten." These were the words with which Robert Platt, the head of personnel in October 1920, concluded a message he wrote for John Goss accompanying a brief account of the three months that had passed since the end of the strike. The message also talked about the reinstatement of most of the workforce that had taken part in the strike into the routine life on the Scovill shop floor. Had there been any examples of discrimination in the rehiring of workers? According to Platt, no more than 5 to 10 percent of the men who had been out on strike had been denied the chance to return to their jobs. This had not happened, continued the official in his report, on the basis of punitive criteria of any kind, but for purely technical reasons. In some cases the positions some were able to fill no longer existed, because they had been taken by others or, more often, because of the lack of relevant orders; in other cases, the foremen had pointed to poor performance by some employees as the reason for turning down their applications.[58]

However, the fact that the Russians and the Lithuanians, who had played such a leading role in the agitation, saw their presence reduced by, respectively, 38 percent and 58 percent cannot fail to raise some suspicions. It is true that large segments of both groups chose, immediately after the strike, to leave the city, presumably to escape the repression and legal consequences that followed in the wake of the numerous disorders that had broken out during the conflict. For many Russians this flight was to become permanent, while most Lithuanians came back as soon as possible. Yet it is also true that, to judge from the messages sent by Goss to the foremen and to the personnel office in the months immediately following the strike, the management's policy of avoiding rehiring "subversives" led to a sizable reduction in the numbers of these two groups in the workforce and the decision by some of these immigrants to leave the city.[59]

Once the strike was over the watchword of the company became clear: back to normalcy. Normalcy meant above all the official restoration of the image of bureaucratic company order, founded on regulations that were equal for all, which John Goss had endeavored to put in place in his fifteen years as manager and which had been so violently called into question by the strike committee with accusations against the foremen to the effect that they were "Huns" and "Kaisers" who ruled their departments arbitrarily and with favoritism. Goss knew very well that these accusations were not without some foundation, because he had before his eyes the files of company spies, which contained, although basically related to the lowest levels of the hierarchy and to not very large groups of recidivists, numerous reports of abuses (discrimination against some individuals and some ethnic groups, small-scale extortion, and verbal and sometimes physical violence). For this reason, at the meetings of the SFA he constantly repeated his appeals to the sense of responsibility that all the middle management ought to show as representatives of the management. What worried him was the fact that those accusations formed one of the clearest demonstrations of the break represented by the strike, however short-lived it might have been. Through the strike the workers had exposed a reality at odds with the bureaucratic model enshrined in the regulations set down in the employees' manual. And the strike had also shown that they preferred autonomous collective bargaining with the management to the small benefits—which were essential for everyday survival, such as easier piece rates, job security, and a temporary lowering of the guard by the supervisors in the case of poor performance—that the vertical relations with the lower levels of the hierarchy could make available to the individual worker. The workers on strike had emphasized only the negative and hostile component of this framework—essentially so similar to the mechanisms of deference and subordination typical of the ethnic communities, and yet so different in terms of language, role, and context in which the relationship took place—comparing it, in a subtle political operation, to an "un-American" conduct, unworthy of the democracy in the name of which people had been mobilized during the war.[60]

Goss's maneuver at the end of the strike can come then as no surprise. The manager called together all the foremen and asked them to make a public statement, which appeared in the papers and in the company bulletin, in which they gave assurances that they would put aside any spirit of vengeance toward the workers, forgetting both the expressions the strike committee had used about them, and the acts of insubordination committed in the plant. The message concluded by arguing that the hallmarks of company practice should now be a sense of partnership and teamwork, productive cooperation based on an acceptance of authority by the workers and impartial recognition of their merits by their superiors. To reinforce this image of the foremen as conscientious and disciplined spokesmen of company legality with an injection of civic virtue, which erased every shadow of "Prussianism" and reaffirmed the perfect right of the Yankee manufacturing world and its trustees to consider themselves the heirs and guarantors of the American political tradition, a pocket edition of the American Constitution was distributed among the foremen. At a moment in world history "when so many millions of people are suffering and dying for lack of a stable government," it was, in the words of the company bulletin, "the workingman's charter to protect his personal liberty," the best proof for everybody of the superiority of the American political and social model—a superiority that in the words of Lincoln quoted in the bulletin, every citizen had to defend and "fortify" against "the caprice of a mob," swearing "never to violate in the least particulars the law of the country" and letting "the reverence of the law . . . become the political religion of the nation."[61]

As always at Scovill, declarations of lofty principle were never without a personal, pragmatic touch. In order to concretely improve the relations between the foremen and the workers, a small educational project was launched that was meant to obviate the friction that the poor knowledge of the new map of Europe on the part of the foremen caused between them and the workers. Perhaps following the example provided some months before in an engineering journal by a manager from the electric industry, the foremen were amply informed about how things were going in the Old World, and thus about how the Poles could no longer be called "Russians" or "Germans" and that they had to be careful not to put next to each other workers belonging to nationalities between whom the war, and even more so the peace treaties, had opened an unbridgeable gap.[62]

Returning to normalcy in the sense of relaunching at full speed the mechanisms of integration tried and tested during the war was not as easy as it had been a year earlier. In September the get together day was a much more low-key event, even though, in the words of the company observers, "the jollification in a general way was every bit as good" as the year before. The program itself offered only a few "homespun" athletics competitions and so no brochure was thought necessary. Then the number of spectators was down by a half, despite the fact that there had been an increase in personnel of almost a thousand employees (from six thousand to seven thousand).[63]

What had happened? Had people been kept away by the continuing aftereffects of the second strike, which had signaled a rupture that was much deeper and broader and whose consequences were much more dramatic than those that followed the 1919 strike? Or was it more simply disappointment at a program that paled beside the previous year's event?

Without any direct testimony as to why fewer workers turned up to the event, all we can do is explain the limitations of the attractions on offer.

These limitations were very probably due to the money-saving efforts that were a decisive factor in the reformulation of company labor policy during the fall and winter of 1920. Under the threat of recession the company had started to cut costs at all levels, an initiative that was soon to take the explosive form of mass dismissals. The workforce shrunk from 7,000 employees in October 1920 to 4,700 at the beginning of the following year and then further to 3,500–4,000 at the end of 1921.[64]

To give an idea of what was going on in the city and the nation, suffice it to say that in the space of a few weeks, the recession brought with it two-digit unemployment rates (21 percent)—figures higher than any period since the 1880s. In Waterbury the numbers employed in industry—34,000 in 1919—fell to 27,000 in December of the following year and then to 16,000 in September 1921. In their end-of-year reports the teachers of the Scovill English courses wrote with regret of "massive dismissals." These they said had been the main reason for the drop in enrollments (from 142 to 77) between October and December 1920. Only a few months later, the course disappeared from the company's budget for good. The updated edition of the employees' manual distributed at the beginning of 1922 did contain the usual section encouraging workers who had problems with the language and who were not American citizens to solve both problems as soon as possible. There was, however, no mention of any company courses, merely a reference to the opportunities that local public evening classes offered to those in need.[65]

After the cancellation of the courses, Robert Platt left the company, remaining, however, an honorary member of the SFA, together with his predecessor, Reverend Gallaudet. The head of personnel was now Alfred J. Wolff, the old head of the plant protection department. The professional profiles and company careers of the two men—one a teacher and organizer of social events, with four years' experience of working for the Gosses, the other an old-style skilled worker, foreman, security supervisor, and "senior" par excellence—reflect, in the passage from one to the other, a crucial moment in the history of Scovill—and at the same time in the history of the business world as a whole. It was a transition from one phase—expansive, and, at least in theory, with an emphasis on the management and potential integration of all human resources—to one of "moderation" and "stagnation," to use the words of a scholar of labor policy in the 1920s. As Wolff declared as he took on his position, his reign sought to continue along the path traced up to that moment, but also reflected a realistic appraisal of the situation in which the company and the national economy found themselves. The profit figures drew a clear picture; from $4.7 million in 1919, profits had plunged to $1.1 million the following year, and then dropped further to half a million in 1921. This situation was reflected in Goss's circulars and in his employees' pay envelopes. The circulars simply repeated, with increasing insistence, the call to save money on everything: raw materials, electricity, office supplies. Between the fall of 1920 and the following spring, pay envelopes were made lighter, nominally by a fourth, and there were progressive reductions generalized for all employees.[66]

The realistic impulse prompted by financial constraints was reinforced by the company's lesser objective need for a personnel structure. The changed situation in the labor market and the climate of social pacification that the workers' defeat in the second strike and the recession had created made labor a less critical factor in the company's scale of priorities. For similar reasons, although continuing to report cases of personnel offices that stood out on account of their selection or training procedures, the managerial journals started to indicate a drop in the entrepreneurial interest in this function, cleverly summarized in a *New York Times* headline from January 1921: "Employers Cut Off Personnel Work." A large electric firm, for example, closed its hundred-strong personnel department almost completely, keeping only a few accounting employees to register hiring and firings. In general, however, the automobile industry was the one where the ax of reductions in this type of expenses was swung most violently. Even Ford dismantled the very symbol of its prewar labor policy—the sociological department—and in the spring of 1921, a General Motors manager declared that it was "time for the discontinuance of many industrial relations activities, which may possibly be termed wartime exigencies, and the getting down to absolute essentials."[67]

John Goss would probably have subscribed to this view. In a few months, Scovill eliminated any initiative aimed at the workforce that did not appear strictly essential or where the company could deploy the technique of outsourcing. The language courses were a typical example of outsourcing. Squeezed by the crisis, the company stopped organizing its own courses and joined the majority of the city's companies, which had never launched any Americanization plans. These companies had instead responded to the appeals for cooperation from the Bureau of Naturalization of the Federal Department of Labor. Already active in organizing evening courses in public schools in 1915, this body, in the period immediately before and after the end of the war, had openly directed its energies toward the local companies (and continued to do so, despite the recession), getting them to urge their employees to enroll for language and civics lessons.[68]

The company services that disappeared as a result of these restrictive policies included at least three classic tools of welfare: the library (which had been opened for all employees in 1918), the singing periods, and the store. In all three cases one reason why the management felt authorized to discontinue these services was economic pressure, but another was the fact that the workers had tried to make relatively autonomous use of the space conceded them by the management, in ascending order of enthusiasm, as it were, from the first to the third. Goss had criticized the tendency of some employees to borrow works of fiction from the library during working hours. Both before and after the open accusation made by the strike committee during the strike of 1920, the immigrant workers in particular had attempted to prolong and enliven the ten-minute singing periods by bringing along their own instruments. They had also started taking over direction from the foremen appointed by the management and asking for free time to practice ahead of performances around the factory. As for the company store, it had not only been used by some of the strikers, but what was perhaps even more galling for the management was the way in which most of the workforce had started to use it after the strike was over: namely, very shrewdly and selectively. Bearing in mind their needs, the immigrant workers' families would carefully choose only those goods that were cheaper than in the neighborhood stores. As a rule, though, the local stores were preferred because they were closer to the workers' houses and especially because of the better credit conditions they offered. The impossibility of running the store without excessive losses ("financially, from the company's standpoint, our whole experience was a big loss," explained a company official when it was decided to put an end to the initiative) induced the management to close it, as they had already done with the cafeterias.[69]

The year 1921 saw the abandonment of the get together day. It was not held that year and was replaced the following year by an initiative we shall look at later. By way of compensation, from the fall of 1920 a new term was introduced in a circular to the foremen and from there it went on to appear in a file, full of questionnaires and tables, that regularly swelled John Goss's massive archives. The word "vacation" was not a complete neologism at Scovill. At least since the turn of the century the term had been used to refer to a paid summer holiday (although there was no clear company provision on this point) granted to certain outstanding individual employees (managers, top managers, and some white-collar workers). With the circular sent out by Goss in the fall of 1920, however, the term came to refer to a benefit regulated by provisions that became generally known and carved out a distinct space within the company.[70]

In that space we find differences founded on the concepts of white collar and seniority repeated, but also reformulated. To be entitled to two weeks of paid vacation a year, employees had to be salary earners (clerks and managers paid on a fixed weekly basis) or be paid by the hour (workers, timekeepers, assistant foremen), and prove company seniority of, respectively, six months and twenty-five years of continuous service. As we have seen, the Scovill management had always treated its veterans with a certain degree of respect. Now this respect became enshrined in regulations, and the formal recognition first seen in the awarding of medals introduced in 1918 took on concrete form. At the same time, however, the dividing line between wage and salary prevailed over seniority as such. Indeed it was a division that, while it presumably corresponded to seniority, increasingly appeared to reflect the presence of new formal skills and qualifications brought into the company by services such as the laboratory and the various technical staffs. Unfortunately, there is no relevant data on this point, with the exception of a list dated December 1917 that refers to fifty-six salaried workers but fails to mention their qualifications. Only a fourth of them had at least twenty-five years of service. However, there can be no doubt that the vacation program reflected both the increasing importance of white-collar workers within the overall company structure (in 1923–25 the salaried workers were never less than 13 percent of the workforce) and the internal divisions within the clerical section. The program confirmed the dividing line defined by the relationship between wage and salary, which also ran through the ranks of supervisors and white-collar workers (assistant foremen and timekeepers, as we said, were not paid salaries).

The principle of selectivity based on seniority and salary was after all the element that characterized, in the positive sense, the labor policies of reduction in expenditure in the recessionary phase nationwide. It was then passed on through the years—in a climate of constant social peace and with a labor market that did not create the problems of the war period and confirmed the signs of an incipient expansion of white-collar and technical jobs. Even after the economic recovery, and the renewed (but contained) expansion of welfare activities that accompanied it, companies focused mainly on provisions such as pensions, vacations, employee shareholding, and internal promotions and on the privileged recipient who deserved them. Moreover, it did so in a selective way that presupposed more stability in terms of emotional investment and mutual expectations between management and workers than was to be found in more generalized forms of welfare.

Vacations were introduced at Scovill first of all as a kind of reward to white-collar workers and foremen for their loyalty during the course of the strike (at American Brass in Ansonia some foremen had in fact taken part in the strike), but at the same time they introduced a selective approach that was to remain. The clause referring to continuity of service was the cause of some debate and, in particular, made it necessary to conduct laborious research into the careers of manual workers. Indeed, the enormous lacunae in prewar documentation became painfully evident when it came to compiling the lists of those entitled to benefits. In many cases the management had to rely on the memory either of the veterans being investigated or their colleagues. The result was a list of about 150 workers (and probably timekeepers and assistant foremen) who in 1921 were entitled to a vacation. Very few of these were "new" immigrants: only 3 out of 146 were Italians (in other words, about 2 percent), although Italians made up the most numerous group of foreign-born employees (17.1 percent) and were the "new" immigrant group with the largest number of names on the list of senior workers.[71]

During the course of the 1920s John Goss developed several plans for another seniority-based initiative, this time for workers' pensions. The basic idea was for a pension scheme backed, as was the usual practice, by an insurance company. However, he himself was not convinced of the economic wisdom of any of these plans and they all came to nothing. Nevertheless, in 1922, for the first time a set of rules was established regulating the paying out of accident pensions in the case of disorders caused by old age and not only in the event of serious accidents. In a reworking of some provisions of the state law on workers' health, the management determined that employees with at least twenty-five years of service who were unable to continue working for physical reasons were entitled to a life pension amounting to half their wage, and in some cases, at the discretion of the management, even those with fewer years of service could receive a fourth of their pay. Consequently, the company started to keep a list of its very few pensioners: a mere sixty-three in 1925. It should be remembered, however, that in the same year the equivalent list at American Brass, which had had an official pension scheme for some time, was even shorter. This can perhaps be explained by the fact that these programs generally contained some extremely severe clauses, which were then also subject to the arbitrary decisions of the management.[72]

The company bulletin had started to emphasize the close connection between seniority and loyalty even more since the years of the recession. Incidentally, unlike many other companies who stopped publishing a bulletin (30 percent did so in 1920–21, plus a further 30 percent in the following three years), Scovill never gave up this useful informational tool, even in the most difficult times; all it did, from January 1921, was to reduce circulation (from seven thousand to five thousand copies) to match the reduction in the workforce. The column "Under the Scovill Lantern," which published short biographies with photographs of employees with twenty-five years of service, occasionally occupied a fourth or even a third of the entire issue. Sometimes written by the people involved, these biographies generally consisted of a short reconstruction of the company career of the veterans. It some cases it was ennobled with a reference to a great event in American history that coincided with the employee's date of birth or with the date of a turning point in that person's professional career.

What may have appeared to be simply local color reflected what in reality other company documentation clearly proved—whether it was Goss's circulars or the data relative to welfare expenditure (which in the middle of the 1920s was about 2 percent of the total for salaries, slightly above the national average of 1.5 percent). Despite a reduction in the staff working in the company hospital, the company did keep up its intensive accident prevention campaign and health care for all. Likewise, it distributed its workers' manual (which now contained a introductory section on the history of the company) and continued to provide some form of assistance to individuals in difficulty. In general, however, the impression one had reading the figures for welfare expenditure and personnel was that the management tended to focus its interest on certain resources, resources already brought together to a large extent in bodies such as the SFA, the SGC, and the Scovill juniors. They were given funds and allowed special conditions in the use of spaces and structures for recreational activities, both those belonging to the company and those owned by others.

In the years after the recession, with a workforce that fluctuated between 4,000 and 4,800 employees, the SFA never had fewer than 550 members, and the women's club kept about 450 to 500 members (equally distributed among blue-collar and white-collar workers). Putting the two figures together, one gets more or less the total number of employees who in 1922 organized the event that permanently replaced the get together day: the excursion to Coney Island. This trip was open to everybody, but no more than 1,100 people went along, confirming that the choice of the program itself—which required a contribution to pay for the train journey and the boat trip—was not meant for those whose pay envelope contained the wage of a general laborer—a wage that was not, as it was for many girls in the club, a supplement to the family income.[73]

With the recession now over and profits starting to rise again (fluctuating between $2.5 and 4 million), the personnel office now embarked on its most ambitious project. Again it was a selective project, confirming the direction already taken, but this time the initiative came from Goss himself and not from Wolff. The idea was to stimulate internally the combined growth of skills and loyalty to the company more systematically than the training programs introduced by Platt during the war. Its innovative character lay in the procedure for selecting candidates for future posts as skilled operators, foremen and technicians. The idea had been suggested to Goss by Millicent Pond, a young psychologist from Yale who had written to him asking to be able to write a doctoral thesis on the applicability of industrial tests. Starting as a university intern, she became first a consultant and then a permanent company employee. As we know, vocational and aptitude tests started, especially after the war, to find widespread application in industry, and were able to exploit the vast amount of experience gathered in selecting recruits during the mobilization. Pond administered at least three thousand tests to newly hired workers over her first two years of work, obtaining some interesting results with regard to turnover levels and the criteria with which the foremen assigned hands to the various positions. In particular, she gained positive results in the selection process for the apprentices' school (attended by an average of fifty to sixty students). The school and, in particular, the techniques used in aptitude tests at Scovill, aroused the interest of various experts at the time, including H. C. Link, one of the founding fathers of work psychology.[74]

These tests and the training plan were the showpieces with which Goss, Pond, and the principal of the apprenticeship school presented themselves during the 1920s and 1930s at the meetings of the American Management Association (AMA) and the Personnel Research Federation (PRF), two of the main national associations that defended the importance of the function of personnel and gathered together the small group of companies with the most sophisticated labor policies. Scovill's lack of a structured pension scheme, employee shareholding schemes or company unions, and a broadly based system of internal promotions undoubtedly excluded the company from the elite of big corporations such as those in the electric sector or Procter and Gamble, which were at the forefront of personnel policies. We should not, however, forget that even though in absolute terms the number of personnel offices was to rise during the 1920s, the vast majority of American companies had none at all. Even among the companies with more than a thousand employees, only half could boast such a service. And the Waterbury company's willingness to enter into dialogue with institutions such as the AMA or the PRF—at one point Goss even held an official position in the PRF—placed it somewhat above the average.[75]

Like a large number of American companies who had a head of personnel, in the 1920s Scovill marked time on the ambitious projects it had developed during the war to centralize the monitoring of hiring, early retirement, and transfers. As we have said, the conditions of the labor market—at Scovill turnover dropped from 100 percent in 1920 to 40 percent in 1928, in large part from the steep drop in voluntary departures—made centralization measures less necessary. In practice, despite the regulations contained in the foremen's and employees' manuals, which again emphasized the need for everything to pass through the personnel office, even these aspects ended up in that tangled gray area where, day by day, management and foremen engaged in informal negotiations that determined the organizational functioning of the company. This bargaining involved the individual foremen and the SFA and centered on the system of benefits and promotions and the tendency to reward the most loyal employees by hiring their children and relatives. On this last point, although there were no written rules, management and foremen were often in substantial agreement, and evidence of this can be seen in a column in the company bulletin under the heading "Fathers and Sons" showing photos of various generations of "Scovillites" from the same family.

More generally, the result was effectively a compromise: The personnel office, although it supervised the medical tests, worked together with the foremen in assigning jobs, and, in particular, reserved itself the right to use tests to select skilled workers and technicians, left the foremen a great deal of room to maneuver. The 1925 edition of the foremen's manual for the first time recognized that department supervisors had the right to "suggest" and "introduce" possible new workers. Two years later, almost two-thirds of new entrants, in the space of about fifteen months, were chosen by the foremen.[76]

Among these workers there was also one young immigrant, little more than twenty years old, who came from the area of southern Italy (Sannio and Irpinia) that had supplied so many inhabitants of Waterbury's Little Italy. His account, which is amply backed up by the interviews carried out in the area by the Works Progress Administration during the period of the New Deal, can perhaps help us to understand what Scovill represented to its ordinary workers in the Jazz Age. His name was John Zampino, and he had arrived in Waterbury from the province of Campobasso through the usual family network in 1921, just managing to escaping the restrictions imposed by the immigration law that had recently been passed, but coming up immediately against the difficulties caused by the recession. At first he had gotten by with casual work in various watch factories, normally a mainly female domain, where the pay was lower than at Scovill. In 1924 he had started working in the brass factory, but had stayed only a few months, the fate of many in a labor market that continued to be, at least until the middle of the 1920s, very unstable and unfavorable to supply. He had to wait another three years in the watch factory before he got the chance to go back to work in Goss's plant, where he was given a permanent job in the polishing department, "all heavy, dirty work."[77]

During his first stay at Scovill, Zampino had encountered the first Italian foremen and assistant foremen who had been appointed around 1922, according to criteria that were a combination of technical, social, and political factors. The son of one of these foremen, who was in charge of the laborers in the yard, remembered his father: he "was one of the very few Italian people who could speak English . . . he helped his fellow countrymen find a job and helped the company find people." Then, "if somebody came over here from Italy and went to work in the factory and became an American citizen . . . my father took him down to the Republican Party hall and had him join the Party." The Republican Party, it should be remembered, was the party of the Goss family, who in the 1920s, while on a local level the tradition of Irish Democratic administrations was reviving, even produced a Republican representative in the state legislature in the person of one of Edward Goss's sons; Edward himself had in the meantime become president of the company. The Italian yard boss worked hard on many occasions between the end of the 1920s and the 1930s to canvas votes for him.[78]

In the 1920s there were, however, still very few foremen among the "new" immigrants. When he came back to Scovill permanently in 1927, in his department, populated with compatriots, Zampino found the usual Irish supervisor. There were time-and-motion study experts from the planning department walking around the factory who were gradually intensifying their efforts to analyze and break down the workers' tasks, at least the most repetitive ones. One of the experts involved in this project was later to recall that what the management was trying to do at that time was to develop the worker's ability "to reach over here and pick up a part without consciously looking. This is what I call muscle-consciousness." Zampino immediately discovered that, if, on the one hand, he had to learn to move quickly, on the other, he also had to unlearn other movements, for example, moving around from one department to another, which was expressly forbidden. However, used as he was to the monotony and low pay of the watch factory, he found the variety of the Scovill products and especially the higher pay ("In the clock shop the work was always the same. At Scovill there were lots of small jobs, cosmetics, carts, lamps, varied work, more experience, more money") sufficient reason to put up with the pace, noise and dirt. The important thing was to learn, patiently and with self-control, what one historian has called the "invisible handshake" with the foreman. According to Zampino, "If you did your work, if you did the time,

I never had problems with the boss." The important thing was "not to talk about unions. . . . If you were in the union, they sent you away." The fact is that few people talked of unions in a city where in the first half of the 1920s local ordinances restricted the use of public spaces for collective demonstrations, which applied to most American industrial towns and cities—a city in which it was enough for De Cicco, now a high school student, to express the opinion that "labor is worthy of his hire" to be suspected of extremism by the principal.[79]

Equally, what could a reader have found at the end of the 1920s in the Italian-language papers which a decade earlier had so ardently supported their striking fellow countrymen? Open praise for the labor policy of Scovill, which did in fact offer a small minority of "ethnics" certain opportunities for advancing up the company ladder. In 1929 out of about thirty internal promotions, mostly within the manual labor section, but in some cases also involving promotions from manual to white-collar work, a fifth and a seventh concerned, respectively, "new" immigrants and Italians; and the latter group now made up 6 percent of administrative staff.[80]

It would go beyond the confines of this present study to reconstruct the paths along which these limited careers took shape, in the intricate relationship between the individual (and increasingly complex) ethnic communities, the production system, and life in the city. Likewise, it would be extraneous to examine the forms of survival and collective support within individual neighborhoods or the political and electoral behavior of the other workers, that is, the mass of laborers and ordinary workers such as Zampino and the colleagues in his department. One thing that is certain is that it took the New Deal to give factory workers the chance to find a way of defending themselves that differed from the "invisible handshake" with theforeman. In the climate of strong social mobilization felt throughout the country and protected by the first federal law that recognized the right to organize unions, between 1933 and 1934 an AFL organizer also reached Waterbury to help the brass workers. Zampino was among the first to respond to the appeal, and during a secret meeting held at Scovill he successfully encouraged his compatriots to join the union: "They were afraid. They remembered 1919, 1920. I said: there's a law, we are all comrades, lots of us were from Campobasso, Italians, they can't send us all away and put students here who don't know how to do the work."[81]

Notes

ABBREVIATIONS

Private and Public Bodies

AFL	American Federation of Labor
AMA	American Management Association
CPI	Committee on Public Information
FMM	Four Minute Men
IAM	International Association of Machinists
IWW	Industrial Workers of the World
NACL	North American Civil League for Immigrants
NCR	National Cash Register
NEWA	New England Workers' Association
NSC	National Safety Council
PRF	Personnel Research Federation
SFA	Scovill Foremen's Association
SGC	Scovill Girls' Club
WWA	Waterbury Workers' Association
YMCA	Young Men's Christian Association

Main Unpublished Primary Sources

Documents kept at the Baker Library, Harvard Business School, Boston

SCI and SCII	Scovill Collection I and II

Documents kept at the Connecticut State Library (CSL), Hartford

CMCR	Connecticut Military Census Records
CSCD	Records of the Connecticut State Council of Defense
PGH	Papers of Governor M. H. Holcomb
WPA-CT	Works Progress Administration—Connecticut

Documents kept at the Homer Babbidge Library, University of Connecticut, Storrs

ABCP	American Brass Company Papers

Documents and oral sources kept at the Mattatuck Museum, Waterbury

BWHP   Brass Workers History Project

Documents kept at the Sterling Library, Yale University, New Haven

SSAR   Sheffield School Administrative Records

Documents kept at the National Archives (NA), various Record Groups (RG), Washington

DJF   Department of Justice Files
DLAR   Department of Labor Americanization Records
FMCS   Department of Labor Federal Mediation and Conciliation Service
MIR   Military Intelligence Records

Documents kept at the New York Public Library

NCFP   National Civic Federation Papers

Documents kept at the Archivio Segreto Vaticano (ASV—Secret Vatican Archives)

DAUS   Delegazione Apostolica negli Stati Uniti (Apostolic Delegation in the
              United States)

NOTES TO INTRODUCTION

1. David Montgomery, *The Fall of the House of Labor: The Workplace, the State, and American Labor Activism, 1865–1925* (Cambridge: Cambridge University Press, 1987), 125; Alfred D. Chandler, Jr., *Scale and Scope: The Dynamics of Industrial Capitalism* (Cambridge, Mass.: Harvard University Press, 1990), 120; Thomas Navin, "The 500 Largest American Industrials in 1917," *Business History Review* 44 (Spring 1970): 374; Charles W. Cheape, *Family Firm to Modern Multinational: Norton Company, a New England Enterprise* (Cambridge, Mass.: Harvard University Press, 1985), ix–x; Mary McCarthy, *How I Grew* (New York: Harcourt Brace Jovanovich, 1987).

2. See my *Dal mestiere alla catena. Lavoro e controllo sociale in America, 1877–1920* (Genova-Ivrea: Hérodote, 1983).

3. On the debate about United States labor history at the time this research was carried out, see *Perspectives on American Labor History: The Problems of Synthesis*, eds. J. Carroll Moody and Alice Kessler-Harris (DeKalb: Northern Illinois University Press, 1989). More recent assessments from a comparative perspective can be found in the special issues of *International Review of Social History* 44 (1999) Supplement, *International Labor and Working-Class History* 57 (Spring 2000), and *Social Science History* 24 (Spring 2000). See also Marcel Van Linden, "Transnationalizing American History," *Journal of American History* 86 (December 1999): 1078–92.

4. A broad summary of all these themes is now to be found in Neill A. Wynn, *From Progressivism to Prosperity: World War I and American Society* (New York: Holmes and Meier, 1986); and Ronald Schaffer, *America in the Great War: The Rise of the War Welfare State* (Oxford and New York: Oxford University Press, 1991).

5. Paul Fussell, *The Great War and Modern Memory* (Oxford and New York: Oxford University Press, 1975), and Eric J. Leed, *No Man's Land: Combat and Identity in World War I* (Cambridge: Cambridge University Press, 1979) are the standard works on the topic.

6. See the pathbreaking works on the American home front by David M. Kennedy, *Over Here: The First World War and American Society* (Oxford and New York: Oxford University Press, 1980); and Stephen Vaughn, *Holding Fast the Inner Lines: Democracy, Nationalism, and the Committee on Public Information* (Chapel Hill: University of North Carolina Press, 1980).

7. Stuart Ewen, *PR! A Social History of Spin* (New York: Basic Books, 1996), chap. 6, and Roland Marchand, *Creating the Corporate Soul: The Rise of Public Relations and Corporate Imagery in American Big Business* (Berkeley: University of California Press, 1998), chap. 3, provide an informative introduction with regard to this point.

8. Alan Trachtenberg, *The Incorporation of America: Culture and Society in the Gilded Age* (New York: Hill and Wang, 1982); V. Lynn Meek, "Organizational Culture: Origins and Weaknesses," *Organization Studies* 9 (Winter 1988): 453–73; Pamela Shockley-Zalabak and Donald Dean Morley, "Adhering to Organizational Culture," *Group and Organization Studies* 14 (December 1989): 483–500.

9. Cecelia Bucki, *Metal, Minds and Machines* (Waterbury: The Mattatuck Museum, 1980); Jeremy Brecher, Jerry Lombardi, and Jan Stackhouse, *Brass Valley: The Story of Working People's Lives and Struggles in an American Industrial Region* (Philadelphia: Temple University Press, 1982); Florence Bartoshesky, "Business Records at the Harvard Business School," *Business History Review* 59 (Autumn 1985): 475–83.

10. On Perlman's position, see Selig S. Perlman, *A Theory of the Labor Movement* (New York: Macmillan, 1928); and Leon Fink, "'Intellectuals' versus 'Workers': Academic Requirements and the Creation of Labor History," *American Historical Review* 96 (April 1991): 395–431. On the creation of the service sector, see Stuart M. Blumin, *The Emergence of the Middle Class: Social Experience in the American City, 1760–1900* (Cambridge: Cambridge University Press, 1989); Ileen A. DeVault, *Sons and Daughters of Labor* (Ithaca, N.Y.: Cornell University Press, 1990); and Olivier Zunz, *Making America Corporate, 1870–1920* (Chicago: The University of Chicago Press, 1990).

11. David Brody, *Steelworkers in America: The Nonunion Era* (New York: Harper & Row, 1960), chap. 9; Daniel Nelson, *Managers and Workers: Origins of the New Factory System in the United States, 1880–1920* (Madison: University of Wisconsin Press, 1975), chap. 8; Melvin Dubofsky, "Abortive Reform: The Wilson Administration and Organized Labor, in Work, Community, and Power: The Experience of Labor in Europe and America, 1900–1925," eds. James E. Cronin and Carmen Sirianni (Philadelphia: Temple University Press, 1983), 197–220; Montgomery, *Fall*, chap. 8. Joseph A. McCartin, *Labor's Great War: The Struggle for Industrial Democracy and the Origins of Modern American Labor Relations, 1912–1921* (Chapel Hill: University of North Carolina Press, 1997) is now the standard account of labor relations during the war. On the tendency in historical studies today to go beyond a basically technical and unilinear vision of productive transformations, see *Masters to Managers: Historical and Comparative Perspectives on American Employers*, ed. Sanford M. Jacoby (New York: Columbia University Press, 1991). On bureaucracy and clans, see William G. Ouchi, "Bureaucracies and Clans," *Administrative Science Quarterly* 25 (March 1980): 129–41. About "factory régimes," see Michael Burawoy, *The Politics of Production* (London: Verso, 1985).

12. On the concept of "work culture," i.e., the set of practices and values worked out by workers on the shop floor, see Susan Porter Benson, *Counter Cultures: Saleswomen, Managers, and Customers in American Department Stores, 1890–1940* (Urbana: University of Illinois Press, 1986), and Patricia M. Cooper, *Once a Cigar Maker* (Urbana: University of Illinois Press, 1987). The idea of working-class "opposition culture," which arises out of the complex tension between ethnic group and social class, has been given its most systematic formulation in Richard Jules Oestreicher, *Solidarity and Fragmentation: Working People and Class Consciousness in Detroit, 1875–1900* (Urbana: University of Illinois Press, 1986).

13. For the formula of *unitary corporatism*, I am indebted to Howell John Harris, letter to the author, 18 March 1988. See also Harris's important works: "The Snares of Liberalism? Politicians, Bureaucrats, and the Shaping of Federal Labour Relations Policy in the United States, ca. 1915–47," in *Shop Floor Bargaining and the State*, eds. Steven Tolliday and Jonathan Zeitlin (Cambridge: Cambridge University Press, 1985); and *Bloodless Victories: The Rise and Fall of the Open Shop in the Philadelphia Metal Trades, 1890–1940* (Cambridge: Cambridge University Press, 2000). For the "corporatist" attempts at stabilizing industrial relations during the First World War, see Larry S. Gerber, "Corporatism in Comparative Perspective: The Impact of the First World War on American and British Labor Relations," *Business History Review* 62 (Spring 1988): 93–127, and the following works by Jeffrey Haydu: "No Change in Existing Standards? Production, Employee Representation, and Government Policy in the United States, 1917–1919," *Journal of Social History* 25 (Fall 1991): 45–64; *Between Craft and Class* (Berkeley: University of California Press, 1988); and *Making American Industry Safe for Democracy: Comparative Perspectives on the State and Employee Representation in the Era of World War I* (Urbana: University of Illinois Press, 1997). An extensive overview of the 1920s is to be found in David Montgomery, "Thinking About American Workers in the 1920s," *International Labor and Working-Class History* 32 (Fall 1987): 4–24.

14. Stuart M. Brandes, *American Welfare Capitalism, 1880–1940* (Chicago: The University of Chicago Press, 1976); Sanford M. Jacoby, *Employing Bureaucracy: Managers, Unions, and the Transformations of Work in American Industry, 1900–1945* (New York: Columbia University Press, 1985); Elizabeth Fones Wolf, "Industrial Recreation, the Second World War, and the Revival of Welfare Capitalism, 1934–1960," *Business History Review* 60 (Summer 1986): 232–57; Gerard Zahavi, *Workers, Managers, and Welfare Capitalism: The Shoeworkers and Tanners of Endicott Johnson, 1890–1950* (Urbana: University of Illinois Press, 1988); Andrea Tone, *The Business of Benevolence: Industrial Paternalism in Progressive America* (Ithaca, N.Y.: Cornell University Press, 1997); Sanford M. Jacoby, *Modern Manors: Welfare Capitalism Since the New Deal* (Princeton, N.J.: Princeton University Press, 1997). See also Kim McQuaid, "A Response to Industrialism: Liberal Businessmen and the Evolving Spectrum of Capitalist Reform, 1886–1960" (Ph.D. diss., Northwestern University, 1975). Definitions of welfare work are to be found in H. M. Gitelman, "Welfare Capitalism Reconsidered," *Labor History* 33 (Winter 1992): 5–31; and Howell J. Harris, "Industrial Paternalism and Welfare Capitalism: 'Where's the Beef?'—or "Show Me the Money!'," unpublished, 2001 (in author's possession). For a comparative perspective on welfare work and company culture, see Charles Dellheim, "The Creation of a Company Culture: Cadburys, 1861–1931," *American Historical Review* 92 (February 1987): 13–44; Robert Fitzgerald, *British Management and*

Industrial Welfare, 1896–1939 (London: Croom Helm, 1990); and the special issue of *International Labor and Working-Class History* 53 (Spring 1998).

15. The three images are outlined, respectively, by Chandler, *Scale;* Martin J. Sklar, *The Corporate Reconstruction of American Capitalism, 1890–1916: The Market, the Law, and Politics* (Cambridge: Cambridge University Press, 1987); and Montgomery, *Fall.*

16. A recent brilliant attempt at capturing the complexities of the rationalization process is provided by Harris, *Bloodless Victories.* On the relationship between corporate power, society, and political power, see Robert F. Burk, *The Corporate State and the Broker State: The Du Ponts and American National Politics* (Cambridge, Mass.: Harvard University Press, 1990). Jerome Bielopera, "The Lower Middle-Classes in Philadelphia, 1850–1920" (Ph.D. diss., Temple University, 1999), contains an informative summary of the burgeoning literature on white-collar workers.

17. Jo Ann Yates, *Control Through Communication: The Rise of System in American Management* (Baltimore, Md.: Johns Hopkins University Press, 1990), and id., "Investing in Information: Supply and Demand Forces in the Use of Information in American Firms, 1850–1920," in *Inside the Business Enterprise,* ed. Peter Temin (Chicago: University of Chicago Press, 1991). Allow me also to point to Ferdinando Fasce, "Immigrazione italiana e fabbrica USA: Il caso Scovill 1915–1920," *Studi storici* 25 (Spring 1985): 1–21; id., "'Sono esclusi i poltroni': Un bollettino aziendale USA nella prima guerra mondiale," *Movimento operaio e socialista* 8 (Summer 1988): 219–47; and id., "Freedom in the Workplace? Immigrants at the Scovill Manufacturing Company, 1915–1921," in *In the Shadow of the Statue of Liberty,* ed. M. Debouzy (Paris: Presses Universitaires de Vincennes, 1988), 107–21.

NOTES TO CHAPTER 1

1. Arundel Cotter, *The Story of Bethlehem Steel* (New York: The Moody Magazine, 1916), 33; Bethlehem Steel annual balance sheet for 1915 and 1916, Bethlehem Steel Archives, Record Group (from now on RG) 15/272, Hagley Museum and Library, Wilmington, Delaware; John H. Goss, "War-Time Manufacture of Fuzes," *Army Ordnance* 9 (January–February 1929): 224–26.

2. William G. Lathrop, *The Brass Industry in the United States* (Mount Carmel, Conn.: Mount Carmel Press, 1926), 122; Joseph W. Roe, *English and American Machine Tool Builders* (New Haven, Conn.: Yale University Press, 1916), 231. On industrial districts, see *Mercato e forze locali: il distretto industriale,* ed. Giacomo Becattini (Bologna: Il Mulino, 1987), 11–48; and *Un paradigma per i distretti industriali: Radici storiche, attualità e sfide future,* eds. Carlo Marco Belfanti and Terenzio Maccarelli (Brescia: Grafo, 1997).

3. Theodore F. Marburg, "Management Problems and Procedures of a Manufacturing Enterprise, 1802–1852: A Case Study of the Origins of the Scovill Mfg. Co." (Ph.D. diss., Clark University, 1945), 324–38; Letter Book 1828–1830, passim, Scovill Collection I (from now on SCI), Baker Library, Harvard Business School, Boston, Massachusetts.

4. Lathrop, *Brass Industry,* 53, 97–98; Thomas R. Navin, *Copper Mining and Management* (Tucson: University of Arizona Press, 1978), 111–16; Christopher Schmitz, "The Rise of Big Business in the World Copper Industry, 1870–1930," *Economic History*

Review 39 (August 1986): 392–410; *Ninth Annual Report of the Bureau of Labor Statistics of the State of Connecticut* (Meriden, Conn.: Press of the Journal Publishing Co., 1893), 40–43; "Points for Brass Founders," *The Foundry* 29 (September 1904): 11.

5. *Boston Commercial Bulletin*, 3 July 1869; *Awards from Philadelphia International Exposition*, Manuscripts M-5/M, Mattatuck Museum, Waterbury, Connecticut.

6. Lathrop, *Brass Industry*, 122–31; Dun & Bradstreet, Waterbury, Connecticut, RG Dun Collection, vol. 32, pp. 400, 412, 437; vol. 34, pp. 826, 865; vol. 37, pp. 130, 228, and 295, Baker Library.

7. Philip W. Bishop, "History of Scovill Manufacturing Company," unpublished typescript, 1952, Scovill Collection II (from now on SCII), case 59, Baker Library, pp. 63–64, 505, 523; American Brass Association, Manuscripts M-5, box 5/P and R, Mattatuck Museum; Frederick J. Kingsbury's handwritten diaries, 1892 and 1893, passim, 1–2 March and 14 December 1899, Manuscripts M-7, box 3, Mattatuck Museum; "The Brass Industry in the Naugatuck Valley," *Iron Age* 65 (15 February 1900): 20. See also Joseph M. McFadden, "Monopoly in Barbed Wire: The Formation of the American Steel and Wire Company," *Business History Review* 52 (Winter 1978): 465–83; Naomi R. Lamoreaux, *The Great Merger Movement in American Business, 1895–1904* (Cambridge: Cambridge University Press, 1985), 2–3; and Chandler, *Scale*, 120.

8. Frederick J. Kingsbury's handwritten diaries, 28 March 1899; Bridgeport Brass Company shareholders' lists, 28 September 1895, 27 January 1898, and 29 November 1902, BB15-1388/1, Bridgeport Public Library, Bridgeport, Connecticut; Scovill shareholders' lists, 9 January 1881, SCII, box 25A, and 1898–1909, SCII, vol. 234; *Connecticut History Makers*, ed. E. Robert Stevenson (Waterbury, Conn.: American & Republican Co., 1929), vol. 1, p. 35.

9. Homer F. Bassett, *Waterbury and Her Industries* (Gardner, Mass.: Lithotype Co., 1889), 26; Alfred D. Chandler, Jr., *The Visible Hand: The Managerial Revolution in American Business* (Cambridge, Mass.: Harvard University Press, 1977), 357. The best historical synthesis of flexible specialization in America can be found in Philip Scranton, "Diversity in Diversity: Flexible Production and American Industrialization, 1880–1930," *Business History Review* 65 (Spring 1991): 27–90 (on Scovill, see p. 34); and id., *Endless Novelty: Specialty Production and American Industrialization, 1865–1925* (Princeton, N.J.: Princeton University Press, 1997).

10. David F. Hounshell, *From the American System to Mass Production, 1800–1932* (Baltimore, Md.: Johns Hopkins University Press, 1984); D. R. Hoke, *Ingenious Yankees: The Rise of the American System of Manufactures in the Private Sector* (New York: Columbia University Press, 1990); Alexander Johnston, *Connecticut: A Story of a Commonwealth Democracy* (Boston and New York: Houghton Mifflin, 1915), 362–65; "Time of Experimentation," *Industrial Management* 57 (June 1919): 505–6; Mark Twain, *A Connecticut Yankee in King Arthur's Court* (New York: W. W. Norton & Co., 1982), 8.

11. *Scientific American* (13 December 1879); U.S. Senate, *Report of the Committee of the Senate Upon the Relations Between Labor and Capital and Testimony Taken by the Committee* (Washington, D.C.: Government Printing Office, 1885), vol. 1, p. 741.

12. For an outline of patents and innovations in Waterbury, see Joseph Anderson, *The Town and City of Waterbury Connecticut From the Aboriginal Period to the Year 1896* (New Haven, Conn.: The Price & Lee Co., 1896), vol. 2, pp. 410–411, 472. The information about the worker John Van Deusen is taken from John Van Deusen's diaries,

December 1864, 10 January and 20 April 1866, 25 March 1870, 1 and 8 January 1874, 12 June 1878, Group no. 181, box 16, vols. 277–99, Sterling Library, Manuscripts and Archives, Yale University. The Blake & Johnson catalogues are kept at the Mattatuck Museum, miscellaneous material. A similar case of a technical innovation developed by workers, managers, and businessmen in the paper industry is presented in a masterly manner by Judith A. McGaw, *Most Wonderful Machine: Mechanization and Social Change in Berkshire Paper Making, 1801–1885* (Princeton, N.J.: Princeton University Press, 1987), 284–315.

13. M. L. Sperry to Economic Light Company, 10 October 1887, SCI, vol. 310, p. 992.

14. On Whitin, see the company letter books7 April 1885–13 July 1891, Whitin Machine Works Collection, AF 1–3, HA1–5, HC 1–2, MA—5, Baker Library. On the textile industry, besides the splendid reconstruction by Thomas Dublin in *Women at Work: The Transformation of Work and Community in Lowell, Massachusetts, 1826–1860* (New York: Columbia University Press, 1979), see the regulations given by Edith Abbott, "History of the Employment of Women in the American Cotton Mills," *Journal of Political Economy* 17 (January 1909): 19–33, and those of such a major company as Dwight Manufacturing Company in the 1840s and 1860s in Dwight Manufacturing Company Collection, HA-1 and HS-1 and 2, Baker Library. On the metal manufacturing industry, see Montgomery, *Fall*, 187; John C. Rumm, "Working Through the Records: Using Business Records to Study the Workers and the Management of Labor," *Archivaria* 27 (Winter 1988–89): 81–82; *German American Workers*, eds. Harmut Keil and John B. Jentz (Urbana: University of Illinois Press, 1988), 87–88. On the railroads, see Walter Licht, *Working for the Railroad: The Organization of Work in the Nineteenth Century* (Princeton, N.J.: Princeton University Press, 1983), 80–88, 93; and Shelton Stromquist, *A Generation of Boomers: The Pattern of Railroad Labor Conflict in Nineteenth-Century America* (Urbana: University of Illinois Press, 1987), 241–43. It should be noted that by the end of the 1840s, written regulations had even reached the big agrarian companies of the West and the cowboys. See David Dary, *Cowboy Culture: A Saga of Five Centuries* (New York: Alfred Knopf, 1981), 303ff. On corporate written communications in general, see Yates, *Control Through Communication.* On industrial conflicts over new regulations, see *Annual Reports of the Bureau of Labor and Industrial Statistics of Michigan,* Lansing, 1885, pp. 18–60, and 1886, pp. 397–432.

15. "Rules and Regulations," *American Machinist* 1 (December 1877): 3–4; M. L. Sperry to Gilbert Clock Co., 13 May 1889, and T. R. Hyde, Jr., to Goddard Co., 16 May 1889, SCI, vol. 323, pp. 655 and 806.

16. Platt Brothers & Co. Records, Manuscripts 33, box 9/9, Mattatuck Museum; SCI, vols. 310, 323, 325, and 429, passim; *Fourth Annual Report of the Bureau of Labor Statistics of the State of Connecticut* (Meriden, Conn.: Press of the Journal Publishing Co., 1888), 48–51, 122–23. On Platt see Matthew W. Roth, *Platt Brothers and Company: Small Business in American Manufacturing* (Hanover, N.H.: University Press of New England, 1994).

17. Egbert P. Watson, *The Modern Practice of American Machinists and Engineers* (Philadelphia: Carey Baird, 1892), 13, 41–43, 269; Edward Kirk, *The Founding of Metals* (Sharon, Pa.: Charles Van Benthutsen & Sons, 1877), 1, 153–57; Joseph Larkin, *The Practical Brass and Iron Founder's Guide* (Philadelphia: Carey Baird, 1876), 44.

18. *Hand Book of the United Brass Workers' Association of North America,* New York, n.d. (although probably c. 1890), 13, 17, 19, 41–43, 51.

19. *Third Annual Report of the Bureau of Labor Statistics of the State of Connecticut* (Meriden, Conn.: Press of the Journal Publishing Co., 1887), 392–433; Jonathan Garlock, *Guide to the Local Assemblies of the Knights of Labor* (Westport, Conn.: Greenwood Press, 1982), 40–41. On the national climate in 1886, see Oestreicher, *Solidarity;* and Bruce L. Nelson, *Beyond the Martyrs: A Social History of Chicago's Anarchists, 1870–1900* (New Brunswick, N.J., and London: Rutgers University Press, 1988).

20. *Third Annual Report,* 282–97.

21. *The American,* 20 October 1884; *Association Work* 1 (October 1885): 1–2; *The Key Note* 2 (March–June 1888), and Waterbury YMCA leaflets 1892–93, kept at Waterbury YMCA; *First Annual Report of the Bureau of Labor Statistics of the State of Connecticut* (Hartford: Press of the Case, Lockwood, and Brainald Co., 1885), 23–24. There are no up-to-date comprehensive treatments of the YMCA on a national scale. But see *Men and Women Adrift: The YMCA and the YWCA in the City,* eds. Nina Mjagkij and Margaret Spratt (New York: New York University Press, 1997); and Morrell Heald, *The Social Responsibilities of Business: Company and Community, 1900–1960* (Cleveland: The Press of Case Western Reserve University, 1970), 35–36.

22. M. L. Sperry to Fahy's Watch Case Co., 8 October 1887, SCI, vol. 310.

23. On subcontracts in the foundry at Scovill, see Bishop, "History of Scovill," 37–42, 150–89; Annual Statement 1894, SCII, vol. 253, p. 190. On the nationwide massive return to this practice in the 1880s, see *First Annual Report,* 71–73; *Sixteenth Annual Report of the Ohio Bureau of Labor Statistics* (Columbus: F. J. Heer Printing Co., 1893), 17; Ernest J. Englander, "The Inside Contract System of Production and Organization: A Neglected Aspect of the History of the Firm," *Labor History* 28 (Fall 1987): 29–46; Montgomery, *Fall,* 20–21; Dan Clawson, *Bureaucracy and the Labor Process: The Transformation of U.S. Industry, 1860–1920* (New York: Monthly Review Press, 1980); Jonathon H. Gillette, "Italian Workers in New Haven: Mutuality and Solidarity at the Turn of the Century," in *Support and Struggle: Italians and Italian Americans in a Comparative Perspective,* eds. Joseph L. Tropea, James E. Miller, and Cheryl Beatie-Repetti (Staten Island, N.Y.: The American Italian Historical Association, 1986), 40–41.

24. U.S. Immigration Commission, *Immigrants in Industries: Reports* (Washington, D.C.: Government Printing Office, 1907–1910), part XXI, vol. 1, p. 257.

25. Samuel Koenig, *Immigrant Settlements in Connecticut: Their Growth and Characteristics* (Hartford: Connecticut State Department of Education, 1936), 25ff.; Census Office, *Statistics of the Population of the United States at the Tenth Census, 1880* (Washington, D.C.: Government Printing Office, 1883), 447ff.; Department of the Interior Census Office, *Compendium of the Eleventh Census, 1890* (Washington, D.C.: Government Printing Office, 1892); *Waterbury Directory for 1875–76* (Bridgeport and New Haven, Conn.: Price & Lee Co., 1875); *Waterbury and Naugatuck Directory for 1890* (New Haven, Conn.: Price & Lee Co., 1890).

26. Anderson, *Waterbury,* vol. 2, pp. 292–295, and vol. 3, pp. 570–1164; Waterbury, Connecticut, *Manual of the City Government* (Waterbury: The Standard Printing Co., 1891).

27. Deirdre Mary Moloney, "Families, Work, and Social Institutions: A Comparative Study of Immigrants and Their Children in Waterbury, CT, 1900–1920" (master's thesis, University of Wisconsin–Madison, 1989), 28–33. Table 1 takes data from the Census

Office, *Census Reports Population* for the years in question (Washington, D.C.: Government Printing Office, 1891, 1901, 1913, 1922). On "queueing," see Nadia Venturini, *Neri e italiani ad Harlem: Gli anni trenta e la guerra d'Etiopia* (Rome: Edizioni Lavoro, 1990), 224, 228.

28. Nicholas Wickenden, "The North West Potentino Since the Napoleonic Age," *Canadian Academic Annals* 5 (1989): 24–26; Giuseppe Casilli, "Dinamica e struttura della famiglia in una comunità dell'Alto Sannio: Pontelandolfo" (master's thesis, University of Cassino, 1984–85); Augusta Molinari and Roberto Sinigaglia, *Stepnjiak Kravcinskji un rivoluzionario russo tra populismo e terrorismo* (Florence: La Nuova Italia, 1977), 41–42, 99–104, 111–14; interviews by Jeremy Brecher and Ferdinando Fasce with G. M. and G. R., Pontelandolfo, 18 and 19 September 1989. A summary of the discussion on the relations between social conflict and emigration can be found in Donna R. Gabaccia, *Militants and Migrants: Rural Sicilians Become American Workers* (New Brunswick, N.J., and London: Rutgers University Press, 1988); and Bruno Ramirez, *On the Move: French-Canadian and Italian Migrants in the North Atlantic Economy, 1860–1914* (Toronto: McClelland & Stewart, 1990). On chain migrations, see Franc Sturino, "Italian Emigration: Reconsidering the Links in Chain Migration," in *Arrangiarsi: The Italian Immigration Experience in Canada,* eds. Roberto Perin and Franc Sturino (Montreal: Guernica, 1989), 63–90.

29. Bishop, "History of Scovill," 210–13, 322–23. Table 2 is based on the data on workforce and capital taken from Scovill's annual balance sheets, SCII, vols. 253, 254, and 284A, whereas the investment index was supplied by Bishop, "History of Scovill," 130ff.

30. *Waterbury and Naugatuck Directory, 1901* (New Haven, Conn.: Price & Lee Co., 1901); *Waterbury and Naugatuck Directory, 1890* (New Haven, Conn.: Price & Lee Co., 1890); Yates, *Control Through Communication,* 164–68; Scovill internal correspondence, 28 June 1879, 28 June 1880, 26 November 1888, SCI, vols. 257, 261 and 480; H. Thomas Johnson and Robert S. Kaplan, *Relevance Lost: The Rise and Fall of Management Accounting* (Boston: Harvard Business School Press, 1987), 80–86.

31. *Scovill Bulletin* (from now on *SB*), February–March 1925, SCII, vol. 316. On *systematic management,* see Joseph A. Litterer, "Systematic Management: The Search for Order and Integration," *Business History Review* 35 (Winter 1961): 461–76; and Daniel Nelson, *Frederick Winslow Taylor and the Rise of Scientific Management* (Madison: University of Wisconsin Press, 1980).

32. Syllabuses and minutes of Faculty Meetings at the Sheffield School, Sheffield School Administrative Records (from now on SSAR), box 9, Sterling Library, p. 241.; 33. SSAR; *Thirteenth Annual Report of the Commissioner of Labor: Hand and Machine Labor* (Washington, D.C.: Government Printing Office, 1899), vol. 1, pp. 149–50, and vol. 2, pp. 646–47; Cost Analysis Sheet, 1911–1913, SCII, vol. 324.

34. J. H. Goss to C. P. Goss, Sr., 22 February 1905, SCII, case 34. John Goss's circulars are kept in SCII, vols. 257 and 258.

35. Ibid.

36. Ibid.

37. J. H. Goss to the foremen and to E. J. Davis, 11 December 1905; 1 October 1906; 1 June and 13 September 1907; 8, 9, 24, 27, and 31 December 1910; 5 June, 3 and 9 October 1912; 1 February 1913. All in SCII, case 34.

38. J. H. Goss to the foremen, 1904–1905, SCII, vols. 257 and 258. On the feminization of white-collar work, see Sharon Hartman Strom, "'Light Manufacturing': The Feminization of American Office Work, 1900–1930," *Industrial and Labor Relations Review* 43 (October 1989): 53–71; id., *Beyond the Typewriter: Gender, Class, and the Origins of Modern American Office Work, 1900–1930* (Urbana: University of Illinois Press, 1992); and Angel Kwolek-Folland, *Engendering Business: Men and Women in the Corporate Office, 1870–1930* (Baltimore, Md.: Johns Hopkins University Press, 1994). For data about clerks in the brass sector at Waterbury, see Department of Commerce Bureau of the Census, *Census of Manufactures, 1914* (Washington, D.C.: Government Printing Office, 1918), vol. 2, p. 303.

39. Stevenson, *Connecticut History Makers*, 109–11; Charles S. Judd, "History of American Brass Co.," unpublished typescript, 1955, Mattatuck Museum; *First Laboratory in the Non-ferrous Metal Industry*, box 4/12, American Brass Company Papers (from now on ABCP), Homer Babbidge Library, Historical Manuscripts and Archives, University of Connecticut, Storrs; "Melting Brass," *Foundry* (July 1901): 213–14.

40. Bishop, "History of Scovill," 214.

41. Bishop, "History of Scovill," 210–16; "Terrill Brass and Copper Notes," unpublished typescript, Works Progress Administration—Connecticut (from now on WPA-CT), RG 33, box 208/8, Connecticut State Library (from now on CSL), Hartford, Connecticut.

42. On the toolmakers' 1901 strike, see *Republican*, May–July 1901; *Iron Age*, 67 (6 June): 25–27, and 68 (25 July): 24–25; Scovill to Dean, Chase & Co., 22 May 1901, Scovill to American Ordnance, 7 June 1901, C. P. Goss, Sr., to G. F. Hardy, International Paper Co., 8 June 1901, E. O. Goss to Frankford Arsenal, 24 June 1901, Scovill to Freeman, Daughaday & Co., 27 June 1901, Scovill to O'Bryan Brothers, 2 July 1901, SCI, vol. 429. On unionization in the town, see *Herald*, 15 February 1903, and *Seventeenth Annual Report of the Bureau of Labor Statistics of the State of Connecticut* (Meriden, Conn.: Press of the Journal Publishing Co., 1901), 147–81. See also Oliver Carsten, "Brotherhood and Conflict in Meriden and New Britain, Connecticut, 1890–1920," in *Confrontation, Class Consciousness, and the Labor Process: Studies in Proletarian Class Formation*, eds. Michael Hanagan and Charles Stephenson (Westport, Conn.: Greenwood Press, 1986), 19–37.

43. On the political system in Connecticut at the turn of the century, see Frederick M. Heath, "Politics and Steady Habits: Issues and Elections in Connecticut, 1894–1914" (Ph.D. diss., Columbia University, 1965); Herbert Janick, "The Mind of the Connecticut Progressive," *Mid-America* 52 (April 1970): 83–101; and Antonia C. Moran, "The Period of Peaceful Anarchy: Constitutional Impasse, 1890–1892," *Connecticut History* 29 (November 1988): 91–115. For a comparison with the overall national picture, see John D. Buenker, *Urban Liberalism and Progressive Reform* (New York: W. W. Norton & Co., 1973), in particular 11–21, 75, 145, 154, 194; and Peter H. Argesinger, "The Value of the Vote: Political Representation in the Gilded Age," *Journal of American History* 76 (June 1989): 59–90. Recent reassessments on the subject of municipal political transformation on a nationwide level can be found in Shelton Stromquist, "The Crucible of Class: Cleveland Politics and the Origins of Municipal Reform in the Progressive Era," *Journal of Urban History* 23 (January 1997): 192–220; and Christopher K. Ansell and Arthur L. Burris, "Bosses of the City Unite! Labor Politics and Political Machine Consolidation, 1870–1910," *Studies in American Political Development* 11 (Spring 1997): 1–43.

44. Frederick M. Heath, "Labor and the Progressive Movement in Connecticut," *Labor History* 12 (Winter 1971): 58–67; Philip S. Foner, *History of the Labor Movement in the United States* (New York: International Publishers, 1964), vol. 3, pp. 35–36; Montgomery, *Fall*, 272–74; Robert J. Embardo, "'Summer Lightning', 1907: The Wobblies in Bridgeport," *Labor History* 30 (Fall 1989): 518–33.

45. A. J. Scopino, Jr., "Community, Class, and Conflict: The Waterbury Trolley Strike of 1903," *Connecticut History* 24 (March 1983): 29–46; *American, Republican* and *Herald*, January–July 1903, passim; William. J. Pape, *History of Waterbury and the Naugatuck Valley, Connecticut* (Chicago and New York: S. J. Clarke Publishing Co., 1918), vol. 1, chap. 2. For a model of the oligarchic structure of power in a medium-sized city with similar characteristics to the one described here, see J. Roger and E. Jane Hollingsworth, *Dimensions in Urban History: Historical and Social Science Perspectives on Middle-Size American Cities* (Madison: University of Wisconsin Press, 1979), 19–22.

46. *Republican*, September–December 1903, passim; *Ordinances of the City of Waterbury* (Waterbury, Conn.: The Standard Printing Co., 1926), 284; *Waterbury, Naugatuck and Watertown City Directory for 1907* (New Haven, Conn.: Price & Lee Co., 1907), 472–73.

47. *Republican*, 23 December 1899; *Report of Proceedings of the 24th Annual Convention of the American Federation of Labor* (Washington, D.C.: The Law Reporter Printing Co., 1904), 74, 211; *Report of Proceedings of the 28th Annual Convention of the American Federation of Labor* (Washington, D.C.: The Law Reporter Printing Co., 1908), 292; *Republican*, 9 and 25 May, 1 and 24 July 1901; G. B. D'Ausilio, *Columbus Day Souvenir, October 12, 1492–1910* (Waterbury, Conn.: D'Ausilio Editore, 1910); *Republican*, 13 October 1910 and 8 October 1911.

48. *Waterbury, Naugatuck and Watertown Directory for 1908* (New Haven, Conn.: Price & Lee Co., 1908); *Waterbury, Naugatuck and Watertown Directory for 1910* (New Haven, Conn.: Price & Lee Co., 1910); interviews by Ferdinando Fasce with S. B., Waterbury, 2 October 1985, and with A. M., Waterbury, 6 October 1985; interview by Jeremy Brecher and Ferdinando Fasce with C. L., Waterbury, 8 October 1985. The only sectors in the city that managed to install and maintain some form of collective bargaining, albeit extremely precariously, were the construction and cigar-making industries. See, for example, *Cigar Makers Official Journal*, March 1909. On ethnic mutual aid societies in general, see Judith Smith, *Family Connections: A History of Italians and Jewish Immigrant Lives in Providence, Rhode Island, 1900–1940* (Albany: State University of New York Press, 1985); Gary Mormino and George E. Pozzetta, *The Immigrant World of Ybor City: Indians and Their Latin Neighbors in Tampa, 1885–1985* (Urbana: University of Illinois Press, 1987); Gabaccia, *Militants*.

49. *Official Convention Book of the Connecticut Federation of Labor, Twenty-Seventh Annual Convention* (Bridgeport: Advocate Print, 1913), 51; *Republican*, 8 October 1911; Brandes, *American Welfare Capitalism*, 92–102; *Dying for Work: Workers' Safety and Health in Twentieth-Century America*, eds. David Rosner and Gerald Markowitz (Bloomington: Indiana University Press, 1987), xiv ff.

50. The American Brass pension scheme is in ABCP, box 1/19.

51. Circular from J. H. Goss, 10 January 1908, SCII, vol. 257.

52. *Waterbury Men*, November 1903, April 1904, January 1906, Waterbury YMCA. On social Christianity and business, see Judith Sealander, *Grand Plans: Business Progressivism*

and Social Change in Ohio's Miami Valley, 1890–1929 (Lexington: University Press of Kentucky, 1988); and Donald K. Gorrell, *The Age of Social Responsibility: The Social Gospel in the Progressive Era, 1900–1920* (Macon: University of Georgia Press, 1988).

53. Montgomery, *Fall*, 318, 324; *Eleventh Annual Meeting of the National Civic Federation* (New York: The National Civic Federation, 1912), 324; *Waterbury, Naugatuck and Watertown City Directory for 1911* (New Haven, Conn.: Price & Lee Co., 1911), 692; Alphabetical Lists: Groups of Foremen, SCII, box 55b; Richard Coopey, "Structures of Control: Changing Role of Shop Floor Supervisors in the U.S. Automobile Industry, 1900–1950" (Ph.D. diss., University of Warwick, 1988), 148–52.

54. See SCII, cases 33 and 34.

55. Ibid.

56. Ibid.

57. Payroll Analysis, SCI, vol. 76.

58. SCII, cases 33 and 34. On the idea of "service" and the tricotomic vision of society underlying it, see Edwin T. Layton, Jr., *The Revolt of the Engineers: Social Responsibility and the American Engineering Profession*, 2d ed. (Baltimore, Md.: Johns Hopkins University Press, 1986); and Zunz, *Making America Corporate*. Zunz also suggests a possible continuity between craft and profession; on this, see also Leon Fink, "Looking Backward: Reflections on Workers' Culture and Certain Conceptual Dilemmas within Labor History," *Perspectives on American Labor History*, 19. On Ford, see the summary in Nelson Lichtenstein, "The Man in the Middle. A Social History of Automobile Industry Foremen," in *On the Line: Essays in the History of Auto Work*, eds. Nelson Lichtenstein and Stephen Meyer (Urbana: University of Illinois Press, 1989), 153–89. More generally, on the processes of the formation of the middle class in the United States, see Blumin, *Emergence of the Middle Class*.

59. SCII, cases 33 and 34 and vol. 330; John H. Goss, "War-Time Manufacture of Fuzes," 224–25. On consumption and the new middle class, see *The Culture of Consumption: Critical Essays in American History, 1880–1980*, eds. Richard Wightman Fox and T. J. Jackson Lears (New York: Pantheon Books, 1983); Andrew R. Heinze, *Adapting to Abundance: Jewish Immigrants, Mass Consumption, and the Search for American Identity* (New York: Columbia University Press, 1990); Kathy Peiss, *Cheap Amusements: Working Women and Leisure in Turn-of-the-Century New York* (Philadelphia: Temple University Press, 1986), chap. 1; Harvey Levenstein, *Revolution at the Table: The Transformation of the American Diet* (New York and Oxford: Oxford University Press, 1988).

NOTES TO CHAPTER 2

1. E. O. Goss to C. P. Goss, Sr., 23 January 1914, SCII, case 58; American Brass balance sheet for 31 December 1913, ABCP, series I, box 2/16; *New York Times*, 12 February 1914; *Twenty-Sixth Report of the Connecticut Bureau of Labor Statistics* (Hartford: Press of the Case, Lockwood, and Brainald Co., 1914), 38–39; Annual Report, 1 January 1914, SCII, vol. 254.

2. E. O. Goss to C. P. Goss, Sr., 14 March 1914, SCII, case 58; Pete Martin, "The Company Car Can't Lick," *Saturday Evening Post* (29 August 1942): 13, 61.

3. On the military orders of the 1880s and 1890s, see SCI, vols. 310, 323, 325, and 429. On the formation of the military-industrial complex, see Robert Hessen, *Steel*

Titan: The Life of Charles M. Schwab (New York and Oxford: Oxford University Press, 1975); Stephen Skorownek, *Building a New American State: The Expansion of National Administrative Capacities, 1877–1920* (Cambridge: Cambridge University Press, 1982), part 2; *Military Enterprise and Technological Change: Perspectives on the American Experience*, ed. Merritt Roe Smith (Cambridge, Mass.: MIT Press, 1985); *Captains of the Old Steam Navy: Makers of the American Naval Tradition*, ed. James C. Bradford (Annapolis, Md.: Naval Institute Press, 1986); Edward M. Coffman, *The Old Army: A Portrait of the American Army in Peacetime, 1784–1898* (New York and Oxford: Oxford University Press, 1986); Edward Hagerman, *The American Civil War and the Origins of Modern Warfare* (Bloomington: Indiana University Press, 1988), chap. 2; Paul A. C. Koistinen, *Mobilizing for Modern War: The Political Economy of American Warfare, 1865–1919* (Lawrence: University Press of Kansas, 1997).

4. SCI, vols. 438 and 439. On "spin-offs" from military to civil industries, see Clive Trebilcock, "British Armaments and European Industrialization," *Economic History Review* 26 (May 1973): 254–72; Roe Smith, *Military Enterprise*, 17–29.

5. *Republican Peace and Victory Edition*, [November 1918], Manuscripts M-30, Mattatuck Museum; John H. Goss, "War-Time Manufacture of Fuzes."

6. "Sco. WWI. Memo about preparation for, 1917," SCII, case 28; Bishop, "History of Scovill," 23; Scovill balance sheet for 1915, SCII, vol. 254; *Twenty-Seventh Report of the Connecticut Bureau of Labor* (Hartford: The State, 1916), 20–28.

7. Douglas T. Hamilton, *Shrapnel Shell Manufacture* (New York: The Industrial Press, 1915), 167ff.

8. Daniel D. Lescohier, *The Labor Market* (New York: The Macmillan Company, 1919), 177–185; G. S. Watkins, *Labor Problems and Labor Administration in the United States During the World War* (Urbana: University of Illinois Press, 1920), 268; *Twenty-Eighth Report of the Connecticut Bureau of Labor* (Hartford: The State, 1918), 51–60. For an attempt to place the American economic and financial situation within an international framework, see William H. Becker, *The Dynamics of Business-Government Relations: Industry and Export, 1893–1921* (Chicago: University of Chicago Press, 1982); Wynn, *From Progressivism*, chap. 4; Paul Fearon, *War, Prosperity, and Depression: The U.S. Economy, 1917–1945* (Lawrence: University Press of Kansas, 1987), chap. 1; Thomas W. Zeiler, "Just Do It! Globalization for Diplomatic Historians," *Diplomatic History* 25 (Fall 2001): 542–51.

9. Lescohier, *The Labor Market*, 177–78; *Bradstreet's*, 7 August 1915; *Corriere del Connecticut*, 25 March and 12 August 1916.

10. Employment Applications Sample, SCII, case 33; *Il Progresso del New England*, 16 October 1915.

11. Ibid.

12. Interview by Jeremy Brecher and Ferdinando Fasce with Pasquale De Cicco, Waterbury, 7 October 1985; Pasquale De Cicco with the author, 14 April 1987; interview by Ferdinando Fasce with Pasquale De Cicco, 14 October 1987.

13. Robert Platt to John H. Goss, 28 November 1917, SCII, case 33; Time Office Count, 1912–26, SCII, vol. 326; Pape, *History of Waterbury*, vol. 1, p. 210. On the question of Ford, use has been made of the correspondence between the managers of the Detroit company and the National Civic Federation during the years 1914–16 contained in Welfare Department General Correspondence, National Civic Federation

Papers (from now on NCFP), box 111, New York Public Library, New York. The path-breaking work by Stephen Meyer III, *The Five Dollar Day: Labor, Management, and Social Control in the Ford Motor Company, 1908–1921* (Albany: State University of New York Press, 1981), is still the standard treatment of Ford's labor policies.

14. On the origins of welfare work, the following sources have been consulted: papers from the National Civic Federation, NCFP, especially boxes 111, 116, and 122; the unpublished typescript "Report by Gertrude Beeks on Factory Inspection Tours, 1901–1902," Nettie Fowler McCormick Papers, box 27/B, State Historical Society of Wisconsin, Madison; as well as the vast literature summarized in note 14 of the Intro-duction. See also Bruno Ramirez, *When Workers Fight: The Politics of Industrial Rela-tions in the Progressive Era, 1896–1916* (Westport, Conn.: Greenwood Press, 1978), 150ff; and Marguerite Green, *The National Civic Federation and the American Labor Movement, 1900–1925* (Westport, Conn.: Greenwood Press, 1978), chap. 6. On National Cash Register, company bulletins have been consulted: *The NCR* (1903–1904) and *Woman's Welfare* (1904), Baker Library. See also Sealander, *Grand Plans,* 34–35.

15. Henry Eilbirt, "The Development of Personnel Management in the United States," *Business History Review* 33 (Fall 1959): 345–64; "The Case for the Employment Manager," unpublished typescript by the War Industries Board, 8 August 1918, Baker Library; Employment Applications 1915–16 Sample, SCII, case 33; interview by Jeremy Brecher and Ferdinando Fasce with Pasquale De Cicco, Waterbury, 7 October 1985.

16. On U.S. Steel and International Harvester, use has been made of, respectively, the steel company's bulletin *U.S. Steel Corporate Committee on Safety Bulletin,* 1910–1914, and numerous pamphlets published by International Harvester, all kept in the Mudd Library, Yale, supplemented with Brody, *Steelworkers in America;* and Richard Ozanne, *A Century of Labor-Management Relations at McCormick and International Harvester* (Madison: University of Wisconsin Press, 1967). For the debate about Amer-icanization, see Gerard Korman, "Americanization at the Factory Gate," *Industrial and Labor Relations Review* 18 (April 1965): 396–41; John McClymer, *War and Welfare: Social Engineering in America* (Westport, Conn.: Greenwood Press, 1980); *American Education and the European Immigrant,* ed. Bernard J. Weiss (Urbana: University of Illi-nois Press, 1982); Maddalena Tirabassi, *Il faro di Beacon Street: Social workers e immi-grate negli Stati Uniti* (Milan: Angeli, 1990); Nancy Gentile Ford, *Americans All! Foreign-Born Soldiers in World War I* (College Station: Texas A&M University Press, 2001), 4–6.

17. *Waterbury, Naugatuck, and Watertown City Directory for 1914* (New Haven, Conn.: The Price and Lee Co., 1914), 604; Employment Applications ca. 1916–17, SCII, case 65. Table 3 is taken from the Annual Report of Accident Statistics, 1918, SCII, case 34.

18. Industrial Services, SCII, case 33; Hospital American Brass, ABCP, series IV, box 1. Table 4 is taken from the Annual Report of Accident Statistics, 1918, SCII, case 34.

19. E. H. Downey, "Workmen's Compensation in the United States," *Journal of Polit-ical Economy* 21 (December 1913): 913–34; Emery R. Hayhurst, "The Brass Moulder's Secret," *Survey* 26 (23 September 1911): 879–82.

20. E. H. Downey, *Workmen's Compensation* (New York: The Macmillan Company, 1924), 159–60; Rosner and Markowitz, *Dying for Work,* 34–53.

21. "Insurance for Workers," *Iron Trade Review* 41 (21 November 1907): 833–34; *Employee Magazines in the United States* (New York: National Industrial Conference Board, 1925), 1–4; E. G. Main to R. E. Platt, 10 October 1919, SCII, case 33.

22. Table 5 is taken from Yates, *Control through Communication,* 193.

23. *SFA News,* December 1915, SCII, vol. 313a.

24. *SFA News,* June 1915, SCII, vol. 313a.

25. The figures about expenses are to be found in SCII, case 33.

26. All quotations are from Descriptions of Serious Accidents, SC II, case 33.

27. Ibid.. On accidents, see also *Iron Age,* 11 July 1918.

28. On working hours, see C. P. Goss to M. C. Roldan, 16 June 1887, SCI, vol. 308; the handwritten copies of the annual reports submitted by Scovill to the Connecticut Bureau of Labor Statistics, SCII, vol. 254; John Goss's circulars, SCII, vols. 257 and 258; Bishop, "History of Scovill," 204–31. Note that the reduction of three hours a year was lower than the already small average reduction in the industry as a whole, which was 4.9 hours for the period 1890–1914. See David R. Roediger and Philip S. Foner, *Our Own Time: A History of American Labor and the Working Day* (London: Verso, 1989), 151.

29. *SFA News,* May 1915, SC II, vol. 313a.

30. Josephine Goldmark and Mary D. Hopkins, *Comparison of an Eight-Hour Plant and a Ten-Hour Plant* (Washington, D.C.: Government Printing Office, 1920), 93–124.

31. *Scovill Bulletin,* September 1916, SCII, vol. 313a.

32. *SFA News,* August 1915, SCII, vol. 313a.

33. *SB,* October 1919, SCII, vol. 314, and various leaflets and correspondence in SCII, case 33.

34. The figures, including those given in Table 6, are taken from SCI, vols. 78 and 312; SCII, vol. 254 and case 36. On women and the brass sector, see Virginia Penny, *The Employments of Women: A Cyclopaedia of Womens' Work* (Boston: Walker, Wise and Co., 1863), 340–42; id., *500 Employments Adapted to Women* (Philadelphia: Potter and Co., 1870), 473–75; Carroll D. Wright, *The Working Girls of Boston* (Boston: Wright and Potter, 1889), 71; Edith Abbott, *Women in Industry* (New York: Appleton, 1910), 75–76. For a comparison with the rest of the metal manufacturing industry during the First World War, see Haydu, *Between Craft,* 135–36.

35. SCI, vols. 62–67 and 76–78; interview by Jeremy Brecher with Modestina De Angelis, Waterbury, 29 December 1985 (my thanks go to J. Brecher for allowing me to use this interview).

36. Moloney, "Families, Work, and Social Institutions," 82–85; Census of Employees, 1918, SCII, case 36; Figures: Labor by Depts., SCII, case 33.

37. Maurine Weiner Greenwald, *Women, War, and Work: The Impact of World War I on Women Workers in the United States* (Westport, Conn.: Greenwood Press, 1980), 155; Alice Kessler-Harris, *A Woman's Wage: Historical Meanings and Social Consequences* (Lexington: University Press of Kentucky, 1990), 23; Brecher, Lombardi, and Stackhouse, *Brass Valley,* passim; interview by Jeremy Brecher with Caroline Nardello, Waterbury, 12 January 1980, Brass Workers History Project (from now on BWHP), tape 41, Mattatuck Museum.

38. State of Connecticut, *Report of the Factory Inspector* (Hartford: The State, 1912), 33–34; State of Connecticut, *Report of the Factory Inspector* (Hartford: The State, 1920), 41–46; Employment Applications Sample, SCII, case 33; Brecher, Lombardi, and Stackhouse, *Brass Valley.*

39. State of Connecticut, *Report of the Department of Labor on the Condition of Wage-Earners in the State* (Hartford: The State, 1918), 32.

40. State of Connecticut, *Report of the Department of Labor on the Conditions of Wage-Earners in the State* (Hartford: The State, 1918), 14–15; Stephen H. Norwood, *Labor's Flaming Youth: Telephone Operators and Worker Militancy* (Urbana: University of Illinois Press, 1990), 15ff.; Bishop, "History of Scovill," 244ff.; *SB,* September 1915, SCII, vol. 313a; Time Office Count, SCII, vol. 326; G. A. Neubauer and Erik Oberg, "Organization of a Munition Plant," *Machinery* 48 (November 1918): 208–12. On Taylor, see Daniel Nelson, *Frederick Winslow Taylor.* On piecework see Simonetta Ortaggi, *Il prezzo del lavoro: Torino e l'industria italiana nel primo Novecento* (Turin: Rosenberg & Sellier, 1988).

41. Brecher, Lombardi, and Stackhouse, *Brass Valley,* 61ff.; Goldmark and Hopkins, *Comparison,* 93–94; SCII, case 63.

42. State of Connecticut, *Report*of the Department of Labor (1918), 7–36; *Four Years in the Underbrush* (New York: Charles Scribner's Sons, 1921), chap. 25; Cornelia Stratton Parker, *Working with the Working Woman* (New York: Harper & Brothers, 1922), 42ff.; Goldmark and Hopkins, *Comparison,* 163ff.; R. E. Platt to E. H. Davis, 24 March 1919, SCII, case 36; *New York Times,* 17 December 1915, 15 December 1916, 29 November 1917. For Table 7, see Bishop, "History of Scovill," 137–59, and the company balance sheets in SCII, vol. 254.

43. Goldmark and Hopkins, *Comparison,* 83–94; William B. Wilson, "Labor Program of the Department of Labor," *Bulletin of the Bureau of Labor Statistics* (1918, no. 247): 166.

44. See note 29 and *SB,* February 1917, SCII, vol. 313a. On the Knights of Columbus, see Christopher J. Kaufman, *Faith and Fraternalism. The History of the Knights of Columbus, 1882–1982* (New York: Harper & Row, 1982).

45. See notes 29 and 39. On housing congestion, see Estelle B. Hunter, *Infant Mortality: Results of a Field Study in Waterbury, CT* (Washington, D.C.: Government Printing Office, 1918); "Where Rent Sharks Prosper and Why," *Survey* 40 (25 May 1918): 218–20; correspondence between Governor M. H. Holcomb and the Honorable W. J. Larkin, February–October 1918, Papers of Governor Marcus H. Holcomb (from now on PGH), RG 5, box 263/160, CSL.

46. *SB,* July 1916 and February 1917, SCII, vol. 313a; *Woman's Welfare,* March 1904; *Eleventh Annual Meeting of the National Civic Federation* (New York: The National Civic Federation, 1912), 324.

47. *Republican,* 20 August 1916. On the 4 July celebrations as a national phenomenon, see Roy Rosenzweig, *Eight Hours for What We Will: Workers and Leisure in an Industrial City, 1870–1920* (Cambridge: Cambridge University Press, 1983), 65–66; Francis G. Couvares, *The Remaking of Pittsburgh: Class and Culture in an Industrializing City, 1877–1919* (Albany: The State University of New York Press, 1984), 108–9; Wilbur Zelinsky, *Nation into State: The Shifting Symbolic Foundations of American Nationalism* (Chapel Hill: University of North Carolina Press, 1988), 72–73; Mary P. Ryan, "The American Parade: Representations of the Nineteenth Century Social Order," in *The New Cultural History,* ed. Lynn Hunt (Berkeley: University of California Press, 1989), 150–51.

48. Procter & Gamble Scrapbook, 1880–1900, Procter & Gamble Archives, Cincinnati; Cheape, *Family Firm,* 134–36; Rosenzweig, *Eight Hours,* 160–62; John Bodnar, *Immigration and Industrialization: Ethnicity in an American Mill Town* (Pittsburgh:

University of Pittsburgh Press, 1977), 120ff. For a comparison with the European experience, see Alan Delgado, *The Annual Outing and Other Excursions* (London: Allen and Unwin, 1977).

49. *SFA News,* December 1915, SCII, vol. 313a.

50. *SFA News,* May 1915, SCII, vol. 313a.

51. *SB,* September 1916, SCII, vol. 313a; Tamara K. Hareven, *Family Time and Industrial Time: The Relationship Between the Family and Work in a New England Industrial Community* (Cambridge: Cambridge University Press, 1982), 62; Employment Applications ca. 1916–17, SCII, cases 65–72.

52. *Republican,* 20 August 1916.

53. On suggestion boxes, see SCII, case 28. On the spread of this measure nationwide, see the works cited by Cheape and Zahavi and also James R. Barrett, *Work and Community in the Jungle: Chicago's Packinghouse Workers, 1894–1922* (Urbana: University of Illinois Press, 1987), 253.

54. John H. Goss, "The Importance of Human Engineering in Industrial Relations," unpublished typescript, 7 December 1937, SCII, case 58; *SFA News,* August 1915, SCII, vol. 313a. The message from Tony Calabrese was taken from this source.

55. The changes in the foundry are illustrated in SCII, vols. 257, 326, and 335, cases 26 and 28; *Brass World,* November and December 1914, January 1915, and July 1916; H. W. Gillett and A. E. Rhoads, *Melting Brass in a Rocking Electric Furnace* (Washington, D.C.: Government Printing Office, 1918), 15–17. For the similar case of American Brass, see the account by an exceptional observer, the future labor sociologist Charles R. Walker, who worked in the foundry in the period immediately after the war and provided a reconstruction of what happened during mobilization, based on the testimony of his colleagues. See "Diary of Charles Rumford Walker, August 20–December 9, 1920," unpublished typescript, BWHP. On the labor market, see Alexander Keyssar, *Out of Work: The First Century of Unemployment in Massachusetts* (Cambridge: Cambridge University Press, 1985), 321.

56. *Seven Centuries of Brassmaking* (Bridgeport, Conn.: Bridgeport Brass Company, 1920), 26–27; various technical and advertising material taken from the archives of Industries—Bridgeport Brass Co., Bridgeport Public Library; *SB,* March–May 1917, SCII, vol. 313a.

57. On the crisis of casters in general, see Margaret Loomis Stecker, "The Founders, the Molders, and the Molding Machine," *Quarterly Journal of Economics* 32 (February 1918): 278–308; Joseph W. Roe, *The Mechanical Equipment* (New York: Industrial Extension Institute, 1918), 61–101; Bureau of Commercial and Industrial Affairs, *The Foundry and Machining Industries of New England* (Boston: Chamber of Commerce, 1926), 5–25. For the role of chemists, see R. H. Chittenden to A. T. Hadley, 19 January 1918, SSAR, box 39/353; Hugh R. Slotten, "Humane Chemistry or Scientific Barbarism? American Responses to World War Poison Gas, 1915–1930," *Journal of American History* 77 (September 1990): 480, 494.

NOTES TO CHAPTER 3

1. *SFA News,* May, October, and November 1915, *SB,* November 1916, June and October 1917, SCII, vol. 313a.

2. Scovill to Emil Pabo, 2 November 1916, SCII, case 28; Bruce Fraser, "Yankees at War: Social Mobilization on the Connecticut Homefront, 1917–1918" (Ph.D. diss., Columbia University, 1976), 88–89, 92–95.

3. Fraser, "Yankees at War," 92–143; various YMCA reports, about the years 1912–15, kept at the YMCA of Greater New York Archives, New York City, file 29; North American Civic League for Immigrants (NACL), *Report 1916–17* (Boston: North American Civic League for Immigrants, n.d.). Fraser shows amply how the publication by the Connecticut Daughters of the American Revolution of one of the most famous guides for immigrants, by Carr (J. F. Carr, *Guida degli Stati Uniti per l'immigrante italiano,* [New York: Doubleday, 1910]), was essentially an isolated event in the state. The booklet was a kind of best-seller in the rest of the country. On the NACL in Connecticut, see also Edward George Hartmann, *The Movement to Americanize the Immigrant* (New York: Columbia University Press, 1948), 43.

4. See the report by the Department of Labor, Bureau of Naturalization, Waterbury, 11 September 1915, U.S. Department of Labor, Immigration, and Naturalization Service, Americanization Records (from now on DLAR), RG 85/54809, 27671-709, National Archives (from now on NA), Washington D.C.; *A Year of Progress* (Waterbury: YMCA Waterbury, 1913), Waterbury YMCA Archives; *Republican,* 5 and 6 July 1915 and 1916; *Immigrants in America Review,* September 1915; *Bulletin No. 2 of the Immigration Committee,* 5 May 1916; *Bulletin No. 14 of the Immigration Committee,* 25 August 1917; Rosenzweig, *Eight Hours,* 160–61.

5. Fraser, "Yankees at War," chaps. 1–3; Heath, *"Politics,"* chaps. 1–2; *Skeleton Copy of the Proceedings of the Twenty-Seventh Annual Convention of the Connecticut Federation of Labor* (Bridgeport, Conn.: Advocate Print, 1913), 7.

6. *Official Convention Book of the Connecticut Federation of Labor Twenty-Eighth Annual Convention* (Bridgeport: Advocate Print, 1914), 2–3; *Official Convention Book of the Connecticut Federation of Labor Twenty-Ninth Annual Convention* (Bridgeport, Conn.: Advocate Print, 1915), 3; Haydu, *Between Craft,* 179; Cecelia Bucki, "Dilution and Tradition: Munitions Workers in Bridgeport, Connecticut, 1915–19," in *The New England Working Class and the New Labor History,* eds. Herbert G. Gutman and Donald H. Bell (Urbana: University of Illinois Press, 1987), 137–40.

7. *Republican,* 10, 15, and 16 January, 6, 7, 9, 22, and 23 February 1917; Ottavio Barié, *L'opinione interventistica negli Stati Uniti, 1914–1917* (Milan: Istituto Editoriale Cisalpino, 1960), 178–79; M. Scully to M. Holcomb, 5 February 1917, PGH, RG 5/80, CSL; Fraser, "Yankees at War," 95.

8. *Hartford Courant,* 22 March 1917; Fraser, "Yankees at War," 114–43.

9. About the census, see the Connecticut Military Census Records (from now on CMCR), RG 29, boxes 12, 24, and 28, CSL. For a comparison with the rest of the nation, see William J. Breen, *Uncle Sam at Home: Civilian Mobilization, Wartime Federalism, and the Council of National Defense, 1917–1919* (Westport, Conn.: Greenwood Press, 1985), 5–7, 39–40; and more recently, Gentile Ford, *Americans All!,* chap. 1.

10. CMCR, RG 29, boxes 24 and 28.

11. CMCR, RG 29, boxes 67 and 68.

12. *SB,* May 1917, SCII, vol. 313a.

13. *Republican,* 29 July 1917; *SB,* August 1917, SCII, vol. 313a. On the role of women in the propaganda activities for mobilization at a national level, see Lettie Gavin, *Ameri-*

can Women in World War I: They Also Served (Niwot: University Press of Colorado, 1997), and especially Kimberley Jensen, "Women, Citizenship, and Civic Sacrifice: Engendering Patriotism in the First World War," in *Bonds of Affection: Americans Define Their Patriotism,* ed. John Bodnar (Princeton, N.J.: Princeton University Press, 1996), 139–59.

14. *SB,* April–September 1917, SCII, vol. 313a.

15. *SB,* July–December 1917, SCII, vol. 313a.

16. Ibid.

17. Fraser, "Yankees at War," 312–22; Kennedy, *Over Here,* chaps. 1 and 2; Meyer, *The Five Dollar Day,* 177, 180.

18. *SB,* October and November 1917, SCII, vol. 313a.

19. Ibid.; *Bulletin No. 17 of the Immigration Committee,* 15 December 1917; internal correspondence in the Connecticut State Council of Defense, October–December 1917, Records of the Connecticut State Council of Defense (from now on CSCD), RG 30, box 74, CSL.

20. George Creel, "The Preparedness with a Punch," *Hearst's* 29 (March 1916): 190, 228–30; Kennedy, *Over Here,* chap. 2; Vaughn, *Holding Fast,* chap. 2; John A. Thompson, *Reformers and War: American Progressive Publicists and the First World War* (Cambridge: Cambridge University Press, 1987), chaps. 5 and 6; Robert B. Westbrook, *John Dewey and American Democracy* (Ithaca, N.Y.: Cornell University Press, 1990), 195–227.

21. The posters are in the Military Collection, box 2, Mattatuck Museum.

22. *SB,* October 1917.

23. Goldmark and Hopkins, *Comparison,* 163ff.; William Leiserson, "The Labor Shortage and the Organization of the Labor Market," *Survey* 40 (20 April 1918): 68–69; "Stabilizing Industrial Employment," special issue of *The Annals of the American Academy of Political and Social Science* 71 (May 1917): 136–55; William J. Breen, "Labor-Market Statistics and the State: The United States in the Era of the Great War, 1914–1930," *Journal of Public Policy History* 8 (Fall 1996): 310–19; U.S. Department of Labor, *Report of the U.S. Housing Corporation* (Washington, D.C.: Government Printing Office, 1920), 5.

24. *SB,* November 1916, SCII, vol. 313a.

25. Ibid.; Bishop, "History of Scovill," chap. 5; C. E. Woods to E. H. Davis, 8 January 1919, SCII, case 36; Goldmark and Hopkins, *Comparison.*

26. Goldmark and Hopkins, *Comparison,* 163–98. On the Bureau of Public Health's inquiry, see Alan Derickson, "Physiological Science and Scientific Management in the Progressive Era: Frederic S. Lee and the Committee on Industrial Fatigue," *Business History Review* 68 (Winter 1994): 483–514. On the origins of personnel offices, see Jacoby, *Employing Bureaucracy;* and "Personnel and Employment Problems in Industrial Management," special issue of *The Annals of the American Academy of Political and Social Science* 65 (May 1916): 76–310.

27. Circulars of the Industrial Service Department, spring 1917, SCII, case 33.

28. On the Kennedy affair, see SCII, case 33, and *Democrat,* 25 January 1917.

29. Circulars of the Industrial Service Department, 1917–1918, SCII, case 33.

30. Goldmark and Hopkins, *Comparison,* 163ff.; H. D. Gallaudet to J. H. Goss, 10 May 1917, SCII, case 33; Meyer, *The Five Dollar Day,* 173ff; Stephen Norwood, "Ford's Brass Knuckles: Harry Bennett, The Cult of Muscularity, and Anti-Labor Terror— 1920–1945," *Labor History* 37 (Summer 1996): 365–77.

31. *Republican,* 7 October 1917.

32. For Goss's view, see an untitled company memo, 14 April 1921, SCII, case 33. On the role and expectations of Progressive intellectuals during the war, see McClymer, *War and Welfare,* and Thompson, *Reformers and War.*

33. E. O. Goss to W. Bryant, 16 July 1918, SCII, case 28; J. H. Goss to M. J. Warner, 20 May 1918, SCII, case 28.

34. R. E. Platt to J. H. Goss, 28 March 1918, R. E. Platt to M. E. Woodruff, 6, 7 and 8 July 1918, M. E. Woodruff to R. E. Platt, 20 and 25 June 1918, SCII, case 33.

35. J. H. Goss to the foremen, 28 March, 2 April, 3, 10, and 14 May 1918, SCII, case 34. On the spread of the planning department (or routing department, as it was sometimes called), see Neubauer and Oberg, "Organization," 208–12.

36. *U.S. Employment Service Bulletin,* 25 June and 4 July 1918; *Il Progresso del New England,* 13 June 1918.

37. *Iron Age,* 11 July 1918.

38. See the files Occupational Lists, SCII, case 58; Census of Employees, 1918, SCII, case 36; Davis E. H. Office, SCII, case 55. On the greater opportunities and prestige of statistics experts during the war and in the years immediately after the war, both inside companies and beyond, see Guy Alchon, *The Invisible Hand of Planning: Capitalism, Social Science, and the State in the 1920s* (Princeton, N.J.: Princeton University Press, 1985), 52–53, 59; and William J. Breen, "Foundations, Statistics, and State-Building: Leonard P. Ayres, the Russell Sage Foundation, and U.S. Government Statistics in the First World War," *Business History Review* 68 (Winter 1994): 451–82.

39. Company memo "Report of Conference on Labor Shortage and Training of New Employees," 7 December 1917, SCII, case 33; B. P. Hyde (Scovill) to L. P. Breckinridge (Sheffield School), 16 June 1920, case 28; U.S. Bureau of Education, *Report of the Commissioner of Education for the Year Ended June 30, 1916* (Washington, D.C.: Government Printing Office, 1916), vol. 1, 217–19; various circulars of the Sheffield School in the summer of 1918, SSAR, series III, box 39/351. On the ties between engineering schools and companies during the war, see David F. Noble, *America by Design: Science, Technology, and the Rise of Corporate Capitalism* (New York: Alfred A. Knopf, 1977); and Clyde W. Barrow, *Universities and the Capitalist State: Corporate Liberalism and the Reconstruction of American Higher Education, 1894–1928* (Madison: University of Wisconsin Press, 1990), chap. 4.

40. See the various files of the Americanization Department, CSCD, RG 30, boxes 166, 169, and 305.

41. See the file Americanization Classes, SCII, case 33. For Ford, see Meyer, *The Five Dollar Day,* 159–61, and on the slaughterhouses, see Barrett, *Work and Community,* 246–47.

42. *Bulletin No. 18 of the Immigration Committee,* 2 January 1918; National Association of Corporation Schools, *Seventh Annual Proceedings* (New York: Kellogg Co., 1919), 471ff.; and *Eighth Annual Proceedings* (New York: Kellogg Co., 1920), 632ff.

43. On the Four Minute Men (FMM) in Connecticut, see CSCD, RG 30, boxes 301–2, 312. For the nationwide picture, see Alfred E. Cornebise, *War as Advertised: The Four Minute Men and America's Crusade* (Philadelphia: The American Philosophical Society, 1984).

44. "The War Work of the Four-Minute Men," *The Touchstone* 6 (September 1918): 507.

45. On rallies and speeches, see the unpublished documentation contained in CSCD, RG 30, boxes 312, 315–19.

46. Kennedy, *Over Here*, chap. 2; Alfred E. Cornebise, *The Stars and Stripes: Doughboy Journal in World War I* (Westport, Conn.: Greenwood, 1984), chap. 1; C. W. Campbell, *Reel America and World War One* (Jefferson, N.C.: McFarland, 1985); Michael Rogin, "The Sword Became a Flashing Vision: D. W. Griffith's *The Birth of a Nation*," *Representations* 9 (Winter 1985): 150–95; Alessandra Lorini, *Rituals of Race: American Public Culture and the Search for Racial Democracy* (Charlottesville: University Press of Virginia, 1999), 234–36.

47. *SB*, February 1918,SCII, vol. 314.

48. Kennedy, *Over Here*, chap. 2; Vaughn, *Holding Fast*, chaps. 2–5; Brett Gary, *The Nervous Liberals: Propaganda Anxieties from World War I to the Cold War* (New York: Columbia University Press, 1999), chap. 1. On mass culture and the process of creating emotions in the first twenty years of the twentieth century, see *An Emotional History of the United States*, eds. Peter N. Stearns and Jan Lewis (New York: New York University Press, 1998), 377–416.

49. Edward L. Munson, *The Management of Men: A Handbook on the Systematic Development of Morale and the Control of Human Behavior* (New York: Holt & Co., 1921), 2ff. See also William Ernest Hocking, *Morale and Its Enemies* (New Haven, Conn.: Yale University Press, 1918), and "Bibliography of Morale," unpublished typescript, 1944, kept at the New York Public Library Annex. An excellent treatment of Munson's activities is provided by Nancy K. Bristow, *Making Men Moral: Social Engineering During the Great War* (New York: New York University Press, 1996), 182–85. For a comparison with the situation in Britain, see J. G. Fuller, *Troop Morale and Popular Culture in the British and Dominion Armies, 1914–1918* (Oxford: Clarendon Press, 1990), chap. 2, which, however, contains no reference to manuals of the kind cited.

50. *SB*, February 1918, SCII, vol. 313a; CSCD, RG 30, box 306; Manuscripts M-30, box 3, Mattatuck Museum.

51. *SB*, February 1918, SCII, vol. 313a.

52. J. T. Hubbell to H. B. Freeman, 5 March 1918, CSCD, RG 30, box 301; James M. Read, *Atrocity Propaganda, 1914–1919* (New Haven, Conn.: Yale University Press, 1941), chap. 1.

53. On the state focus of mobilization, see Fraser, "Yankees at War," 319–25; and Breen, *Uncle Sam*, 200ff. See also Robert Cuff, "American Mobilization for War, 1917–45," in *Mobilization for Total War: The Canadian, American, and British Experience*, ed. N. F. Dreisziger (Waterloo, Ont.: Wilfried Laurier University Press, 1981), 71–86.

54. The interweaving of the various spheres emerges from the extensive material contained in CSCD, RG 30, especially boxes 300–2. On Wolff, see the file Selective Service, SCII, case 28, and the correspondence about the draft in PGH, RG 5, box 247.

55. See the periodic notes contained in the Plant Protection Service Records, RG 165, War Department, NA; the *Journal of the Board of Aldermen of the City of Waterbury for the Year 1917* (Waterbury, Conn.: The Standard Printing Co., 1917), 15, 311; and the *Journal of the Board of Aldermen of the City of Waterbury for the Year 1918* (Waterbury, Conn.: The Standard Printing Co., 1918), 140ff.

56. *SB*, May and June 1918, SCII, vol. 314.

57. The extant files are in SCII, box 33A. On similar spying practices in other companies, see Meyer, *The Five Dollar Day,* 187–93; Cheape, *Family Firm,* 130–31; and David J. Goldberg, *A Tale of Three Cities: Labor Organization and Protest in Paterson, Passaic, and Lawrence, 1916–1921* (New Brunswick, N.J., and London: Rutgers University Press, 1989), 205. An overview of antiunion and antiworker espionage in the early twentieth century is presented in Gary M. Fink, "Efficiency and Control: Labor Espionage in Southern Textiles," unpublished typescript, January 1989 (in author'spossession).

58. SCII, box 33A.

59. *Republican,* 5 July 1915; *Skeleton Copy of the Proceedings of the Twenty-Eighth Annual Convention of the Connecticut Federation of Labor* (Bridgeport, Conn.: Advocate Print, 1914), 2; *Official Convention Book of the Connecticut Federation of Labor Thirtieth Annual Convention* (Bridgeport, Conn.: Advocate Print, 1916), 3; William Francis Sullivan, "Turmoil in the Brass City: A Study of Working Class Consciousness During the Waterbury Strikes of 1919 and 1920" (master's thesis, Trinity College, 1997), 35–36.

60. State of Connecticut, *Twenty-Eighth Report of the Bureau of Labor* (Hartford: The State, 1918), 48–49; SCII, box 33A; Elisabetta Vezzosi, *Il socialismo indifferente: Immigrati italiani e Socialist Party negli Stati Uniti del primo Novecento* (Rome: Edizioni Lavoro, 1991), 25–27, 46. On the great wave of labor struggles in the United States during the war, see Montgomery, *Fall,* chaps. 7–8; Philip S. Foner, *History of the Labor Movement in the United States* (New York: International Publishers, 1987), vol. 7: *Labor and the World War, 1914–1918;* and McCartin, *Labor's Great War,* 137–41, 150–80; interview by Jeremy Brecher with Mario De Ciampis, Waterbury, 26 November 1984, BWHP.

61. SCII, box 33A.

62. On these processes on a national level, see especially David Montgomery, "Nationalism, American Patriotism and Class Consciousness among Immigrant Workers in the U.S. in the Epoch of WWI," in *Struggle a Hard Battle: Essays on Working-Class Immigrants,* ed. Dirk Hoerder (DeKalb: Northern Illinois University Press, 1986), 327–51; John J. Bukowczyck, "The Transformation of Working Class Ethnicity: Corporate Control, Americanization, and the Polish Immigrant Middle Class in Bayonne, New Jersey, 1915–1925," *Labor History* 25 (Winter 1984): 53–82; Linda Schneider, "American Nationality and Workers' Consciousness in Industrial Conflict: 1870–1920. Three Case Studies" (Ph.D. diss., Columbia University, 1975), chap. 7; John Bodnar, *Remaking America: Public Memory, Commemoration, and Patriotism in the Twentieth Century* (Princeton, N.J.: Princeton University Press, 1992), 81–85; Gary Hartman, "Building the Ideal Immigrant: Reconciling Lithuanism and 100 Percent Americanism to Create a Respectable Nationalist Movement, 1870–1922," *Journal of American Ethnic History* 18 (Fall 1998): 55–60.

63. H. B. Freeman to L. Roversi, 28 May 1918, CSCD, R6 30, box 302, CSL.

64. On the Italian community in the prewar period, see chap. 1, no. 43, and also the correspondence about life in the local parish, both taken from the Delegazione Apostolica in the United States (from now on DAUS), IX/15, 30, 56 and 79, Archivio Segreto Vaticano (from now on ASV), and from the diocese papers kept in the Archives of the Archdiocese of Hartford. On the subject of the war, I consulted the extant issues of *Il Progresso del New England* that cover the period January–November 1918; the local English-language papers, especially the *Republican;* and the material about the mobilization in CSCD, RG 30, boxes 302–304. See also the interview by J. Brecher with De Ciampis;

interviews by J. Brecher and F. Fasce with P. De Cicco (see chap. 2, note 11); NACL, *Annual Report 1918–1919* (Boston: North American Civic League for Immigrants, n.d.); and "Address given by Judge Edward Mascolo at the Dedication of the Italian House," unpublished typescript, Waterbury, 1 September 1935, Mattatuck Museum.

65. On the Lithuanian community, see Brecher, Lombardi, and Stackhouse, *Brass Valley,* 13–39; Moloney, "Families, Work, and Social Institutions," 32–46; William Lawrence Wolkovich-Valkavicius, *Lithuanian Pioneer Priest of New England* (Brooklyn: Franciscan Press, 1980), 51–179; Dolores Ann Liptack, "European Immigrants and the Catholic Church in Connecticut, 1870–1920" (Ph.D. diss., University of Connecticut, 1979); *Republican,* 10 September 1911 and 20 July 1919; material on mobilization in CSCD, RG 30, boxes 305 and 307; shorthand versions of interviews with members of the community carried out in the 1930s by the Works Progress Administration, in WPA-CT, RG 33, boxes 68, 74, and 92.

66. SCII, box 33A; J. H. Goss to M. J. Warner, 20 May 1918, and A. J. Wolff to Camp Devens military authorities, 7 August 1918, SCII, case 28.

67. SCII, case 33; State of Connecticut, *Report of the Department of Labor (1918),* 102–3; State of Connecticut, *Report of the Department of Labor and Factory Inspector on the Conditions of Wage-Earners in the State* (Hartford: The State, 1920), 66; SCI, vol. 87.

68. On the housing problem, see the vast company documentation in SCII, cases 28 and 33. For the national picture, see Cheape, *Family Firm,* 138–39; "Housing of Workmen," unpublished typescript of the War Industries Board, 1918, Baker Library; *Nation's Business,* April 1918; Morton C. Tuttle, *The Housing Problem in Its Relation to the Contentment of Labor* (New York: National Housing Corporation, 1920).

69. *Republican,* 29 July 1917; *SB,* December 1919, SCII, vol. 314; SCII, case 28; SCI, vol. 87. On "war kitchen gardens," see Wynn, *From Progressivism,* 156; and Cornebise, *War as Advertised,* 96. On the Food Administration and propaganda, see Levenstein, *Revolution at the Table,* 145ff.

70. SCII, case 33; Cooper, *Once a Cigar Maker,* 178, 193, and 196; *Forbes,* 19 April 1919; *Industrial Management,* June 1920; National Industrial Conference Board, *Rest Periods for Industrial Workers* (Boston: National Industrial Conference Board, 1919), 2–3.

71. U.S. Treasury Department, 4th *Liberty Loan—Handbook for Speakers* (Washington, D.C.: Government Printing Office, 1918), 27.

72. *SB,* May 1918, SCII, vol. 313a.

73. *SB,* June 1918, SC II, Vol. 313a.

74. *SB,* July and September 1918, SCII, vol. 314; James B. Gilbert, *Work Without Salvation* (Baltimore, Md.: The Johns Hopkins University Press, 1977), 69–79.

75. *SB,* August and December 1918, SCII, vol. 314; J. H. Goss to the foremen, 16 July 1918, SCII, case 34.

76. SCII, case 36.

77. The manuals are in SCII, case 34. For a comparison with American Brass, see ABCP, series IV, box 23/8. On the manuals on a national level, see Heinz Diemer, *Factory Organization and Administration* (New York: McGraw-Hill, 1910), 250–51; and Yates, *Control Through Communication,* 66–74.

78. On relations with the National War Labor Board, see SCII, case 28, and on wage increases, see the interview by Jeremy Brecher with John Hollingworth, Waterbury, 25

November 1980, BWHP, tape 35. On the policy of the National War Labor Board, see Valerie J. Connor, *The National War Labor Board* (Chapel Hill: University of North Carolina Press, 1983).

79. *SB,* September 1919, vol. 314.

80. The teachers' reports are in SCII, case 33. See also CSCD, RG 30, boxes 166, 169, and 170. About the other companies, see *Iron Age,* 18 July 1918; and National Association of Corporation Schools, *Eighth Annual Proceedings* (New York: National Association of Corporation Schools, 1920), 610–11.

81. *Republican Peace and Victory Edition;* State of Connecticut, *Report of the Department of Labor,* 49–54; National Civic Federation Welfare Department, NCFP, box 116. On the National Civic Federation, see chap. 2, notes 12 and 13, and also James Weinstein, *The Corporate Ideal in the Liberal State, 1900–1918* (Boston: Beacon Press, 1968). On the Cheney Brothers, see the company brochure *Plans Proposed by Cheney Brothers for Social Insurance and Old Age Pensions* (Hartford: The Case, Lockwood, and Brainald Co., 1910); and National Industrial Conference Board, *Industrial Relations Activities at Cheney Brothers* (New York: National Industrial Conference Board, 1929), kept in the Mudd Library, Yale.

82. SCII, vol. 254; ABCP, series I, box 2/16; *Republican,* 16 November 1919.

NOTES TO CHAPTER 4

1. State of Connecticut, *Report of the Department of Labor and Factory Inspector (1920),* 25–26.

2. Ibid.; U.S. Public Health Service, *Epidemic Influenza* (Washington, D.C.: Government Printing Office, 1918), 1–4; U.S. Public Health Service, *Spanish Influenza* (Washington, D.C.: Government Printing Office, 1918); Alfred W. Crosby, *America's Forgotten Pandemic: The Influenza of 1918* (Cambridge: Cambridge University Press, 1989), 45–69; E. J. Webb to C. A. Woods, 18 and 25 November 1918, SCII, case 33.

3. "Extent and Control of the Influenza Epidemic," *Survey* 40 (19 October 1918): 63–64, 74–76; *Il Progresso del New England,* 26 October and 2 November 1918.

4. Interviews by Jeremy Brecher and Ferdinando Fasce with P. De Cicco (see chap. 2, note 11).

5. Ibid.; *SB,* November 1918, SCII, vol. 314.

6. *U.S. Employment Service Bulletin,* 31 December 1918, 10 January and 7 February 1919; General Assembly—State of Connecticut, typewritten minutes of the meetings of the Joint Standing Committee on Labor, 14 March 1919, CSL; *Republican,* 13 and 18 March 1919.

7. *SB,* October 1918 and June 1919, SCII, vols. 314 and 315.

8. Brecher, Lombardi, and Stackhouse, *Brass Valley,* 61, 64; U.S. Department of Labor, Women's Bureau, *Home Work in Bridgeport, Connecticut* (Washington, D.C.: Government Printing Office, 1920), 18; State of Connecticut, *Seventh Biennial Report of the Factory Inspection Department to the Governor* (Hartford: The State, 1920), 32.

9. State of Connecticut, *Report of the Department of Labor and Factory Inspector (1920), 102–5;* National Industrial Conference Board, *Wages and Hours in American Industry* (New York: National Industrial Conference Board, 1925), 43–44.

10. H. T. Wayne and H. R. McCory to R. E. Platt, 13 March 1919, SCII, case 33.

11. J. H. Goss to the foremen, 24 and 27 June 1919, SCII, case 33.

12. E. O. Goss to I. B. Clark, 4 June 1918, SCII, case 28; Figures: Labor by Departments, 1919–1920, SCII, case 33.

13. SCII, vols. 335 and 336 and case 36; Brass and Copper and Tobacco Notes, 1938, WPA-CT, RG 33, box 205/22, CSL.

14. Figures: Labor by Departments, 1919–1920; Census of Employees, 1921, SCII, case 35. On the feminization of office work, see Hartman Strom, "'Light Manufacturing,'" 67–71; Zunz, *Making America Corporate,* 117; Mary Christine Anderson, "Gender, Class, and Culture: Women Secretarial and Clerical Workers in the United States, 1925–1955" (Ph.D. diss., Ohio State University, 1986).

15. Reports from foremen to J. H. Goss in SCII, case 26; Yates, *Control Through Communication,* 187, 191.

16. Foremen's Lectures, 1919, SCII, case 35; Lathrop, *Brass Industry,* 158–59; ABCP, series I, box 1/7.

17. Foremen's Lectures, 1919; various reports from C. E. Woods to J. H. Goss, January–June 1919, SCII, case 36.

18. J. H. Goss to the foremen, 17 and 23 January, 17 March, 15 April, and 16 May 1919, SCII, case 34; reports from the foremen to Goss, 1919–1922, SCII, case 26.

19. Foremen's Lectures—Scovill Mfg. Co.—Year 1919—Inventing Control and Storekeeping—Lecture No. 2, 9, SC II, Case 35.

20. J. H. Goss to the foremen, 17 June and 23 July 1919, SCII, case 36; correspondence between W. Monagan and J. H. Goss, 26 September 1918, 10 April, 14 and 21 September, and 21 October 1919, SCII, case 26. For similar administrative and technical initiatives, see Charles E. Fouhy, "Employment Department Routine of the Curtiss Aeroplane and Motor Company," *Industrial Management* 57 (November 1918): 350–52; Edward J. Benge, "Personnel Department Filing System," *Industrial Management* 59 (February 1920): 84–86. On the currents within accounting rationalization on which the Scovill consultants drew, see Johnson and Kaplan, *Relevance Lost;* Joseph A. Litterer, "Alexander Hamilton Church and the Development of Modern Management," *Business History Review* 35 (Winter 1959): 461–76; Mariann Jelinek, "Toward Systematic Management: Alexander Hamilton Church," *Business History Review* 54 (Spring 1980): 63–79; Paul J. Miranti, *Accountancy Comes of Age: The Development of an American Profession, 1886–1940* (Chapel Hill: University of North Carolina Press, 1990).

21. Time Office Count, 1911–1926, SCII, vol. 326.

22. Ibid.; Enumeration of Employees, SCII, case 36; *Journal of the Board of Aldermen of the City of Waterbury for the Year 1919* (Waterbury: The Standard Printing Co., 1919), 18, 58, 167.

23. *Republican,* 6 and 9 February 1919. On the national political climate, see William Preston, Jr., *Aliens and Dissenters: Federal Suppression of Radicals, 1903–1933* (New York: Harper & Row, 1963), chap. 8; John Higham, *Strangers in the Land: Patterns of American Nativism, 1860–1925* (New York: Atheneum, 1963), chap. 8; McClymer, *War and Welfare,* 209–30; David R. Colburn, "Governor Alfred E. Smith and the Red Scare," *Political Science Quarterly* 88 (September 1973): 423–43; David M. Rabban, "The Emergence of Modern First Amendment Doctrine," *The University of Chicago Law Review* 50 (Fall 1983): 1207–1351. On Connecticut and Waterbury, see Bruce B. Shubert, "The Palmer Raids in Connecticut, 1919–1920," *Connecticut Review* 12 (October

1971): 53–69; and David Edward LaMontagne, "The Mad Men Among Us: Bolsheviki and Brass City Hysteria. Waterbury, 1919–1920" (master's thesis, Trinity College, 1985).

24. *Republican,* 10, 11, and 14 March 1919. On the Lawrence strike, see Rudolph J. Vecoli, "Anthony Capraro and the Lawrence Strike of 1919," in *Pane e lavoro: The Italian American Working Class,* ed. George E. Pozzetta (Toronto: The Multicultural History Society of Ontario, 1980), 3–27; and Goldberg, *A Tale of Three Cities,* chaps. 5 and 7.

25. *Republican,* 30 March, 13 and 20 April 1919; Socialist Revolution - Russian Echoes - Anonymous Letters, SCII, case 63.

26. On the files, see SCII, box 33A. On the company school ceremonies, see NCFP, box 111; CSCD, RG 30, box 166; and *SB,* September 1919, SCII, vol. 315.

27. The teachers' reports are in SCII, case 33.

28. *Herald,* 6 and 7 June 1919; *New York Times,* 18 and 20 June 1919.

29. "Untitled Scovill brochure, 17 June 1919, SC II, Case 33.

30. Ibid.; information reports of the Bureau of Investigation of the Department of Justice, 19, 20, and 21 June 1919, Department of Justice Files (from now on DJF), RG 65, Roll 799 M-1085/363529, NA; *American,* 18 and 19 June 1919. On the Bureau of Investigation, see Lorin Lee Cary, "The Bureau of Investigation and Radicalism in Toledo, Ohio: 1918–1920," *Labor History* 21 (Summer 1980): 430–40; and David Williams, "The Bureau of Investigation and Its Critics, 1919–1921: The Origins of Federal Political Surveillance," *Journal of American History* 68 (December 1981): 560–82.

31. SCII, box 33A; reports by Department of Justice informers, February–May 1919, DJF, RG 65, Roll 799 M-1085/363529, NA.

32. *American,* 20, 21, and 23 June 1919; *Herald,* 22 June 1919; *Republican,* 22 and 23 June 1919; *The First Battalion Bugle,* 26 June 1919. On the participation of housewives and workers' wives in the strikes at that time, see Ardis Cameron, "Bread and Roses Revisited: Women's Culture and Working-Class Activism in the Lawrence Strike of 1912," in *Women, Work, and Protest: A Century of U.S. Women's Labor History,* ed. Ruth Milkman (London: Routledge & Kegan Paul, 1985), 54–61; Philip J. Leahey, "Skilled Labor and the Rise of the Modern Corporation: The Case of the Electrical Industry," *Labor History* 27 (Winter 1985–86): 31–53; William Scheuerman, "The Politics of Protest: The Great Steel Strike of 1919–20 in Lackawanna, New York," *International Review of Social History* 31 (Spring 1986): 121–46.

33. *American,* 24–27 June 1919; *Republican,* 26–27 June 1919; reports by Department of Justice informers, 24 and 26 June 1919, DJF, RG 65, Roll 799 M-1085/363529, NA.

34. *Herald,* 29 June 1919; *Republican,* 28 June 1919; *Official Proceedings: Thirty-Fifth Annual Convention of the Connecticut Federation of Labor Held in Waterbury, Connecticut* (Hartford: Allied Printing, 1921), 9; reports by Department of Justice informers, July 1919, DJF, RG 65, Roll 799 M-1085/363715.

35. *Il Progresso del New England,* 28 June 1919.

36. "SB," June 1919, SCII, vol. 315.

37. On welfare and recreational projects, see SCII, case 33; *SB,* June–September 1919, SCII, vol. 315; S. W. Gisriel to W. Monagan, 24 September 1919, SCII, case 26; some YMCA brochures from the period 1919–20, Waterbury YMCA.

38. "Scovill Employees Fourth Annual Get Together Day," SCII, case 28; *Il Progresso*

del New England, 18 January 1919. For an exposition on the problem of dating, see Beth L. Bailey, *From the Front Porch to Back Seat: Courtship in Twentieth-Century America* (Baltimore, Md.: Johns Hopkins University Press, 1989), chap. 1.

39. See the works cited at note 22 and also Stanley Coben, "A Study in Nativism: The American Red Scare of 1919–20," *Political Science Quarterly* 79 (March 1964): 52–53; reports and bulletins of the Military Intelligence Division, 8–21 February and 1–13 March 1920; *U.S. Military Intelligence Reports: Surveillance of Radicals in the United States, 1917–1941* (from now on MIR), University Publications of America microfilms, reel 16; *Republican,* 8 March 1920.

40. *Bradstreet's,* 8 May 1920; *New York Times,* 24 June 1920; *The American Labor Year Book, 1921–1922,* eds. Alan Trachtenberg and Bernard Glassberg (New York: Rand School of Social Science, 1922), 431.

41. *Il Progresso del New England,* 1 May 1920; State of Connecticut, *Report of the Department of Labor* (1920), 76; typewritten reports of the Waterbury Chamber of Commerce, "Cost of Living—Waterbury," spring 1920, SCII, vol. 284A; National Industrial Conference Board, *Cost of Living, 1914–1930* (New York: National Industrial Conference Board, 1931), 98, 140; Diary of Charles Rumford Walker, 23, 30–31.

42. *Il Progresso del New England,* 21 February, 13 and 20 March 1920; *Herald,* 20 June 1920; final report by T. J. Williams, Department of Labor official, on the Waterbury strike, 31 July 1920, Department of Labor, Federal Mediation and Conciliation Service (from now on FMCS), RG 280, case file 170–1133, NA.

43. *American,* 16 April 1920; *Democrat,* 23 April 1920; *Republican,* 3 May 1920; *SB,* September 1919 and June 1920, SCII, vol. 314; interview by Jeremy Brecher with James Tiso, Waterbury, 2 December 1980, BWHP, tapes 38 and 39.

44. On the dynamics of the strike, see SCII, cases 33 and 58.

45. *Democrat,* 24 April 1920.

46. See the numerous local newspaper clippings kept in SCII, vols. 244–248; Department of Justice informers' reports, 14, 16, 22, and 24 June, DJF, RG 65, Roll 799 M-1085/363703; and the weekly reports by Department of Labor officials, May–June 1920, FMCS. On the subject of the workers' use of democratic rhetoric on citizenship during the war and at this time, see Montgomery, *Fall,* chap. 8; McCartin, *Labor's Great War,* 105–7; Mormino and Pozzetta, *The Immigrant World,* 128, 140; David Brody, *Labor in Crisis: The Steel Strike of 1919* (Urbana: University of Illinois Press, 1987), 73, 153; Gary Gerstle, *Working-Class Americanism: The Politics of Labor in a Textile City, 1914–1960* (Cambridge: Cambridge University Press, 1989), 45ff; James R. Barrett, "Americanization from the Bottom Up: Immigration and the Remaking of the Working Class in the United States, 1880–1930," *Journal of American History* 79 (December 1992): 1014–15.

47. Correspondence between W. Bergin, A. J. Wolff, and J. H. Goss, February 1921, SCII, case 33; *Herald,* 20 and 27 June 1920; *Republican,* 24 and 27 June 1920; *Il Progresso Italo-Americano,* 23 June 1920; *Il Progresso del New England,* 26 June 1920; Rev. G. Valdambrini to Mons. J. Bonzano, 5 July 1920, DAUS IX/93.

48. *Il Progresso del New England,* 21 May 1920.

49. *Il Progresso del New England,* 1, 15, 22, and 29 May 1920; *Herald,* 4 and 25 May 1920; *Republican,* 24 May 1920. On similar cases of ethnic support for the strikers in this period, see Mormino and Pozzetta, *The Immigrant World,* 117; Barrett, *Work and*

Community, 173ff.; Bukowczyck, " Transformation," 70–72; Ewa Morawska, *For Bread with Butter: Life-Worlds of East Central Europeans in Johnstown, Pennsylvania, 1890–1940* (Cambridge: Cambridge University Press, 1985), 180–81.

50. A. S. O'Brien, "The Psychology of *Lo Sciopero,*" *Herald,* 16 May 1920.

51. Ibid.; *Democrat,* 27 April 1920; *Republican,* 27 April, 7 June, and 5 July 1920; *Herald,* 6 June 1920; *American,* 26 June 1920; B. P. Hyde to W. McBride, 7 July 1920, SCII, case 58; Scovill company circulars on the development of the strike in some departments, May–June 1920, SCII, case 33. On the perception of the strike as "festival" and "holiday" in various European and American contexts, see Michelle Perrot, *Les ouvriers en grève: France, 1871–1890* (Paris: Mouton, 1974), vol. 1, 140ff.; Norwood, *Labor's Flaming Youth,* 8; Peppino Ortoleva, "Una voce dal coro: Angelo Rocco e lo sciopero di Lawrence del 1912," *Movimento operaio e socialista* 4 (January–June 1981): 23–24.

52. SCII, box 33A; O'Brien, "Psychology."

53. *Il Progresso Italo-Americano,* 15 July 1920; *Republican,* 18 July 1920; *Democrat, American,* and *La Verità,* 1 May 1920; *Herald,* 2 and 9 May 1920.

54. Reports by T. J. Williams and H. J. Skeffington to H. L. Kerwin, 15 and 22 May, 1, 8 and 10 June 1920, FMCS.

55. Ibid.

56. *Il Proletario,* 19 June 1920; "Connecticut Brass," unpublished typescript, 1935, WPA-CT, box 208/8, 14–15.

57. LaMontagne, "The Mad Men Among Us," chap. 3; Goldberg, *A Tale of Three Cities,* 205–12.

58. R. E. Platt to J. H. Goss, 4 October 1920, SCII, case 33.

59. The data about the Lithuanians and the Russians is in SCII, case 33. See also LaMontagne, "The Mad Men Among Us," chaps. 3 and 4; Shubert, "The Palmer Raids," 65ff.; Jerome Davis, *The Russians and Ruthenians in America: Bolsheviks or Brothers?* (New York: G. Doran, 1922), xi ff.

60. For reports about the behavior of the foremen, see SCII, box 33A.

61. *Herald,* 18 July 1920; *Republican,* 27 July 1920; *SB,* June and July 1920, SCII, vol. 314.

62. J. H. Goss to the foremen, July 1920, SCII, case 35; William Talbot, "Who's Who in Industry in America?" *Industrial Management* 59 (February 1920): 138–42.

63. *SB,* September 1920, SCII, vol. 315.

64. See the file Census 1921, SCII, case 36.

65. Department of Commerce, Bureau of the Census, *Fourteenth Census of the United States Taken in the Year 1920* (Washington, D.C.: Government Printing Office, 1923), vol. 9, p. 208; *U.S. Employment Service Bulletin,* December 1921; for company teachers' reports, see SCII, case 33; *Employees' Manual, 1922,* SCII, case 34.

66. Company circulars dated 21 February, 8 April, 26 May, and 9 September 1921, SCII, case 33; company balance sheets for 1919–1921, SCII, vol. 254; *American,* 8 February 1926, in SCI, vol. 439.

67. Jacoby, *Employing Bureaucracy,* 178; Joyce Shaw Peterson, *American Automobile Workers, 1900–1933* (Albany: State University of New York Press, 1987), 27, 51–59; Meyer, *The Five Dollar Day,* 197–99; Ruth Milkman, *Gender at Work: The Dynamics of Job Segregation by Sex During World War II* (Urbana: University of Illinois Press, 1987), chap. 2.

68. *Revolutionary Radicalism: Its History, Purpose, and Tactics* (Albany: Lyon Company, 1920), part 2, vol. 2, 4299–4300; reports by those in charge of the Waterbury school units to the Bureau of Naturalization of the Department of Labor, 27 June, 4 October, 3 November 1921, 21 January and 1 February 1922, DLAR, RG 85/54809, 27671-709; reports and flyers of the New Haven Americanization Committee, March 1921, February 1922, Farnam Family Papers, Group 203, box 255/3294, Sterling Library.

69. J. H. Goss to R. E. Platt, 15 August 1919, SCII, case 34; circular sent by J. H. Goss, 5 August 1921, SCII, case 34; *SB*, August 1920, SCII, vol. 315; reports by foremen and company officials about the store, 23 September and 5 November 1920, 15, 17, 19, and 21 March 1921, SCII, case 58.

70. J. H. Goss to the foremen, 2 September 1920, SCII, case 34; correspondence between the foremen and J. H. Goss about vacations, November 1920–March 1921, SCII, case 28.

71. J. H. Goss to B. P. Hyde, 15 November 1920, and list of employees entitled to vacations, June–July 1921, SCII, case 35. On the spread of paid company vacations on a national level, see National Industrial Conference Board, *Vacations with Pay for Wage Earners* (New York: National Industrial Conference Board, 1935), 1–11; and "Pertinent Facts About Vacations," *Factory and Industrial Management* 79 (June 1930): 1340–42. On the selective nature of labor policy, see Montgomery, *Fall*, 454–57; Jacoby, *Employing Bureaucracy*, chap. 6; and Laura J. Owen, "Gender Differences in Labor Turnover and the Development of Internal Labor Markets in the United States during the 1920s," *Enterprise and Society* 2 (March 2001): 41–71.

72. The discussion and information about pensions are in SCII, cases 35, 37, and 41. The figures relative to American Brass are in SCII, case 33. On industrial pensions on a national level, see *Industry*, 3 September 1921; and Murray Webb Latimer, *Industrial Pension Systems in the United States and Canada* (New York: Industrial Relations Counselor, 1932), 2–58. For an overview, see William Graebner, *A History of Retirement: The Meaning and Function of an American Institution, 1885–1978* (New Haven, Conn.: Yale University Press, 1980). In particular, about the 1920s, see Jacoby, *Employing Bureaucracy*, 199; and N. Sue Weiler, "Industrial Scrap Heap: Employment Patterns and Change for the Aged in the 1920s," *Social Science History* 13 (Spring 1989): 65–88.

73. On leisure policy in the 1920s, see SCII, cases 33 and 38, boxes 34A and 55B.

74. On Millicent Pond and her tests, see SCII, cases 38 and 58; Henry C. Link, "Psychological Tests in Industry," *Annals of the American Academy of Political and Social Science* 90 (November 1923): 37–39; and the writings of Millicent Pond, "Selective Placement of Metal Workers I," *Journal of Personnel Research* 5 (January 1927): 345–68; "Selective Placement of Metal Workers II," *Journal of Personnel Research* 5 (February 1927): 405–17; "Selective Placement of Metal Workers III," *Journal of Personnel Research* 5 (February 1927): 452–66; "How Shall We Measure the Trained Man?" unpublished typescript, 1930, SCII, vol. 299; and "The Value of Mental Tests," *Scovill Standard* 3 (January–February 1932): 15–17, SCII, vol. 322. In general, on the subject of industrial psychology, see the studies by Sanford M. Jacoby, "Employee Attitude Testing at Sears, Roebuck and Company, 1938–1960," *Business History Review* 60 (Winter 1986): 602–33; Paul Davis Chapman, *Schools as Sorters: Lewis M. Terman, Applied Psychology, and the Intelligence Testing Movement, 1890–1930* (New York: New York University Press, 1988);

and Richard Gillespie, *Manufacturing Knowledge: A History of the Hawthorne Experiments* (Cambridge: Cambridge University Press, 1991), chap. 1.

75. On Goss and the Personnel Research Federation, see SCII, case 58. On this organization, see Jacoby, *Employing Bureaucracy,* 184; and Gillespie, *Manufacturing Knowledge,* 33–34. On Procter & Gamble, see Herbert Feis, *Labor Relations: A Study Made in the Procter and Gamble Company* (New York: Adelphi Company, 1928), and the company documentation about employee shareholding kept in the Procter & Gamble Archives, Cincinnati. On the electromechanical companies, see the important workby Ronald W. Schatz, *The Electrical Workers: A History of Labor at General Electric and Westinghouse, 1923–1960* (Urbana: University of Illinois Press, 1983), part 1; and David E. Nye, *Image Worlds: Corporate Identities at General Electric, 1890–1930* (Cambridge, Mass.: MIT Press, 1985).

76. The data relating to turnover are in SCII, case 36. On foremen, see SCII, case 33 and vol. 316a.

77. Interview by Ferdinando Fasce with John Zampino, Waterbury, 8 October 1985.

78. Ibid.; interview by Ferdinando Fasce with Arthur Finelli, Waterbury, 8 October 1985. On factory life in the 1920s, see SCII, cases 37 and 58; and Connecticut Brass, unpublished typescript (1935), WPA-CT.

79. Interview by Ferdinando Fasce with John Zampino; interview by Jeremy Brecher with Jim Cusack, Waterbury, 30 October 1980, BWHP, tapes 24 and 25; interviews by Jeremy Brecher and Ferdinando Fasce with Pasquale De Cicco (see chap. 2, note 11). On the rationalization of production, see SCII, vol. 345. The city ordinances are in *Ordinances,* 284. For a comparison with the national picture, see David Montgomery, "Liberty and Union: Workers and Government in America, 1900–1940," in *Essays from the Lowell Conference on Industrial History, 1980 and 1981,* eds. Robert Weible, Oliver Ford, and Paul Marion (Lowell, Mass.: Lowell Conference on Industrial History, 1981), 151–52; and Stanley Coben, *Rebellion Against Victorianism: The Impetus for Cultural Change in 1920s America* (New York and Oxford: Oxford University Press, 1991), 137ff. On the "invisible handshake," see Michael Huberman, "The Economic Origins of Paternalism," *Social History* 12 (May 1987): 177–92.

80. *La Verità,* 13 February 1929; *American,* 23 August 1929; M. Pond to J. H. Goss, 27 May 1932, SCII, case 36. On the political climate and the antiunion atmosphere in the city in the 1920s, see the numerous newspaper clippings kept in SCI, vols. 438 and 439; "The Story of Waterbury," *Republican,* 14 June 1953; interview by Jeremy Brecher with Michele Russo, 29 March 1988, BWHP; interviews by Ferdinando Fasce with H. L. and R. L., Waterbury, 23 November 1990.

81. Interview by Ferdinando Fasce with John Zampino; Brecher, Lombardi, and Stackhouse, *Brass Valley,* 157–90.

Note on Sources

The main body of primary unpublished sources comes from the Scovill papers kept in the manuscript section of the Baker Library, Harvard Business School. This is a vast collection comprising 927 volumes of letter books, 171 boxes, and 81 cases. The collection is divided into two parts (Scovill Collection I and II), corresponding roughly to the nineteenth and twentieth centuries. For the purposes of a general examination of the development of the company during the nineteenth century, this material has been supplemented by papers (also kept in the Baker Library) of the R. G. Dun Collection. In the same archive I also examined the papers of the Whitin Machine Works, a large metal manufacturing company, and Dwight Manufacturing Company, to shed comparative light on the phenomena of internal subcontracting and the spread of written rules in companies in the nineteenth century. The Baker Library was also the source for brochures from various companies (including, in particular, National Cash Register) that were at the forefront of the welfare movement. Other company brochures that were consulted in relation to this phenomenon were taken from U.S. Steel, International Harvester, Westinghouse, and General Electric, kept in the Yale University Mudd Library. Again, in order to place the question in the broadest possible context of company neopaternalism, I examined the National Civic Federation Papers kept in the New York Public Library; further material from the Nettie Fowler McCormick Papers, State Historical Society of Wisconsin, Madison; and the papers of Procter and Gamble, kept in the Procter and Gamble archives in Cincinnati.

For the purposes of making a close comparison with other companies in the brass industry, the papers of American Brass, Scovill's main competitor, were consulted (to be found in the Homer Babbidge Library, University of Connecticut in Storrs), as well as those of smaller companies such as Platt Brothers (kept at the Mattatuck Museum in Waterbury). Here I also looked at the unpublished diaries of F. J. Kingsbury, president of Scovill until the beginning of the twentieth century. References to Kingsbury were also found in the papers of Bridgeport Brass Company, another company where he had strong interests, and in papers kept in the section on the corporate world in the manuscript section of the Bridgeport Public Library—a section that proved to be rich in material on technological innovation in the brass industry during the period of the First World War. Unfortunately, it was not possible to find references to Scovill in the archives of its main partner in war contracts, Bethlehem Steel. This archive, to

179

be found at the Hagley Museum and Library in Wilmington, Delaware, did, however, provide numerous suggestions for a definition of the general character of the arms market and the growing military-industrial complex.

With regard to engineering and technical sources, I consulted the papers of the Sheffield School, the prestigious Yale engineering school where John H. Goss, the manager who occupies center stage in this book, studied. This school cooperated constructively with Scovill in the field of technical and managerial training. These sources were supplemented by the main technical journals, from inside and outside the industry (from American Machinist to Brass World), for details that can be found in the notes at the end of each chapter. These notes also provide references to management and economic journals (including Iron Age, Nation's Business, and Industrial Management) consulted for the period from 1900 to 1930.

The complex dynamics of mobilization have been reconstructed with the aid of the vast documentation to be found in state and federal archives. At the Connecticut State Library in Hartford I consulted in particular the Connecticut Military Census records; the papers of the Connecticut State Council of Defense and those of the governor in office during the mobilization and in the immediate postwar period; and the Papers of Governor M. H. Holcomb. The search for information about Scovill in the papers of the War Industries Board in the National Archives in Washington, D.C., unfortunately proved to be fruitless. I had more success, however, with the Military Intelligence Records, the papers of the Federal Mediation and Conciliation Service, the Plant Protection Service Records, and the Americanization Records. All this material, together with the Department of Justice Files, allowed me to describe the industrial conflict in the period from 1919 to 1920.

The area where the primary sources proved to be most lacking about this conflict, and more generally about the world of labor during the period covered by this study, was in fact in the world of unions and workers. The investigations I carried out at the state archive of the AFL-CIO union in Hamden or at the aforementioned Homer Babbidge Library (the most important center for union material in the whole of Connecticut) were of almost no use. Very useful, on the other hand, were the transcripts of interviews with workers conducted by the Works Progress Administration in the 1930s, which were available in the aforementioned Connecticut State Library. Another approach that proved to be extremely useful, besides scanning local papers and press reports for information about all the annual conventions of the individual unions and union federations, at the state and national level, was the examination of the unpublished written sources and the tape library, made up of interviews with former workers, kept in the archives of the Brass Workers' History Project (BWHP) at the Mattatuck Museum in Waterbury. The oral sources collected there have been supplemented by about a dozen interviews carried out by the author, mostly with members of the still sizable Italian community in Waterbury. In my attempt to define the general characteristics of this community, I have profitably examined papers about the local Catholic church, found in the Archivio Segreto Vaticano and the archive of the Archdiocese of Hartford.

With regard to the unpublished material of the BWHP, one need only recall the diary written by Charles Walker, the future labor sociologist employed by American Brass in the immediate postwar period. Again, in relation to unpublished labor material, I should mention the diary of John Van Deusen, a skilled worker in Waterbury who was able to shed a great deal of light on the craft world of the nineteenth century.

I found this in the Sterling Library at Yale, where I also consulted the Farnham Papers (Farnham was an economics scholar who came from a wealthy New Haven family), which contain documentary evidence of great importance about the bodies responsible for dealing with immigrants in Connecticut. Again on this topic I examined periodicals and correspondence preserved at the Waterbury branch of the YMCA and in the national archives of the same organization, to be found at one of its New York Headquarters (YMCA of Greater New York).

Index

U. S. Steel, 46, 47, 49, 53, 162n16
uniforms, 59
Union of Russian Citizens, 120, 127,
128–29, 130
unions.: alternatives to, 32; and the
American Federation of Labor (AFL),
28, 97, 124, 133–34, 170n59, 180; and
blacklists of workers, 28, 170n57; collective bargaining by, 133–36; and the
Democratic Party, 29–31; groups
formed in opposition to, 29, 30; and
immigrants, 122–27; Knights of
Labor, 12–13, 38, 156n19; Lady Brass
Workers, 28; and mediation, 135;
Metal Polishers, 28–29, 31, 32; and
politics, 29–31, 123–24, 170nn59–63,
178n80; and the psychology of lo
sciopero, 132, 176n50; and the
Republican Party, 30–31; and Scovill,
121–27; and violence, 29; and work
hours, 53–54. *See also* skilled labor;
strikes
United Brass Workers' Association of
North America, 12
United States: census, 74–75, 166n9,
176nn64–65; Committee on Public
Information (CPI), 90–91, 94, 96;
effect of World War I on, 43, 70–74;
entry into World War I, 73–74, 75;
immigrants to, 2, 14, 16–18, 29–32,
31, 35, 43–48, 47, 71–72, 107–9,
128–33; and Liberty Bonds, 76–77,
92, 130; patriotism in, 71–72, 130,
137–38, 164n47; and the Progressive
movement, 47, 49, 77, 83–84; and the
Red Scare, 119–20, 127, 175n39; relationship with Great Britain, 91
unskilled labor, 31–32

vacations, worker, 142–43, 178n73
Van Deusen, John, 7–8, 180
vertical integration, 2
violence and strikes, 29, 123–24, 131
Vittorio Emanuele Society, 32

wages: and bonuses, 79; at Ford Motor
Company, 80; overtime, 54, 107; and
piecework, 58–60, 118; regulation of,

32–33, 107, 141–42; at Scovill, 34, 44,
54, 140; and seniority, 141–42; of
skilled workers, 2, 10–11, 14, 36,
171–72n78; and union control,
28–29, 125; of white collar workers,
36
Walker, Charles, 180
WASPs (White Anglo-Saxon Protestants),
29–30, 71, 74, 98, 130, 135
Water and the Naugatuck Valley, 2
Waterbury (Connecticut): elections,
29–31; entrepreneurs and leaders in,
3, 5, 8, 29–31; growth of the middle
class in, 31–38; immigration to,
16–18, 97–98, 146; and Liberty
Bonds, 76–77; and new patents, 7–8,
154–55n12; patriotism and anti-
Bolshevism in, 100–101; population
growth, 44; public health, 82–83,
110–12; and recession, 39, 139; and
the Red Scare, 119–20; and the Scovill
Manufacturing Company, 1–2, 7, 95,
154n9; social activities in, 63–66,
93–94; strikes in, 12–13, 28, 127,
128–30, 159n45; unions in, 28, 29–30;
and the YMCA, 13–14
Waterbury SavingsBank, 3
Waterbury Workers' Association (WWA),
122–24, 128–29
welfarism, 33–34, 81, 102, 109, 144,
156n21, 159n49
Westinghouse, 108, 179
white collar workers, 35, 36, 110–11, 114,
141–42
Whitin Machine Works, 9, 155n14, 179
Whitney, Eli, 6
Wilson, Woodrow, 73, 77, 94
Wolff, Alfred J., 35, 95–96, 139
women: and domestic work, 58–59;
employed in manufacturing, 7, 25,
56–63, 102, 114, 126–27, 144, 163n34,
163n37, 164n42; and the feminization
of office work, 25, 58, 114, 158n37;
and housing, 102; Irish, 63; and
piecework, 58–60; and the Scovill
Girls' Club, 56, 62–63, 144; and uniforms, 59
woodworking industry, 13